INTERNATIONAL ECONOMIC LAW AND DEVELOPING STATES

An Introduction

Edited by
Hazel Fox

FIAT LVX

The British Institute of International and Comparative Law
London, 1992

British Library Cataloguing in Publication Data

International economic law and developing states.
Vol.2 : An introduction
I. Fox, Hazel
341.75

ISBN 0 903067 33 1

Published by
The British Institute of International and Comparative Law
Charles Clore House, 17 Russell Square, London WC1B 5DR
Printed by Burrups Ltd, St Ives plc London and Tokyo.   B853468/SH

TABLE OF CONTENTS

Page

iii

TABLE OF CONTENTS

PREFACE

Pieter Ver Loren van Themaat[1]

As a continental lawyer I felt, of course, both honoured and challenged by being asked to write a preface to this book. I understand from the second and third paragraphs of the Introduction that I owe this invitation to the fact that continental or 'civil' lawyers are being considered as 'system-builders'. This is in contrast to the more 'typically English pragmatic approach to questions of international economic law'. I do not deny that in my publications on comparative national economic law, on European Community Law and on international economic law I have tried, indeed, to systematise those new and often seemingly incoherent branches of law. Since Grotius' works on the law of war and peace and on the freedom of the sea it is, however, largely for **pragmatic** reasons that Dutch lawyers have often tried to be system-builders in the field of international law. After the sea-wars with England in the second half of the seventeenth century, the Dutch Republic of that time was no longer strong enough to defend its international trade interests (the main source of its wealth up to that time) by power diplomacy and wars alone. Not only did it seek international co-operation with England,

---

1. The author worked successively from 1945–1958 in the Dutch Ministry of Economic Affairs (where he had to deal with price regulation, control of restrictive business practices and the establishment of self-regulating agencies of industry, mainly for agricultural products), from 1958–1967 as Director-General of Competition for the EEC Commission (responsible for the implementation of Articles 85–102 and 220 of the EEC Treaty), from 1967–1981 as Professor of national and international economic law and the substantive law of the European Communities at the University of Utrecht and from 1981–1986 as Advocate-General at the Court of Justice of the European Communities. From 1980 onwards he was also one of the rapporteurs of the ILA Committee on Legal aspects of a New International Economic Order.

in particular from 1688 onwards. It also looked for protection by means of effective rules of public international law. In the field of international economic relations, the disastrous effects of the chaotic nationalistic and protectionist experiments between the two world wars, therefore, quite naturally incited the Netherlands to support strongly the development of a coherent system of international economic organisations after the Second World War, as described in this book. Its greater dependence on economic relations with other European countries rather than with non-European countries was also the main reason for the Dutch initiative (the Beyen initiative which led to the Benelux memorandum of 1955) to prepare for the EEC as a still more developed international organisation. 70% of Dutch exports (about 35% of its GNP) are now going to other Member States of the EC and therefore prove the wisdom of this initiative. With regard to international economic organisations like the GATT, as well as with regard to the European Communities, the Netherlands, in conformity with Dutch tradition since the second half of the seventeenth century, is moreover strongly in favour of a 'government by rules' of international economic relations, and, since the Second World War, of independent common institutions for their management. As a small country it distrusts 'power diplomacy' and intergovernmental procedures of decision-making, where not common interests, but purely national interests dictate the attitudes of the participating countries and where the interests of the more powerful countries tend to prevail. Dutch lawyers and politicians applaud therefore that, for example, in GATT even the US now tends to recognise the greater merits of a 'government by rules' with regard to the **management** of international trade relations. Not yet, to be sure, with regard to the innovations of the GATT rules themselves during the Uruguay Round. The Dutch considered it shortsighted that this same intergovernmental attitude, looking not for the added value of common interests, but for a compromise, based on the lowest common denominator of purely national interests, tended to prevail during the ongoing inter-governmental conferences mandated to strengthen the European Communities.

It is against this pragmatic background of the Dutch tradition of systematisation and promotion of the development of public international law in general and of public international economic law in particular, that I now submit some general observations, inspired by this book. These observations will deal in turn with (1) the overall concept of the book, (2) the notion 'international economic law', (3) the dialectic relationship between law and economics in this branch of law and (4) its 'hard law' or 'soft law' character. At the end I draw some conclusions, which I hope may contribute to encourage the preparation of new volumes of this series. All of my comments are mainly based on my own experiences, both in practice and during my academic career, as indicated in footnote 1.

Let me state immediately with regard to the **first point** that I consider this book as an excellent introduction to the subject. This favourable judgment is based on its combination of an admirable doctrinal chapter written by the editor, on the definition and sources of international economic law, with chapters on future developments (the new international economic order), the legal limits to effective national control of international economic relations, the three most important existing worldwide international economic organisations, the poor prospects of managed international trade on an intergovernmental basis as exemplified by the Multifibre Arrangement and the Sovereign Debt Crisis. I will come back to some of these chapters in my next observations, but I want to stress at once, that I support wholeheartedly the 'world focus' of the overall concept of this book, as explained in its first chapter.

My **second observation** deals with the notion of 'international economic law'. In the first chapter of the book the editor presents an excellent summary of the various definitions one finds in literature. While I agree with the definition used in this book, I do not believe that I disagree with the editor, when I add that in my opinion this does not exclude that for other purposes other definitions might be more appropriate. Lawyers working for export firms or for transnational corporations, for example, may be interested in the first place in international and comparative private law (property law, contract law, company law) and parts of the public economic, fiscal, social and other legislation in the countries concerned, which may have relevant economic effects on their activities in these countries. An overall view of national systems of merger control or investment regulation might be more relevant to them than a detailed study of the hardly existing multilateral rules in these areas. It follows from available data, that even the recent EEC merger control regulation only covers a very low percentage of the number of national and international mergers affecting interstate trade and which are covered by national systems of merger control. From an academic point of view, the comparative study of internationally relevant parts of private economic law and/or of public economic law affecting international relations of the most important countries in various parts of the world may also be rewarding. For the purpose of the implementation and further development of public international law, however, the notion underlying this book is obviously more appropriate.

My **third observation** deals with the dialectic relationship between law and economics in (national or international) economic law. This relationship can be subdivided into a relationship between economic facts and forces on one hand (national economic policies included) and legal norms on the other; and the relationship between economic policy objectives and principles on the one hand and legal objectives, principles **and institutions** on the other hand. Most of the chapters of this book underline the decisive importance of various aspects of these relationships. The chapter on extraterritorial jurisdiction makes clear that in a world where transnational corporations, investments and trade have increased to such a vast extent, their effective national regulation is doomed to be severely affected by the territorial principle as an inherent element of the powers of the sovereign state. The chapters on international financial institutions, GATT, the MFA and the debt crisis illustrate to what extent market forces and national economic interests and policies can frustrate the attainment of the objectives of international economic organisations. This is especially true if their institutions are weak and based too much on traditional inter-governmental procedures. With regard to the relationship between economic objectives and principles on the one hand and legal objectives, principles and institutions on the other, my experience at the Dutch Ministry of Economic Affairs has already made clear to me that lawyers run the risk of being considered as mere instruments for the implementation of the economic policy objectives, formulated by economists. I presume that many business lawyers will have had the same experience. The chapter on the Sovereign Debt Crisis shows, however, that provided there is a good understanding of economic analysis of the underlying economic **and** national legal facts (in this case the macro-economic and micro-economic prospects of the debtor country and the bank regulations of the creditor countries) a lawyer can contribute creatively to find the most effective solutions for the problems to be solved. This, in my experience, is also true for the role of lawyers in the implementation or interpretation of economic regulations. With regard to price regulations (such as those of the European common agricultural policy), antitrust policy, the control of national subsidies and anti-dumping measures, both their implementation and the defence of the parties before administrative agencies or courts require from the lawyers involved a good understanding of economic analysis, prepared by economists. They also require the ability of a constructive dialogue with economists on both the analysis of the facts and the objectives to be achieved in order to translate these facts and objectives into legal terms, which, in combination with purely legal arguments, can overcome restraint by the competent courts. In other terms: without close co-operation with economists and a mutual understanding of each other's terminology, lawyers are often helpless in this branch of law. If these conditions are fulfilled, however, they can become managers in business, in government or in international organisations just as well as economists and they can defend their clients with optimum results before the administration or the courts. For these reasons I have actively promoted during the academic part of my career a substantial place for courses on the basic micro- and macro-economic issues and methods and their interplay with economic (private and public) law. A good illustration of the usefulness of such an interdisciplinary approach of the interplay of economics, law and politics in the field of 'trade policy and development' can be found in a small book under the quoted title, edited by Gerrit Faber (University Press Rotterdam, The Hague 1990) and reviewed in (1990) 27 Common Market Law Review, 617–623.

My **fourth observation** deals with the 'hard law' or 'soft law' character of international economic law. When I followed courses on public international law at the University of Leiden just before the Second World War, my admired teacher Professor Telders emphasised in his courses that even 'hard law', to be found in treaties and other binding sources of public international law, was 'imperfect law'. Whilst its norms certainly had to be respected, there were – generally speaking – no sanctions or other effective means of enforcement available in case of their violation. He illustrated this by the vain efforts of the League of Nations to stop the illegal Italian aggression of Abyssinia. From this point of view it appears that the borderline between 'hard law' and 'soft law' norms of public international economic law is rather fluid. While for example the agreement within the European Monetary (exchange rate) System not to change the central rates without the agreement of the other partners is a purely political and not a legally binding agreement, it has always been respected. Many of the GATT clauses on the other hand, as this book shows, whilst being 'hard law' in character, are frequently violated.

More generally speaking, Röling noted in one of This' works, quoted in my book on *The Changing Structure of International Economic Law* (Martinus Nijhoff 1981, p.44), that the 'collective legitimation of certain expectations' by the United Nations General Assembly may lead to 'resolutions which can acquire the status of "hard law" through state practice when they are confirmed in later resolutions referring back to them'.

The ILA, in its 'Seoul Declaration' of 1986 (adopted after six years of intensive discussion between lawyers from many developed and developing countries within its competent committee), considered it more cautiously 'appropriate that the declaration should include principles in the sense of generally recognised legal principles, as well as others that need acceptance by treaty or as customary international law in order to obtain binding force'.

One of the principles mentioned in this Declaration, which seems of particular importance in the context of the present observation, is the interpretation in paragraph 4.1, of the duty to co-operate, to be found in Articles 55 and 56 of the UN Charter, as implying 'the progressive development of this duty **in proportion to the growing economic interdependence** between states which should lead therefore in particular to a reinforced co-operation in the fields of international trade, international monetary and financial relations'. (There follows a list of ten other subjects, including the 'co-ordination of the various activities with a view to a coherent implementation of a new international economic order'.)

The Declaration also includes many other principles, including principles of equity and solidarity; a generally accepted formulation of the famous principle of permanent sovereignty over natural resources, economic activities and wealth; the right to development; the principle of a common heritage of mankind; three principles of equality or non-discrimination, including the preferential and non-reciprocal treatment of developing countries; the right to benefit from science and technology; a call for strengthening of the rule of law in international economic relations; and a principle of peaceful settlement of disputes, in particular by recourse to international adjudication, international or transnational arbitration or other international procedures for the settlement of disputes.

A further resolution, proposed by its committee on legal aspects of a new international economic order and adopted by the ILA in 1988 at its Warsaw Conference, more specifically called for a strengthening of the GATT dispute settlement system. Interestingly, in the context of the mentioned lack of effective sanctions in international economic law, and almost as an elaboration of a duty to be found already in Article X.3 of GATT, the resolution on this point adds that 'because of the inherent limits of dispute settlement proceedings among governments ... the Uruguay Round agreements should ... include requirements for the incorporation of precise and unconditional GATT obligations into domestic trade legislation and for national judicial review of executive trade restrictions which tax domestic citizens and restrict their individual freedom of choice and real income'. As one knows, such enforcement by national courts is already the most effective way of enforcement of many rules of the EEC (the doctrine of direct applicability of Community law). It might also be a way to strengthen the GATT discipline.

I end this part of my observations with two more general remarks:

(1)   Not only the last resolution, but also most of the principles to be found in the Seoul Declaration, are drawn from a careful study of principles in existing 'hard law', case law of courts and arbitration tribunals, with varying degrees of extrapolation from general principles, as found only in a specific context. The method of reasoning of the European Court of Justice is not very different from such an approach with regard to general principles of law. The ILA principles merit study, in particular, by lawyers from developing countries involved in the implementation of 'soft law' principles by 'hard law' rules. Such principles may indeed be considered to be at least evolving principles of 'hard law' and could then be implemented by rules of 'hard law'. A seminar, organised by the ILA in Calcutta in March 1991 on the 'implementation of the right to development' has already found an encouraging response.[2]

2.   See for the reports: Subrata Roy Chowdhury, Eric Denters and Paul J.I.M. de Waart (eds.), *The right to development in international law*, Martinus Nijhoff Publishers 1992.

(2) The quoted principle 4.1, in combination with some of the other principles of the Seoul Declaration, could constitute an excellent starting point for a study of the actual and the potential role of the EEC in its implementation. Between its heavily interdependent Member States it constitutes an interesting laboratory of new forms of effective international co-operation, which forms a pole of attraction to Central and Eastern Europe and which can serve as an example for GATT and other international organisations as well by some of its characteristics. It is now finding ways and means for the 'progressive development of co-operation in proportion to the growing interdependence' with EFTA countries, some of the countries of Central Europe, Mediterranean countries outside Europe and – in particular in the Uruguay Round and in specific forms of co-operation with developing countries – with the rest of the world. As the editor rightly observes in the first chapter of this book, the EC rules have also to be set in a world context, even if additionally I submit that principles 4.1 and 4.4 of the Seoul Declaration are quite realistic in their call for a network of more or less intensive forms of co-operation in proportion to different degrees of interdependence at various geographical levels. In order to remain a pole of attraction to the rest of the world, however, the EEC, in my opinion, although continuing to strengthen the added value of pooling parts of the national sovereignty of its Member States, should remain an international organisations *sui generis*. Certainly with particular responsibilities towards its Member States and towards their populations, represented in the European Parliament; but also recognising its responsibility towards the rest of the world and contributing to the establishment of more effective forms of the prevalence of the rule of law in all its international economic relations.

Some conclusions

The various observations made in this Preface tend to suggest that a variety of new subjects offer themselves for treatment in new volumes of this series. The dialectic relationship between law and economics as well as the territorial limits of national regulation of international phenomena, for example, could be illustrated by a study of the growing network of national and supranational systems of control of international mergers with their challenges for close co-operation between lawyers and economists and for eliminating the gaps and conflicts resulting from these networks. Data about the rapid growth of the number of transnational mergers should be included in such a study. The legal problems arising from the growing role of transnational corporations in international economic relations could be studied on the basis of the latest draft of a UN Code of Conduct for transnational corporations, the practical importance of which should be illustrated by some statistical materials on their share in world trade and foreign investments. The general problems of developing countries in the international economic order could also be illustrated by statistical materials about, *inter alia*, the development of their GNP, their foreign debts, the development of foreign and domestic investments, the decline in price of their exported commodities and their share in world trade during the last decade. Such statistical materials, to be found, *inter alia*, in the annual reports of the World Bank should then be accompanied, however, by conclusions about the challenges for the further development of international economic law resulting from these statistics. In order not to prolong this list of potential new subjects for study, I would refer again in conclusion to the two suggestions made at the end of my observations on 'hard law' and 'soft law' principles.

LIST OF CONTRIBUTORS

DAMIAN CHALMERS
Lecturer in Law, University of Liverpool

S.K. CHATTERJEE
Reader and Lecturer in Law, City of London Polytechnic

JONATHAN M. CLARK, JR
Associate, White & Case, London

HENRY G. DARWIN
Barrister, 4/5 Gray's Inn Square, London; Former Second Legal Adviser,
Foreign and Commonwealth Office

HAZEL FOX
Editor, The British Institute of International and Comparative Law;
Honorary Fellow of Somerville College Oxford, Barrister, Lincoln's Inn

IOANNIS TZIONAS
Attorney at Law, Bar of Thessaloniki; LL.M. (London), Ph.D. student
(Institute of Advanced Legal Studies, London); Scholar of the State Schol-
arship Foundation of Greece

GILLIAN WHITE
Professor of International Law, University of Manchester, 1975–1991, now
Emeritus Professor, University of Manchester; Barrister (Gray's Inn)

LIST OF ABBREVIATIONS

AJIL	American Journal of International Law
ASIL	American Society of International Law
BISD	Basic Instruments and Selected Documents
BYIL	British Yearbook of International Law
Can.YBIL	Canadian Yearbook of International Law
CERDS	Charter for Economic Rights and Duties of States
EEC	European Economic Community
GATT	General Agreement on Tariffs and Trade
Germ.YBIL	German Yearbook of International Law
Hag. Rec.	Hague Recueil
IBRD	International Bank for Reconstruction and Development
ICJ	International Court of Justice
ICLQ	International and Comparative Law Quarterly
ICSID	International Centre for Settlement of Investment Disputes
IDA	International Development Association
IFC	International Finance Corporation
ILM	International Legal Materials
IMF	International Monetary Fund
JWT(L)	Journal of World Trade Law
LDC	Less developed country
MFA	Multifibre Arrangement
MFN	Most-favoured-nation
MIGA	Multilateral Investment Guarantee Agency
NIEO	New International Economic Order
OECD	Organisation for Economic Cooperation and Development
OMAs	Orderly marketing arrangements
OPEC	Oil Producing and Exporting Countries
SDRs	Special Drawing Rights
UKTS	United Kingdom Treaty Series
UNCTAD	United Nations Committee for Trade and Development
UNGA Res.	United Nations General Assembly Resolution
UNTS	United Nations Treaty Series
VERs	Voluntary export restraints
VRAs	Voluntary restraint arrangements

INTRODUCTION

THE first volume in this series *International Economic Law and Developing States: Some Aspects* was published in 1988. Both it and the present book are the product of the annual Commonwealth Students' Conferences organised by The British Institute of International and Comparative Law. When I joined the Institute in 1982 as Director, by reason of my own public international law interests and partly in response to those who ran university courses for overseas students, I planned the conferences on the theme of international arrangements relating to natural resources. Over the next ten years we addressed this subject in a number of different ways. We examined the international and municipal law concerning foreign investment and the development of natural resources; we studied the existing instruments - treaty, memorandum of understanding, loan and credit agreements and the new methods advocated in the programme of the NIEO and CERDS by which developing States might more effectively exploit their resources; we identified the actors involved in international economic transactions, global and regional financial institutions, the sovereign borrower, the commercial banks; and we also turned our attention to the machinery for settlement of disputes between exporter and importer States, ICSID, ICC, the London Court of Arbitration and most recently the operation of GATT panels.

In a manner typically English, pragmatic and *ad hoc* we came in these years to study many of the building blocks which civil lawyers with their ability to abstract general characteristics have systematised into the branch of law known as international economic law. The title of the first volume in this series was our first tentative acknowledgement that the topics studied possessed sufficient internal coherence and order to be treated as a separate branch of law. That book has been found useful both by teachers and students in English universities and polytechnics for courses relating to the international regulation of the economies of States.

Encouraged by its success we have now prepared a second volume, a more systematic introduction to international economic law, which brings together the papers given at the Commonwealth Students' Conference held in Brighton in November 1990, supplemented by two papers commissioned expressly for the book. As before the papers are provided by a wide variety of experts drawn from university teachers, lawyers in government service, in the World Bank and in private commercial practice.

In editing the book I have borne in mind that this branch of law remains largely unfamiliar to the average law student in the United Kingdom, even to one who has included a public international law, EC law or international relations course in a three or four year law degree. A number of questions puzzle the newcomer to this branch of law. Is it a public or private law course? how does it differ from a course on international trade or the private international law of commercial transactions? Does the subject primarily involve a study of international banks? if so is it a specialist chapter in the law of international organisations? Or is it more concerned with the exercise of power by States? Should one, then, treat it as an extension of the regulation of the use of force and the law relating to sanctions? How can economic theories and their application in the management of the economies of States, whether singly or in collectivity, generate rules of a legal nature and if they can, what causes them to differ from the rules found in other branches of the law?

These are some of the difficult questions which have to be addressed in any introduction to international economic law and I hope answers or pointers to possible answers will be found in the papers here collected. The book attempts a systematic introduction to the subject. The first two chapters are concerned with the question of sources. In the first chapter 'Definition and Sources' I endeavour to locate this branch of law in relation to general public international law and to identify its distinguishing features, objectives and the materials on which it draws. In the second chapter 'Some Principles of the New International Economic Order and recent trends in International Economic Law', Professor White, until 1991 Professor of International Law, University of Manchester, examines how the principles and programmes of the New International Economic Order have survived the debt crisis and to what extent they have given rise to rules of law in the current measures adopted for debt relief. Any discussion of international regulatory powers must take account of the principles of international law which govern the allocation of jurisdiction between States. Here, the third chapter, 'Extraterritorial Jurisdiction in Economic Transactions' will be of assistance; Henry Darwin, former Second Legal Adviser at the Foreign and Commonwealth Office, provides a brief but comprehensive survey of the different types of dispute, antitrust, international transport, foreign policy goals which have led to assertions of extraterritorial jurisdiction, measures of opposition resisting exorbitant claims and, increasingly, measures of co-operation by States realising that they have reciprocal interests in such jurisdiction.

The next four chapters in the book are concerned with international financial regulatory machinery. Dr S.K. Chatterjee, Senior Lecturer at the City of London Polytechnic, has worked for a period in the World Bank, and his exposition in Chapter IV of the International Monetary Fund, the World Bank and in Chapter V of its associated institutions, the International Development Association and the International Finance Corporation, concentrates on their operational aspects. Dr Chatterjee explains how all these institutions have adapted their original structures to meet changing economic conditions. Our first volume gave some account of the differential and more favourable treatment accorded to developing countries by the General Agreement on Tariffs and Trade (the GATT). In this second volume we have considerably strengthened the coverage of the GATT; Ioannis Tzionas, preparing a doctorate at the Institute of Advanced Legal Studies, achieves a remarkably comprehensive survey of the GATT, its origins and objectives, the sources of GATT law, its institutional framework and the substantive legal foundations upon which the GATT law is based. In the next chapter Damian Chalmers, Lecturer in Law at Liverpool University, provides a case study of the operation of GATT mechanisms in the international trade in textiles and examines how the Multifibre Arrangement provides an alternative legal model to the 'most favoured nation' principle, the cardinal rule of the GATT. Finally Jonathan Clark Jr., who is in practice with the Washington law firm, White and Case and currently based in their London office, reviews the 'Sovereign Debt Crisis' from a commercial lawyer's perspective. This chapter explains the nature of the concern for security of commercial bank creditors and how initial rescheduling of sovereign debt was designed merely to afford a respite of time and temporary deferral of overdue obligations, whereas debt renegotiation, after the Brady initiative and US government's change of position in 1989, was directed at sufficient reduction in debt stock to enable the sovereign borrowers to service their remaining debt without further restructuring.

Throughout all the chapters of the book particular attention has been paid to the interests of developing States. Professor White's chapter assesses the extent to which economic recession and the debt crisis of the 1980s has led to revision of Third World programmes for reform of the legal mechanics of international trade. The chapters on the IMF, World Bank, and the Multi-fibre Arrangement demonstrate the perception of and response of those institutions to developing States' economic needs. Jonathan Clark's chapter reveals the ingenuity of lawyers in devising new loan devices to strike an acceptable balance between the reluctant commercial bank and the hard pressed sovereign borrower.

Students who attended the Institute's annual conferences on international economic law found them hard work, but rewarding for the insight they gave into the international regulation of economic affairs. I hope readers of this book will also find the effort demanded in understanding new material and international finance structures to be equally rewarding.

I am particularly grateful that Professor Ver Loren van Themaat has consented to write the Preface. As the footnotes throughout this book demonstrate, his writings on international economic law have been an inspiration to all the contributors. Sarah McAleer, Publications Officer at the Institute has prepared the manuscript for publication and Anne Goldstein has carried out the typesetting. My thanks go to them and to the Institute for making this second volume possible.

Hazel Fox

Chapter I

THE DEFINITION AND SOURCES OF INTERNATIONAL ECONOMIC LAW

Hazel Fox

Chapter I

THE DEFINITION AND SOURCES OF INTERNATIONAL ECONOMIC LAW

Hazel Fox

I. INTRODUCTION

INTERNATIONAL economic law is not a familiar branch of law to English lawyers.

Yet there is no denying the increase in international co-ordination of economic activity since World War II and the active involvement of the United Kingdom in that process. John Maynard Keynes, the British economist, was a key figure in the planning of the Bretton Woods system, which established the International Monetary Fund (IMF) to ensure economic stability in post-war monetary relations between States and the International Bank for Reconstruction and Development (the World Bank) to provide the development assistance to enable all States to participate in world trade. Britain was a founder member of both organisations and party to the aid arrangements which enabled the economic recovery of Western Europe after the war and to the later aid given on attainment of independence to former colonial territories in Africa, Asia and the Caribbean. The third institution envisaged in the Bretton Woods system, the Trade Organisation, was never set up, due, significantly, to its failure to gain the approval of the Congress of the United States of America. (That State emerged from the Second World War as the free world's most important economic player, at any rate for the next 25 years. During which same period Britain came reluctantly to terms with the realisation that she herself no longer enjoyed that status). It fell to the General Agreement on Tariffs and Trade (the GATT) to fill the gap left by the failure over the Trade Organisation; it was brought into effect provisionally and Britain, as a founder member, along with other Western industrialised States, promoted through its procedures the liberalisation of world trade. In 1973, somewhat belatedly, the United Kingdom became a party to the treaties founding the three European Communities, the European Coal and Steel Community (ECSC), the European Atomic Energy Community (Euratom) and the European Economic Community and thus is now a member State of the world's most important regional grouping of States, the European Economic Community (EEC).

II. WRITINGS ON INTERNATIONAL ECONOMIC LAW

A. English Writers

These events clearly suggest that international regulation of trade and monetary matters have direct relevance to Britain's present and future economic welfare. Why, then, does direct regulation of the international economy take up so little space in current English writings on public international law? Does this omission derive from some obstacle of principle which excludes international law from matters relating to regulation of the economy or from some thinking which considers indirect methods of regulation of economic interests, as in the law of the sea or the law of neutrality, to be the sounder approach? The question is clearly relevant when one is seeking to identify the sources of international economic law.

To some extent the omission of reference to such matters is not surprising because works such as Oppenheim, Brierly, McNair and, to a lesser extent, Fitzmaurice and Waldock, on which much of current English teaching of public international law is based, were written at a time before the international financial institutions and trade regulatory procedures had established themselves. So we find in the last edition of Brierly edited by Waldock, three pages given up to the International Labour Office (ILO), described as 'an agency with a particular structure which gives a peculiar interest'[1] and the

---

1. Brierly, *Law of Nations* ed. Waldock (6th edn 1963) p.122.

IMF and the World Bank only appear in a list of specialised agencies of the United Nations. Lauterpacht, with the assistance of Dr C.W. Jenks, Assistant Director of the ILO, attaches an Appendix with brief sections on the IMF, World Bank and the GATT to his last edition of Oppenheim.[2]

O'Connell, in *International Law* (1970) offered a more sophisticated treatment in a chapter entitled 'Responsibility with respect to monetary sovereignty' giving an account of international law rules relating to monetary policy and the organisational machinery at the international level for the control of financial policy. His first sentence identifies the problems of the subject: 'Money is an economic concept, the juridical characteristics of which are controversial' and explains the role of public international law 'In a work of public international law money is of interest only to the extent to which monetary policy ceases to be a matter of domestic concern and engages the security of nations'.[3] This approach appears to remove from international law the study of the normal regulation of economic conduct of States and confines it to the abnormal use of economic regulation to control conduct of States which is contrary to non-economic norms.

In later years, even though economic regulation through the meetings of the GATT and the work of the IMF and the World Bank had become an established feature of the international scene, this same approach appears to continue to be adopted. More recent writers have applied it in a restrictive manner to exclude any reference to trade or monetary matters save where a threat to or breach of international peace is controlled by the application of economic sanctions or the treatment of aliens results in the expropriation of assets and payment of inadequate compensation. Thus neither Harris nor Shaw have any specific section relating to the IMF, the World Bank or the GATT.[4] The omission of the General Agreement on Tariffs and Trade 1947 in Harris' lists is particularly curious; lack of formal ratification disqualifies it technically from inclusion in the list of treaties but surely it might appear under Other Documents? Brownlie in his *Principles of Public International*

2.   Oppenheim, *International Law Vol. I, Peace* ed. H. Lauterpacht (8th edn 1955).
3.   D.P. O'Connell, *International Law* Vol.II (2nd edn 1970) p.1095.
4.   D.L. Harris, *Cases and Materials on International Law* (3rd edn 1983); M.N. Shaw *International Law* (2nd edn 1982).

Law follows the same line. Foreign investment and expropriation are dealt with under injury to person and property of aliens. The application of trade restrictions to non-nationals is treated shortly under jurisdictional competence. There is no separate heading for economic sanctions. The IMF and the World Bank are scarcely mentioned but his treatment of the United Nations, by reference to specific resolution or activity rather than to examination of its general role, suggests that he views none of these organisations as falling within the purview of principles of international law. After setting out the law of the sea, Brownlie proceeds to Chapter V, Common Amenities and Co-operation in the Use of Resources, which contains a short paragraph entitled Restrictive Practices, in which the following sentences appear:[5]

> The General Agreement on Trade and Tariffs [sic] and the International Monetary Fund regulate respectively trade and currency exchange ... There has been a move away from generalised laissez-faire principles, which favoured the economically strong, towards regimes of sophisticated balance between control and flexibility. The relativity of freedom in economic matters is indicated by the European Economic Community which promotes free interchange internally while appearing externally as a multilateral protectionist arrangement.

In fairness to British writers it must be said that fuller treatment is to be found in specialist works (Mann, Fawcett)[6] but, apart from the pioneer work of Schwarzenberger which stands alone,[7] even here there has been a tendency, as in Bowett's *Law of International Institutions*,[8] to describe constitutional features and structure and not to analyse function and operation, for instance, by reference to the enormous difference of the administrative forms of co-operation of the nineteenth century such as the Universal Postal Union, the International Telecommunications Union, the International Meteorological Organisation and the post-war policy making international financial institutions and trade groupings.

---

5.   Brownlie, *Principles of Public International Law* (4th edn 1990), p.262.
6.   F.A. Mann, *The Legal Aspect of Money* (4th edn 1982); J.E.S. Fawcett, (1971-I) 132 Hague Recueil 365.
7.   G. Schwarzenberger, 'The Principles and Standards of International Economic Law' (1966-I) Hague Recueil 7; *Economic World Order* (1970).
8.   D.W. Bowett, *The Law of International Institutions* (4th edn 1982).

B. Other Writers

When we turn to writings abroad we find more extensive coverage of the subject. Foreign writers consider the normal regulation of economic relations between States, as well as the use of economic measures to prevent illegal use of force, to be a matter for international lawyers. Even here it is always necessary to be aware that the subject is a dynamic one and one to which each writer contributes his own explanation of economic events and their regulation by law. In France after the seminal Colloque d'Orleans of the Société française de droit international held in 1979,[9] a number of student books have been published on international economic law such as Carreau, Juillard, Flory and Michel Belanger.[10] General textbooks provide an introductory account of the international machinery for trade and monetary policy; Quoc, Daillier, Pellet for instance devotes some 70 pages to its treatment.[11] In the United States the focus is significantly different with space being devoted to description of private law trade transactions between individuals and enterprises and of the constitutional powers of the President and Congress on trade; a number of course books have been published, those of Lowenfeld and Jackson being particularly readable and instructive.[12]

9. *Aspects du droit international économique, Colloque d'Orleans*, Société française de droit internationale (1972).

10. D. Carreau, P. Juillard, T. Flory, *Droit international économique* (2nd edn 1990); M. Belanger, *Institutions économiques internationales* (3rd edn 1987).

11. N. Quoc, P. Daillier, A. Pellet, *Droit international public* (3rd edn 1987).

12. A. Lowenfeld, *International Economic Law* Vol.I, International Private Trade (1981); Vol.II, International Private Investment (1982); Vol.III, Trade Controls for Political Ends (1983); Vol.IV, The International Monetary System (1984); Vol.V, Tax Aspects of International Transactions (2nd edn 1984); Vol.VI, Public Controls on International Trade (1983); John H. Jackson, *Legal Problems of International Economic Relations*: Case Materials and Texts on National and International Regulation (1986).

II. THE CONCEPT OF ECONOMIC LAW

A. *National Economic Law*

One explanation, certainly for the coverage of French and Germany public international lawyers, is a tradition of study of economic law in their national systems. Central economic planning has a long history in France: the term 'droit économique' was first employed by Proudhon (1865) and seen as a complementary branch of law to public and civil law.[13] French and German writers have subsequently debated the meaning and scope of the subject,[14] some emphasising the constitutional aspects in the allocation of power between public and private agencies, or examining the juridical nature of property, contract and the ability to engage in economic activities; others seeing it as the means to concentrate and collectivise the production and distribution of goods and performance of services, or stressing the administrative law aspects of the subject as concerned with the machinery and procedures of public powers. It is this last aspect which seems the most relevant to our present discussion – namely the direction of the economy by the State, that is the powers of public authorities to intervene in the running of the economy, the organisation of certain sectors such as transport and agriculture, the protection of national industries, external trade, subsidies, price control, monopolies and restrictive practices. Transposed to the international plane this aspect becomes the legal machinery by which the international economy is directed by States and international organisations and as such broadly corresponds to the subject of international economic law which we are here examining.

There is no similar study of economic law in England.[15] Trade law has essentially been a matter of private law and improvements in trade regulation such as the Hague-Visby and Warsaw-Montreal rules for carriage of goods by

---

13.   Pierre J. Proudhon, *De la capacité politique des classes ouvrières*.

14.   G. Rinck, *Wirtschaftsrecht* (3rd edn 1972); G. Farjat, *Droit économique* (1971); A. Jacquemin and G. Schrans, *Le droit économique* (1970). For a brief English account of this literature see D. Lasok, *The Law of the Economy in the European Communities* (1980).

15.   C. Schmitthoff, 'The Concept of Economic Law in England' [1966] Jo. of Business Law 309; T. Daintith, *The Economic Law of the United Kingdom* (1975).

sea and air,[16] the Antwerp rules relating to salvage,[17] the ICC terms for documentary credits,[18] have been made as much on the initiative of the practitioners in the laws of shipping, banking and commerce in association with foreign colleagues as on the direction of the government. It seems probable that the widespread support for the principles of free trade given by both the British government and British commercial interests in the nineteenth and first half of the twentieth century largely explains this 'hands-off' approach to any discussion of economic law.[19] Lack of basic grounding in economics and mistrust of the unreliable and ephemeral nature of economic theories of State regulation may be additional reasons for this approach. Lawyers can be deterred by the volatility of economic factors – their changeability and difficulty of ascertainment as well as the difficulty of gauging the effect of human intervention on their operation.

Certainly regulation by government of economic matters has not, until Britain's entry into the Common Market, been seen in terms of law. Unlike the US Constitution which allocates trade powers between the President and Congress,[20] the unwritten English constitution appears to vest the trade power unrestrictedly in the executive, and largely to treat it as a non-justiciable matter controlled solely by political action; only where government

---

16.   International Convention for the Unification of Certain Rules of Law relating to Bills of Lading (The Hague Rules) 1924, 120 LNTS 155, UKTS 17 (1931) Cmnd 3806, Protocol to amend the Hague Rules (The Hague-Visby Rules) 1968 UKTS 83 (1977) Cmnd 6944: Convention for the Unification of Certain Rules Relating to International Carriage by Air, Warsaw, 1929 137 LNTS 11, UKTS 11 (1933) Cmd 4284, Montreal Protocols Nos.1 to 4 to amend the Warsaw Convention as amended by Protocol No.1 at the Hague 1975, UK Misc. Nos.12, 15, 16, 17 (1976) Cmnd 6480-3. See generally C. Schmitthoff, *The Law of Export Trade* (9th edn 1990).

17.   See Carver/Colinvaux, *Carriage of Goods by Sea*, (13th edn 1982) Appendix, York Antwerp Rules.

18.   ICC Uniform Customs and Practice for Documentary Credits, 1983 Revision, Publ. No.400.

19.   R.M. McIver, *The Modern State* (1926); Hayek, *The Constitution of Liberty* (1963), chaps. 15 and 16.

20.   US Restatement of the Law Third (1987) Vol.12, pp.266–267; *United States v. Curtis-Wright Export Corp.* (Supreme Ct. of the US, 1936) 299 US 304, 57 S.Ct. 216, *Youngstown Sheet & Tube Co. v. Sawyer* (Supreme Ct. of the US, 1952) 343 US 579, 79 S.Ct. 863; *United States v. Guy W. Capps. Inc.* (US Ct. of Appeal, 4th Cir., 1953) 204, F.2d 655; *Consumers Union of US Inc. v. Kissinger*, (US Ct. of Appeals, District of Columbia, 1974) 506 F.2d 136, Cert.denied, 421, US 1004, 95 S.Ct. 2406 (1975).

regulation changes existing private rights or imposes a financial charge is legislation required to give it effect.[21]

B. Regional and International Economic Law

With decision-making on economic matters now largely transferred to Brussels, to decisions of the Council of Ministers on the proposals of the European Commission, the position has altered; UK membership of the EC is increasingly resulting in the regulation of trade and monetary matters by legal means; regulations of the Council apply directly within the UK and directives in certain circumstances have direct effect, enabling enterprises and individuals to invoke EC law against the government in English courts. The legality of such regulations, directives and decisions of national courts relating to economic matters are all subject to the supervisory jurisdiction of the European Court of Justice.[22]

In these circumstances it seems difficult, if not impossible, for English lawyers to continue their disregard of the subject of the regulation of the economy by governments. English lawyers expert in EC law have an increasing familiarity with regulatory mechanisms of EC law by which Member States take appropriate measures to implement their obligations arising under the removal of obstacles to freedom of movement of persons, services and capital and the co-ordination of economic policies. Yet there is a risk of lopsidedness in this study of regulatory economic mechanisms which have effect in the UK if the EC rules are not set in a world context and considered by reference to international regulation of trade and monetary matters. Historically, by reason of her Empire Britain has considered trade in global terms. Her relations with the United States, her links with her former Dominions, Australia, Canada, India, Pakistan and New Zealand and other more recently independent members of the Commonwealth, have developed an ability to view economic problems in world terms. New

---

21. Phillips and Jackson, *Constitutional Law and Administrative Law* (7th edn 1987) p.217; Daintith (1976) 92 LQR 62 at 72, 77–78.

22. D.A.O. Edwards and R.C. Lowe, *European Community Law, an Introduction* (1991); T.C. Hartley, *The Foundations of European Community Law* (2nd edn 1988); Kapteyn and Ver Loren van Themaat, *The Law of the European Communities* (4th edn 1990).

developments – the emergence of Japan as leader in foreign investment in United States and Western Europe, the economic growth of other States around the Pacific Rim – China, Indonesia; the dismantling of the Russian Empire – require for their appraisal a similar world vision. This world focus is precisely the impetus for the study of international economic law. The presence of the international lawyer with a global focus on the machinery of international economic regulation will provide the necessary corrective to any regional parochialism of the EC lawyer or national protectionism on the part of the US trade lawyer.

III. INTERNATIONAL LAW INCLUDES ECONOMIC REGULATION

A further argument supporting the study of international economic law comes from the international lawyer's own area of competence, the security of nations. It being largely accepted by States, though by no means always observed, that the use of force to change the international status of recognised States is illegal, the time would seem ripe to shift the lawyer's attention to developing principles and rules to regulate the economic conduct of States. In addition to the aims expressed in the preamble 'to maintain international peace and security' and 'to ensure armed force should not be used save in the common interest', the UN Charter also declares the aim 'to employ international machinery for the promotion of the economic and social advancement of all peoples'. Article 1 identifies it to be a purpose of the United Nations 'to achieve international co-operation in solving international problems of an economic ... character' and Chapter IX provides in Article 55 that 'with a view to the creation of conditions of stability and well-being which are necessary for peaceful and friendly relations among nations ... the UN shall promote higher standards of living, full employment and conditions of economic and social progress and development'. By Article 56 Member States pledge themselves to take joint and separate action in co-operation with the UN for the achievement of these purposes and Article 57 provides for the establishment of specialised agencies with wide responsibilities to assist them in these ends. The Friendly Relations Declaration 1970 reiterates the duty of States to 'co-operate in the economic growth throughout the world, especially that of the developing countries'.[23] The IMF, the World Bank, the GATT procedures and operation of free trade areas, notably with the EEC, are the contemporary international machinery by which this third aspect of international security is being pursued. Their impact on the economic welfare of States and peoples of the world is equal to if not exceeding that of the activities of the UN, Human Rights machinery and other forms of co-operation which international lawyers study. This, then, is surely a compelling reason for lawyers to turn their attention to international economic law.

IV. DEFINITION OF INTERNATIONAL ECONOMIC LAW

LET us then see how public international lawyers define their subject. Some definition is particularly essential for the English lawyer before embarking on the subject's study because he enjoys no background familiarity from national law with concepts of economic law.

Definitions fall into three groups; they may be determined by the source of legal authority, the content of the subject or the objective to be achieved. Once again, it must be borne in mind that the subject is under constant change; change in the international economy itself, and in the regulatory mechanisms adopted to deal with it. Definitions will inevitably alter to accommodate these changing facts.

A. Source of Legal Authority

Writers who adopt a definition based on the origin of the rules governing the topic include Schwarzenberger, Carreau, Juillard, Flory, VerLoren van Themaat and Seidl-Hohenveldern.[24] For them international economic law

23. General Assembly Declaration on Principles of International Law Concerning Friendly Relations UNGA Res.2625 (XXV) 24 Oct. 1970, reprinted in Harris, *Cases and Materials on International Law* (1983 edn), Appendix III.

24. G. Schwarzenberger, 'The Principles and Standards of International Economic Law (1966-I) 117 Hague Recueil 7; D. Carreau, P. Juillard, T. Flory, *Droit international économique* (2nd edn 1980); P. Ver Loren van Themaat, *The Changing Structure of International Economic Law* (1981), p.9; I. Seidl-Hohenveldern, 'International Economic Law' (1986) 198 Hague Recueil 11, reprinted

is defined as public international rules for international economic relations. Ver Loren van Themaat speaks of 'the total range of norms (directly or indirectly based on treaties) of public international law with regard to transnational economic transactions'.

B. *Content of Subject*

The second group defines by reference to the content of the subject.[25] Petersmann speaks for writers supporting this method, contrasting 'the international law of the economy' of the first method with his own preferred definition of 'the law of the international economy', 'a functional unity of the private, national and international regulations of the world economy' and consequently including private law, State law and public international law.[26] Schwarzenberger offered, as early as 1966, a definition spanning both these methods:[27]

International economic law is the branch of public international law which is concerned with:
   i.   ownership and exploitation of natural resources;
   ii.   production and distribution of goods;
   iii.   invisible international transactions of an economic and financial nature, currency and finance, related services;
   iv.   status and organisation of those engaged in such activities.

Zamora also adopts a list approach: 'the main subject is international trade in goods and services, international financial transactions and monetary affairs, foreign investment'.[28]

Any definition on a list basis, however, can be criticised as open-ended, quickly becoming out of date and hence requiring continual additions.

and updated as *International Economic Law* (1989), p.1.
   25. E.g. Jackson, *Legal Aspects of International Economic Relations* (1986), p.xix.
   26. E.-U. Petersmann, 'International Economic Theory and International Economic Law: on the Tasks of a Legal Theory of International Economic Order' in R.St.J. Macdonald, D.M. Johnston (eds.), *The Structure and Process of International Law* (1983), at p.251.
   27. G. Schwarzenberger, (1966-I) 117 Hague Recueil 7 and *Economic World Order* (1970) p.4.
   28. S. Zamora, 'Is There Customary International Economic Law?' (1990) 32 Germ.YBIL 9 at 15.

C. Objective

The third group, that of the objective to be achieved, is best illustrated by proponents of the New International Economic Order who see the topic as one of regulation of the international economic order to give a proper place to Third World Developing States. Flory equates international economic law with 'le droit du développement', the law of development,[29] which, as Pellet phrases, concerns the third stage of the three Ds; after decolonisation and (self-)determination of Third World States the law of development will enable these States to attain economic quality with Western industrialised States.[30]

The economic advancement of developing States is not, however, the sole goal pursued by adherents of international economic law. Some see it as a mechanism to curb the domestic protectionism of their own States, the long-term interests of which, in their view, lie in liberalisation of world trade.[31] Others emphasise accountability of both State and international organisation in the management of the world economy to the individual and the private trader and seek to develop procedures to protect the latters' interests.[32] Yet another school of thought would emphasise the shared use of world resources for the common good; the concept of the common heritage applied to outer space and the deep seabed,[33] the moratorium on minerals exploitation in Antarctica,[34] the protection of the environment by restriction of economies

29. M. Flory, *Droit international du développement* (1977).

30. A. Pellet, *Le droit international du développement* (1978). See generally F. Snyder and P. Slinn, *International Law of Development: Comparative Perspectives* (1987).

31. E.-U. Petersmann, *Aussenwirtschaft* (1986), pp.433–434; Hausser, 'Foreign Trade Policy and the Function of Rules for Trade Policy Making' in Detlev, Dicke and Petersmann, *Foreign Trade in the Present and a New International Economic Order* (1988), pp.18–38.

32. See P. Slinn (ed.), *Law and Development for the 1990s: Towards New Dimensions of Accountability* (forthcoming).

33. The Agreement Concerning the Activities of States on the Moon and other celestial bodies 1979, (1979) 18 ILM 1434; Arts.1 and 5 UN Convention on the Law of the Sea 1982, (1982) 21 ILM 1261, Chap.XI.

34. Bonn Protocol for Moratorium on Mineral Activities in Antarctica 1991.

to sustainable growth[35] – all these concerns would be brought within the scope of international economic law.

D. Characteristics of International Economic Law

What are the characteristics of international economic law which these definitions seek to capture? Prosper Weil, in a well-argued paper, identified the original features of the subject.[36] He wrote that it employed novel techniques of fact collection, monitoring of State conduct, and consultation; it abandoned the principle of equality of States in order to reflect the divergent weight which the economic policies of countries have on world development; rules of the GATT and regional economic free trade areas were applied with flexibility, hedged with safeguards and exceptions with their content expressed in vague, temporary and constantly modified terms; dispute settlement by third party adjudication was seen as too adversarial, rigid and slow to be resorted to – a convergence of viewpoints, rather than a clarification of legal rights or a crystallisation of a rule, was sought. These features – lack of certainty, of formality or precision, impermanence of any general rule, absence of judicial sanctions – did not, however, in his view, entitle international economic law to qualify as an independent branch of law. They were more the marks of an immature legal system; and he explained them as due to a lack of cohesiveness in the international community which it was sought to regulate, inability to control or fully understand the economic factors at work resulting in consequent weakness in the community's sanctions, and non-justiciability of its rules.

35. International Union for the Conservation of Natural and Natural Resources and the World Wildlife Fund, *World Conservation Strategy* (1980); World Commission on Environment and Development, *Our Common Future* (1987), p.43.
36. See P. Weil, 'Le droit économique: mythe ou realité' in *Colloque d'Orleans* op. cit. supra n.9 at 1.

V. SOURCES OF INTERNATIONAL ECONOMIC LAW

BEARING these strictures in mind, let us look at the definitions to see how they draw the boundaries of the subject and what source material they rely upon. All the definitions have to deal with the problems which the peculiar characteristics of the subject give rise to. They can be dealt with by reference to the three elements which the title of the subject includes.

A. International

1. States and international organisations

Under 'international' we need to know who are the actors or subjects of this branch of law. Writers who define the subject by source of authority would reply States and international organisations.[37] The study is consequently concerned with their acts, the agreements of States and the constitutions establishing international economic institutions. Source material will, therefore, include international agreements, universal, regional and bilateral: universal agreements include the General Agreement on Tariffs and Trade,[38] international commodity agreements;[39] regional agreements include the European Free Trade Area (EFTA),[40] the Canada–US Free Trade Area,[41] ASEAN,[42] ANDEAN[43] and other agreements relevant to

37. Seidl-Hohenveldern, op. cit. supra n.24.

38. The General Agreement on Tariffs and Trade 30 Oct. 1947 effective 1 Jan. 1948, 55 UNTS 187; Protocol of Provisional Application, 55 UNTS 308. The text of the GATT in its current form is contained in IV GATT Basic Instruments and Selected Documents (BISD).

39. E.g. International Natural Rubber Agreement 1987. For the list of international Commodity agreements see UN Multilateral Treaties deposited with the Secretary-General Status as at 31 Dec. 1990 Chap.XIX. See also McDade, 'The Institutional and Legal Developments of International Commodity Agreements in the Light of the Tin Collapse' in Fox (ed.), *International Economic Law and Developing States*, Vol.I, Some Aspects, chap.VI p.113.

40. Convention establishing the European Free Trade Association 1960, 370 UNTS 3 EFTA Bulletin.

41. Canada–US Free Trade Area (1988) 27 ILM 289.

42. Association of South East Asean Nations comprising Brunei, Indonesia, Malaysia, the Philippines, Singapore and Thailand.

43. (1969) 8 ILM 910.

Central and South America and the Caribbean.[44] (The decision to include these other regional arrangements may turn on whether the criterion is comprehensive coverage of attempts at economic co-operation or the effectiveness of that co-operation). Bilateral agreements would include treaties of friendship, navigation and commerce,[45] investment protection treaties[46] and lump sum agreements settling inter-state claims.[47] There will be some overlap with the constitutions of international economic institutions; the universal group of these will include the articles of association of the IMF,[48] of the World Bank[49] and its ancillary bodies, the International Development Association (IDA),[50] the International Finance Corporation (IFC),[51] the Centre for Settlement of Investment Disputes (ICSID),[52] the Bank for International Settlements (BIS);[53] among the regional constitutions would be those relating to the Organisation for Economic Co-operation (OECD),[54] and to the European Economic Community (EEC). A further category of functional arrangements might

44. See documents in Mutharika, *International Law of Development*, Vol.4, chap.XVI pp.2071–2339; Vol.6, chap.XVII pp.517–597.

45. E.g. Treaty of Friendship, Navigation and Commerce between the United States and Nicaragua 21 Jan. 1956 367 UNTS 3; generally see White in Fox (ed.), *International Economic Law and Developing States*, Vol.I, chap.I p.9 and infra this volume, chap.II p.25.

46. E.g. UK/People's Republic of Bangladesh Agreement for the Promotion and Protection of Investments 19 June 1980, UKTS No.73 (1980). See E. Denza and S. Brooks, 'Investment Protection Treaties – UK Experience' (1987) 36 ICLQ 908.

47. E.g. People's Republic of China/United Kingdom, Concerning the settlement of mutual historical property claims 5 June 1987, UKTS No. 37 (1987) Cmd 198, (1988) 37 ICLQ 1010 and generally Lillich and Weston, *International Claims: Their Settlement by Lump Sum Agreements* (1975).

48. J. Gold, *The Rule of Law in the International Monetary Fund*, IMF Pamphlet Series No.32 (1980).

49. For World Bank see further Chatterjee infra chap.V and Silard in Fox (ed.), *International Economic Law and Developing States*, Vol.I, chap.II p.27.

50. Articles of Agreement of the IDA, 26 Jan. 1960, 439 UNTS 249.

51. Agreement of the International Finance Corporation 25 May 1955, 264 UNTS 117.

52. Convention on the Settlement of Investment Disputes between States and Nationals of other States 18 Mar. 1965, 575 UNTS 159.

53. International Convention respecting the Bank for International Settlements 1930, 104 LNTS 441, UKTS 6 (1931) Cmd. 3484.

54. Convention on the Organisation of Economic Co-operation and Development, 14 Dec. 1960, 88 UNTS 179.

include on a world basis UN specialised agencies such as the Food and Agriculture Organisation (FAO)[55] and ILO,[56] the International Atomic Energy Agency (IAEA) and the World Intellectual Property Organisation (WIPO).[57]

If we add to this body of international agreements secondary material relating to acts of States implementing the agreements or decisions of the financial institutions, and thus include the GATT codes,[58] the MultiFibre Arrangement,[59] decisions of IMF relating to conditionality, the extended fund facility and general agreements to borrow,[60] we will find that we have already a considerable corpus of material to study.

2.   Other actors

But supporters of the other types of definition would extend the range of materials. Petersmann, for instance, sees one of the purposes of international economic regulation as the reduction of the unilateral power of the State to control trade matters.[61] He would extend the study to other actors who have impact on the international economy such as multinational corporations, agencies or sub-units of governments working together, such as the Committee of Central Bankers,[62] the Basel-Mulhouse Airport project,[63] non-governmental organisations such as ICC and IUCN.[64] In doing so he would

55.   TIAS No. 1554, 60 Stat. 1946.

56.   15 UNTS 35; 191 UNTS 143; 466 UNTS 323; 958 UNTS 167.

57.   Statute of the International Atomic Energy Agency 26 Oct. 1956, 510 UNTS 161; Convention establishing the World Intellectual Property Organisation 14 July 1967, 828 UNTS 3. See generally Bowett, *The Law of International Institutions* (4th edn 1982).

58.   BISD 26S.

59.   The Arrangement regarding International Trade in Textiles, BISD 215 3; see Chalmers infra chap.VII.

60.   J. Gold, *Conditionality*, IMF Pamphlet Series No.31 (1979).

61.   Op. cit. supra n.26, p.251.

62.   Committee on Banking Regulations and Supervisory Practices (1986) 25 ILM 978.

63.   French/Swiss Agreement concerning the Basel-Mulhouse Airport 4 July 1949, OJ 3 June 1953; Adam, *Les établissements publics internationaux* (1957), pp.223–247.

64.   International Union for Conservation of Nature and Natural Resources, Morges, Switzerland established October 1948: for resolutions of its Assembly see Rüster/Simma, *International Protection of the Environment* Vol.V, pp.2309–2392 and later volumes.

extend the scope of the materials, particularly in the field of foreign investment; thus documents relating to the conduct of transnational enterprises such as the ICC Guidelines for International Investment 1972, the ILO Tripartite Declaration of Principles relating to Multinational Enterprises and Social Policy 1977, the OECD Declaration on International Investments and Multinational Enterprises 1976, the UN ECOSOC Draft Code of Conduct on Transnational Corporations 1987, would all become relevant.[65] Statements of intent in communiqués of political groupings such as G7 (Canada, France, Germany, Italy, Japan, UK and US) would also be included.

3.   Objectives of international law

Supporters of a policy-orientated definition would extend the material even further. Those who see international economic law in terms of a law of development would include UN General Assembly Resolutions such as Resolution 1803(XVII)[66] on Permanent Sovereignty over Natural Resources, the 1974 Declaration on the Establishment of a New International Economic Order,[67] and the Charter of Economic Rights and Duties of States,[68] the documentation relating to the regional and functional commissions of ECOSOC, UNCTAD's establishment in 1964 and work relating to commodities,[69] UNCITRAL's programme from 1966 for the unification of the law of international trade.[70] Not all collections of documents of international economic law include such material. For instance such documentation is notably absent from the American Society of International Law's database of basic materials set up by its interest group in international economic law. It is presumably excluded on the ground that it is policy not law. Its inclusion

---

65.   For texts see Kunig, Law, Meng (eds.), *International Economic Law. Basic documents* (1989), pp.559–598.

66.   (1963) 2 ILM 223.

67.   (1974) 13 ILM 715.

68.   (1975) 14 ILM 251.

69.   Proceedings of the UNCTAD, First Session, Vol.III, Commodity Trade (UN Publications), Sales No.64 II.B.13.

70.   Report of UNCITRAL on the work of its first session, *Official Records of the General Assembly, Twenty-third session Supplement No.16* (A/7216).

requires a consideration of the second element 'law' in the subject of our study.

B. Law

1.   Treaty

International lawyers are already familiar with the distinction between 'hard' and 'soft' law, and the distinction needs to be re-examined in relation to international economic law. International agreements between States are clearly recognised as a source of law in Article 38 of the ICJ Statute; decisions of international organisations are not specifically mentioned; some derive their legal force expressly from their member States' agreements, others may be treated as evidence of State practice and hence evidence of custom or as themselves constituting international customary law.

2.   Custom

International custom is not frequently invoked as a source of international economic law, it being widely accepted that this subject still today remains largely treaty-based. The international law of expropriation is perhaps one instance of customary economic law.[71]

3.   Soft law

Recommendations of the UN General Assembly and other international organisations, guidelines and programmes for action vary in their authority.[72] Some may rank as declaratory or interpretative of existing law; others' persuasive force will depend on the content, the wording of the text, the voting pattern by which they are adopted, subsequent repetition and practice of States and use by other international agencies – for example, the ICJ's use of the UN General Assembly Resolutions to interpret the UN Charter in the

71.   Zamora, op. cit. supra n.28, p.23.
72.   Sloan, 'General Assembly Resolutions Revisited' (1987) 58 BYIL 39.

Nicaragua v. United States of America (Merits) Case lent the authority of that tribunal to those resolutions.[73]   Lawyers engaged in the study of international economic law will need to assess their sources, to be aware that much may be models, optional standards, or tentative drafts of emerging law rather than crystallised law.   They should keep in mind Sir Hersch Lauterpacht's words in the *Voting Procedure* Case:[74]

> The State ... while not bound to accept the recommendation is bound to give it due consideration. If ... it disregards it, it is bound to explain its reasons.

4.   Private and public law

We also need to understand what is meant by an international transaction. Does it cover any commercial act which takes place across frontiers?   The Third Restatement of the Foreign Relations of the United States seems to be of that view, declaring the law of international economic relations to cover 'all the international law and international agreements governing economic transactions that cross State boundaries or that otherwise have implications for more than one State'.[75]   There is a division of opinion among teachers and writers whether transnational private law transactions are to be totally excluded.   On one view they do not involve international actors; they relate to bilateral commercial matters between private traders adjudicated by private law courts and even where the rules are internationally harmonised by treaty they remain of private law character to be applied by national courts with, in some exceptional cases, the possibility of an appeal to a regional court to provide a uniform ruling.   On this view national commercial laws relating to sale, supply and transport of goods and the financing of foreign sales, and the private international law rules governing such transactions are to be excluded; as also is any *lex mercatoria* or customary rules followed by merchants[76] or any international harmonisation of such substantive rules such as the UN

---

73.   *Case concerning Military and Paramilitary Activities in and against Nicaragua. Nicaragua/United States Merits,* [1986] ICJ Rep. 14 at 99–102, paras.188–192.

74.   *Voting Procedure in Questions relating to reports and petitions concerning the territory of S.W. Africa* [1955] ICJ Rep. 67 at 129 (sep. opinion).

75.   US Restatement of the Law Third (1987) Vol.2, p.261.

76.   Berthold Goldman, *Lex Mercatoria,* Forum Internationale, No.3, 1983.

Uniform International Sales Convention,[77] or internationally harmonised private international law rules such as the Hague Conventions on Service Abroad of Judicial Documents and on Taking Evidence Abroad[78] and international enforcement rules such as the New York Convention on the Recognition of Foreign Arbitral Awards[79] and the Brussels Convention on Jurisdiction and Judgments 1982.[80] On another view, which is the view frequently adopted in US law courses on international trade and that followed in the database of basic documents set up by the ASIL interest group in international economic law, documents governing private law commercial transactions, international litigation and arbitration are relevant to the subject. This view approximates to that noted above as the English viewpoint which considers that if the rules governing the transnational operation of these private law transactions are properly drawn, the unrestricted pursuit of these transactions will be the best means to achieve international economic prosperity.

C. Economic

However, to reduce the subject to manageable proportions for study, both in relating to the private law of international trade and to other branches of international law, we must remind ourselves of the third element in its title, 'economic'. Its inclusion does not require the fashioning of legal concepts to implement the latest economic theory, planned, mixed, privatised, federal, corporatist, or whatever. (Lawyers should follow Dean Colliard's advice and beware of basic concepts, whether economic, mathematical or physical and confine their attention to the consequences of their application). But it does mean that the subject is concerned with the direct legal regulation of the economy by international means. Indirect means through private law transactions or through other branches of international law which protect or

---

77. John O. Honnold, *Uniform Law for International Sales under the 1980 United Nations Convention* (1989).
78. Reproduced in S. O'Malley and A. Layton, *European Civil Practice* (1989) at pp.1781 and 1790 respectively.
79. 330 UNTS 3.
80. Civil Jurisdiction and Judgments Act 1982, Current Law Statutes Annotated 1989 c.27.

balance economic interests of States as in the law of the sea, of the air, of neutrality, or as in international environmental law are therefore to be excluded.

VI. CONCLUSION

To sum up, international economic law may be defined as the law of regulation of the economy by States, international organisations and other international means. Its sources are primarily the treaties and constitutions of international economic institutions which have been referred to in the preceding pages and the consequential decisions and acts implementing the objectives of these treaties and constitutions. The extent to which other material is studied will depend on its classification as a source of law, on the type of definition applied to the subject, and above all, on its suitability for legal analysis and development of legal concepts. The student should never forget his role as a lawyer in handling such material.

As a conclusion to this first chapter which has sought to indicate the definition and source material of this area of law, let me offer some suggestions as to the areas which the subject may cover.

First, the identification, examination and testing by reference to the materials identified in the preceding pages of the fundamental assumptions on which the law must be based. Those assumptions will surely include economic sovereignty and mutual interdependence. The core of the problem lies in striking a balance between these two principles and in applying them in a uniform and fair way to the very different economic situations of large and small States, developed and developing, North and South. Account must also be taken of the position of the private individual or enterprise. This may call for recognition of freedoms of economic action exercisable by all and of internationally derived prohibitions to enforce such freedoms. Part of this enquiry will go to the extent to which such freedoms are to be vested in the State or directly in private enterprises and individuals, thereby bypassing the State.

Second, the subject must cover the manner in which economic mechanisms and international economic institutions regulate the use of natural resources and investment. This may call for a comparative analysis of the major international economic institutions, their objectives, structure, the form and content of the legal means which they use, their co-ordination of action and resolution of disputes internally with Member States, and externally with non-Member States and other international institutions.

Finally, the subject will concern itself with the identification of legal values (often longer-term than transient economic targets) which should control the exercise of economic regulatory powers; such legal values include proper notification, record-keeping and transparency of any action taken, observance of jurisdictional limits, non-retroactivity, proportionality, equity, the recognition of the individual's rights or reasonable expectations relating to the action regulated. The agenda is a lengthy one, but one which by reason of its application of legal techniques to a novel and unchartered territory offers a rewarding challenge to international lawyers entering the twenty-first century.

Chapter II

THE NEW INTERNATIONAL ECONOMIC ORDER: PRINCIPLES AND TRENDS

Gillian White

Chapter II

THE NEW INTERNATIONAL ECONOMIC ORDER: PRINCIPLES AND TRENDS

Gillian White

DESPITE evidence of a distinct lessening of emphasis by developing States on the New International Economic Order (NIEO), the General Assembly still has the matter on its agenda. The 46th session, 1990, included the following agenda item: progressive development of the principles and norms of international law relating to the NIEO, and in a resolution of the 45th session the General Assembly recommended that the Sixth Committee should consider making a final decision at the 46th session on the question of the appropriate forum within the GA framework which would undertake the task of completing this codification and progressive development. Progress here would seem to be at the proverbial snail's pace.

In a perceptive essay Judge Manfred Lachs proposed that world order must rest primarily on three pillars: disarmament and security; equitable economic relations among nations; the protection of humankind and nature from dangerous consequences of science and technology. The second pillar, which aims at putting international economic relations on a more equitable basis 'whether we call it a NIEO or otherwise', would amount only to a continuation and logical development of certain basic principles already adopted by States. He cited Article 55 of the UN Charter, a series of GA resolutions including the Declaration on the Establishment of a NIEO[1] and

---

1.   Res.3201 (S-VII), May 1974.

the Charter of Economic Rights and Duties of States (CERDS),[2] the actions
of international bodies such as UNCTAD, and the concept of the common
heritage of mankind.[3]   In 1988 in a contribution to the debate at the
International Law Association's 63rd Conference on the Report of its
Committee on Legal Aspects of a NIEO, Lachs argued that equity certainly
calls for the recognition of 'the right to development' but that only some
elements of this right have become part of positive law. We are in the midst
of an important law making process, to reinforce existing rules and to make
the law grow so that the existence of this right may become universally
recognised.[4]

In the latest edition of his textbook Ian Brownlie submits that there 'is
probably also a collective duty of member states [of the United Nations] to
create reasonable living standards both for their own peoples and for those
of other states'.[5]

At the level of the GA Sixth Committee, then, and in academic discourse,
the NIEO is by no means defunct. However, one can but agree with the
comment that the original NIEO instruments were very general, abstract and
programmatic.   They were perhaps overloaded and hence unworkable.
Subsequent development has seen a diversion of various topics under
different organisations or forums.[6]

This chapter aims to examine, in the light of recent State practice, some
selected principles from the 1974 Declaration on the Establishment of a
NIEO[7]and to attempt to demonstrate the degree to which these principles
are applied by States and international institutions in their economic
relations. It may be that other legal principles must now be brought into the
frame, to supplement those enunciated in 1974. The subject of international

2.   Res.3281 (XXIX), Dec. 1974; Brownlie, *Basic Documents in International Law* (3rd edn),
p.235.
3.   M. Lachs, 'Law in the World of Today', in A. Boos and H. Siblesz (eds.), *Realism in Law-
Making: Essays in International Law in Honour of Willem Riphagen* (1986), pp.101, 105.
4.   *ILA, Report of 63rd Conference, Warsaw 1988*, p.824.
5.   Brownlie, *Principles of International Law* (4th edn 1990), p.259.
6.   C. Chinkin in ASIL Proceedings 1988, pp.390–391, a valuable contribution to the debate
on international 'hard' and 'soft' law forms. See the same author's 'The challenge of soft law ...'
(1989) 38 ICLQ 850.
7.   Hereafter 'the 1974 Declaration'.

economic relations is so vast, complex and fast-moving that it would be small wonder if the cumbrous and conservative international law making processes have been unable to keep up.

The first area for examination is that of external debt and debt relief. Second, some of the controversial issues surrounding foreign direct investment and permanent sovereignty over natural wealth and resources will be addressed, and finally issues relating to development assistance, internal reform and human rights will be reviewed.

I. DEBT AND DEBT RELIEF

A. The Background

External debt and the various measures of debt relief developed over recent years constitute a major aspect of current State practice in areas of international economic relations covered by NIEO principles. The background to the situation as it stands at the beginning of the 1990s is familiar. The South Commission's 1990 Report stated:[8]

> The most prominent feature of the external environment for development in the 1970s was the large expansion of the volume of international commercial bank loans to developing countries ... [M]any of these countries were experiencing persistent trade imbalances and large fiscal deficits. The correction of these required domestic reforms which involved politically difficult choices, and also risked slowing economic growth temporarily. For the less poor of the developing countries, the abundant supply of foreign credit at low, or even negative, real interest rates therefore offered a way out which avoided the need for economic contraction and hard political choices.

For the least-developed countries the debt burden, owed mainly to governments of developed market economy countries and to the multilateral financial institutions (as private banks have not seen these countries generally to be suitable commercial borrowers), had become in the 1980s equally as crippling to their weaker economies as it had for middle-income heavily indebted States such as Brazil and Mexico. Recognition of the external debt

---

8. *The Challenge to the South, The Report of the South Commission* (hereafter, *Challenge*) (OUP, 1990) pp.55–56.

situation as 'a major development issue' came in the fourth Lomé Convention 1990, between the European Community and its Member States, on one hand, and 69 African, Caribbean and Pacific States on the other.[9] Article 239 states:

> The ACP States and the Community share the view that the external debt situation of ACP States has emerged as a major development issue, and that the associated heavy debt-servicing obligations contribute to constraints on import capacity and the level of investments in these States, thus affecting their growth and development.

Taking the developing States as a group, debt-related transfers were reversed in direction from 1983, when service repayments of principal and interest charges exceeded loan disbursements.[10] By 1988, the only developing States that were still net recipients of debt-related resources were those of South Asia. The South Commission singled out debt issues as paramount among those on which action is urgent:[11]

> Achieving a durable solution to this problem has become an absolute prerequisite for any resumption of growth, not only in the heavily indebted countries, but in most parts of the South.

Several Central and Latin American States unilaterally suspended all or part of their debt service between 1985[12] and 1988.[13] Brazil made the first challenge by a major debtor when it suspended payments for 19 months in 1987–88 on its medium- and long-term debt of $110.5 billion.[14] This challenge ended when Brazil requested rescheduling negotiations with creditor banks and agreement was reached with them in 1988.

9.   Hereafter 'Lomé IV'. Text in (1990) 23 ILM 783 and *The Courier*, No. 120, March-April 1990.

10.   See *Challenge*, pp.57–58, 60; *IBRD World Debt Tables 1989–90*; ILA Committee on Int'l Monetary Law, in *Report of 63rd Conference 1988*, pp.419–421; J.E. Spero, *The Politics of International Economic Relations* (4th edn 1990), pp.185–188 (hereafter *Spero*); S. George, *A Fate Worse than Debt* (Penguin Books, 1988) pp.13, 63, 236 (hereafter *George*).

11.   *Challenge*, p.226.

12.   Peru's newly elected government limited debt service for a time to 10% of export earnings, *Spero*, p.190; *George*, pp.216–218, 238.

13.   Eg. Bolivia, Costa Rica, Dominican Republic, Ecuador, Honduras: see *Spero*, p.191.

14.   *Spero*, p.191; *George*, pp.238–239.

From the perspective of this chapter, which seeks to illustrate from State practice the continuing existence and viability, or otherwise, of some of the normative principles in the 1974 Declaration, response of private banks to such moves by debtor governments and the numerous sophisticated restructuring or 'exit' devices developed in the late 1980s are of secondary significance. Limitations of space preclude analysis of this aspect of the debt crisis and its management by creditor banks with some input from, in particular, the US administration.[15] Rather, the Toronto Summit of 1988 and related developments merit attention, as these were moves on the inter-State level with minimal or ancillary involvement of private banks.

B. Relevant Principles of the NIEO

The initial step in examining this practice must be the 1974 Declaration. Which of the 20 principles formulated as the foundation of the NIEO are relevant to the developing States' external debt problems and the responses of developed States? Principles (1) and (o) appear to be centrally relevant:

---

15. See the accounts in *Spero*, pp.178–195; the Baker plan, from the then Secretary of the US Treasury, (1985) 25 ILM 412 and IMF Press Release No.13, Joint Ann. Discussion, Board of Governors, 1985; *George*, pp.189–193; the Brady initiative of March 1989 by US Treasurer Nicholas Brady, *Treasury News*, 10 March 1989, *IMF Ann. Rep. 1989*, pp.23 et seq and *Spero* pp.193–195; *Challenge*, pp.227–228.

For criticism of Baker and Brady plans see D. Suratgar, 'A Call for Renewed Liberal Internationalism', (1990) 20 Ga.J. Int'l & Comp.L. 571.

On restructuring, re-purchasing and swap schemes see, *inter alia*, Sperber, 'Debt-Equity Swapping', (1988) 26 Colum. J. Transnat'l. L. 377, a detailed and fully referenced account of this process with case studies; Gibson and Curtis, 'A Debt-for-Nature Blueprint', (1990) 28 Colum. J. Transnat'l. L. 332, on schemes developed by US banks and several Central and Latin American governments; Burton, 'Debt for Development: A New Opportunity for Non-profits, Commercial Banks and Developing States', (1990) 31 Harv. Int'l. L.J. 233. On similar, but more radical lines see *George*, chap.14, 'The 3-D Solution: Debt, Development, Democracy', especially pp.244–258.

Few, if any, of these devices are original conceptions. See B. Eichengreen and P.H. Lindert, *The International Debt Crisis in Historical Perspective* (1989) *passim*, and F.G. Dawson, *The First Latin American Debt Crisis* (Yale UP, 1990), p.2. See generally chap.VIII infra p.219, 'The Sovereign Debt Crisis: A Lawyer's Perspective'.

(l) Ensuring that one of the main aims of the reformed international monetary system shall be the promotion of the development of the developing countries and the adequate flow of real resources to them;[16]

(o) Securing favourable conditions for the transfer of financial resources to developing countries;

Two other principles, (k) and (r), also speak to certain aspects of the overall debt problem, at least in some instances:

(k) Extension of active assistance to developing countries by the whole international community, free of any political or military conditions;

(r) The need for developing countries to concentrate all their resources for the cause of development.

C. Other Legal Concepts and Principles

A second step is to note the entry into the discussion of these issues of the concepts of shared or co-responsibility, and 'equitable burden sharing'.[17] At its 1986 Conference in Seoul the International Law Association adopted a Declaration on the Progressive Development of Principles of Public International Law relating to a NIEO.[18] The ILA Committee on Legal Aspects of a NIEO in its Report to the 1988 Conference of the Association commented on the recognition by all participating States in UNCTAD VII of the shared responsibility of the main parties concerned in the debt

---

16. For the events between 1971 and 1974 which led ultimately to the reform of the IMF system for multilateral management of the international monetary system embodied in the Second Amendment to the IMF Articles of Agreement, 1976, see *Spero*, pp.45–48.

17. See *ILA Report of 63rd Conference 1988*, Committee on Legal Aspects of a NIEO, p.798; UNCTAD VII 1987, Final Act para.48: 'There has been an evolving response of the international community to the debt problem. It recognises the shared responsibility of the main parties concerned (developing debtor countries, developed creditor countries, private and multilateral financial institutions).' In para.44 of the Final Act the States declare that the response to the crisis 'should continue to evolve, through continuous dialogue and shared responsibility'. They then set out 13 elements in the strategy of response, calling on parties involved to undertake specified acts and policies.

See also *Challenge*, p.269; *Spero*, pp.352–353, 355, with strong notes of caution on probable responses of developed States.

18. Hereafter 'Seoul Declaration'.

problem.[19] The Committee called for a more stable international economic environment and the strengthening of 'even handed multilateral surveillance' to extend to developed States' economic and financial arrangement.[20] The Committee pointed to paragraph 3.2 of the Seoul Declaration as relevant to possible solutions in this difficult area:

> The principle of solidarity reflects the growing interdependence of economic development, the growing recognition that States have to be made responsible for the external effects of their economic policies and the growing awareness that underdevelopment or wrong development of national economies is also harmful to other nations and endangers the maintenance of peace ... all States whose economic, monetary and financial policies have a substantial impact on other States, should conduct their economic policies in a manner which takes into account the interests of other countries by appropriate procedures of consultation. In the legitimate exercise of their economic sovereignty, they should seek to avoid any measure which causes substantial injury to other States, in particular to the interests of developing States and their peoples.

The same Committee in its Report to the 1990 Conference highlighted this principle of solidarity and noted that the Mexican debt accord of 1989, under the Brady plan, involved a reduction of $7 billion from the State's debt to US banks and the reduction of the interest rate on a second block loan of $22.5 billion from an average of 10% to a fixed 6.25%. A working paper by Professor Peter Sarcevic interpreted this agreement[21] as a move in the direction advocated by the 1988 Warsaw Report and as an application of the principles of solidarity and of *sic utere tuo ut alienum non laedas*, expressed in the final sentence of paragraph 3.2 of the Seoul Declaration.[22] Certainly the Mexican agreement was the first time that private banks accepted debt forgiveness and reduced overall debt levels. Whether the involvement of the international institutions and Japan can be viewed as placing this example into the category of State practice is problematic. Even if such a categorisation were justified, evidence that the decisions of any creditor government

19. See supra n.17.
20. For recent developments in surveillance in the GATT see A. Qureshi in (1990) 24 JWT 147.
21. The agreement involved new loans by the Japanese government, funds from the IMF and World Bank, credits of the Bank for International Settlements and guarantee funds from Mexico itself, see *Spero*, p.194.
22. See paras.34 and 40 of the Committee's 1990 Report.

or international body in agreeing to the arrangement were based on any sense of *opinio juris* is lacking. Professor Sarcevic's evaluation must be treated with some caution.

Third, the relevance of certain other established principles from private law and the international law of treaties and State responsibility may be undisputed at the theoretical level, but again it may be hard to discover evidence that the international actors involved regarded themselves as applying these principles to their negotiated reschedulings or debt forgiveness decisions. The principles are those of binding contract subject to supervening impossibility of performance, the plea of fundamental change of circumstances,[23] the plea of necessity as precluding wrongfulness of an act which would otherwise be in breach of a State's international obligation,[24] and the proposition that there is a legal duty on creditors to renegotiate a loan agreement at the request of the debtor.[25]

D. *The Toronto Summit and Other Developments*

At the June 1988 Toronto summit the G7 Heads of State and government[26] reached consensus on new terms for rescheduling the debt owed to official creditors by the poorest developing States who were also undertaking internationally approved adjustment programmes. A 'framework of comparability' was created, within which government creditors could choose among the following debt relief measures:[27]

(1) concessional interest rates, usually on shorter maturities;
(2) longer repayment periods at commercial rates of interest;
(3) partial write-offs of debt-service obligations;
(4) a combination of the above.

23. As in the V.C. on the Law of Treaties, Art.62.
24. See ILC Draft Articles on State Responsibility, Art.33, YBILC 1980, Vol.II, Part Two, p.34.
25. See ILA Committee on Int'l Monetary Law, in *Report of 63rd Conference 1988*, pp.422–426, 461.
26. The G7 comprises the USA, Federal Republic of Germany, Japan, France, Canada, the UK and Italy.
27. *IMF Survey*, 27 June 1988, pp.219–223.

'The understanding was that concessions of different kinds should involve comparable burdens'.[28] Later in 1988 the Paris Club of official creditors[29] agreed on how the various options would work:[30]

(a) **Partial write-off:** one-third of debt service originally due during the renegotiated period would be forgiven; the remainder would be rescheduled under fairly standard terms for low-income countries; viz. 14 year maturity with an 8 year grace period, at market rates;
(b) **Extended maturities:** the full amount of debt service being renegotiated would be rescheduled at market rates, but with 25 year maturity and 14 year grace period;
(c) **Concessional interest rates:** the full amount would be rescheduled as in (b) but at the short term of (a) and at a rate 3.5% points below market rates or one-half of market rates, whichever gave the *smaller* reduction.

The short-term cash flow benefits for debtor States under these concessionary deals were not large. The World Bank estimated that for countries in its Special Programme for Africa debt-service payments in 1989–90 would fall by less than 5% compared with other recent reschedulings.[31] Nevertheless, the Toronto move was 'the first recognition of a need for debt relief ...'.[32] Previously, official creditors had resisted any proposal for writing off part or all of even the poorest countries' debts.

In March 1990 it was reported that the US Agency for International Development had signed agreements relieving ten African States of some US

28. *World Economic Survey 1989* (UN publication), p.67.
29. The Paris Club has no fixed membership or institutional structure. It represents practices and procedures which have evolved since the first ad hoc meeting was convened for Argentina in 1956. Meetings are open to all official creditors accepting these practices and procedures. The IMF, IBRD, UNCTAD and regional development banks are invited to make presentations. See P. Keller and N. Weerasinghe, *Multilateral Official Debt Rescheduling – Recent Experience* (IMF, May 1988) p.20.
30. Options (a) and (c) are considered to carry comparable degrees of concessionality. Option (b) involves no concessionality in terms of discounted present value *if* the longer-term claims are paid, but it clearly is more risky for creditors.
31. IBRD, *World Debt Tables 1990*; F. Palanza, 'Africa's Debt: How Much Progress ... in the last Three Years?'; Eur. Investment Bank Papers No.15, Dec. 1990, p.41 at 45, 46; OECD, *Financing and External Debt of Developing Countries – 1989 Survey* (July 1990); and *George*, p.242. For earlier Paris Club reschedulings, always on a case-by-case basis, see Keller and Weerasinghe, *passim*.
32. *Spero*, p.192.

$305 million official debt.[33] A further step in this direction came at the September 1990 annual meeting of Commonwealth Finance ministers when a UK initiative, supported by Canada and others, was carried through to the meeting of G7 finance ministers later the same month. This plan envisaged a cut of US $18,300 million from the $27,500 million official debt owed by 19 low-income countries, all in sub-Saharan Africa except Bolivia and Guyana, and all qualified for relief under the Toronto summit terms. The 1990 'enhanced' Toronto terms included four elements:[34]

(1) Paris Club creditors would write off two-thirds of rescheduled debt;
(2) These creditors would deal with the total debt of an eligible State in one operation rather than in one-year maturities;
(3) Interest payments would be capitalised for the first 5 years of rescheduling, *with debt repayments linked to the debtor State's export capacity*; [emphasis added]
(4) Repayment period would be extended from 14 to 25 years.

These proposals were welcomed by IMF Managing Director, Michel Camdessus, at the 1990 annual joint meeting of Fund and Bank governors.

A fourth example of cancellation (or forgiveness) of official debt was the European Community's decision early in 1991 to cancel the debt owed by ACP States to the Community, as distinct from debts to individual Member States.[35] These debts arose from special loans under Lomé provisions, including SYSMIN and European Development Fund loans; repayment of STABEX transfers; and EDF risk capital loans. The Commission Vice-President proposing cancellation stressed that in the spirit of ACP–EC relations under successive Lomé Conventions the Community should not be cast merely in the role of creditor but rather as a co-partner in development.[36] It should be noted that this write-off amounts to only 2% of the total debt of the ACP countries, which now reaches some 130 billion ECUs.

---

33.   The States were Benin, Cameroon, Ghana, Guinea, Kenya, Madagascar, Malawi, Mali, Nigeria and Zaire. Agreements with Ivory Coast, Niger and Uganda were anticipated; these would extend total reductions to $745m. out of a total sub-Saharan African debt to the US Government of $6.600m. To qualify, debtor States had to be undertaking IMF or World Bank approved economic reforms.
34.   These developments are summarised in *Keesing's Record of World Events*, 1990, p.37894.
35.   Pursuant to policies reflected in Arts.239–241, Lomé IV.
36.   *The Courier*, No.125, Jan–Feb. 1991, p.9.

The write-off excludes loans from the European Investment Bank's own resources, supplied through the financial markets.

E. Evaluation of Debt
Relief Measures

An interim evaluation by UNCTAD in 1989 noted that several countries had benefited from concessional relief in the Paris Club since October 1988 but that the Toronto terms had major shortcomings. Eligibility seemed to be confined to States within the World Bank Special Programme for sub-Saharan Africa, thus excluding some of the most debt-distressed low-income countries; the debt service reduction was small; not all obligations to Paris Club creditors were covered, and the share of Paris Club debt in these States' total debt was limited. A final criticism was that some creditor governments were financing debt relief by transferring funds from their aid budgets to their export credit agencies. More positively, UNCTAD observed that in recent years an increasing number of creditor countries had converted Official Development Assistance (ODA) debt of poorer developing countries into grants in line with UNCTAD resolution 165 (S-IX) of 1978.[37] The USSR, France and the USA were mentioned as having so acted.[38]

F. The World Bank's Debt
Reduction Facility

As for the commercial debt burden of the low-income least-developed States,[39] the World Bank introduced a Debt Reduction Facility (DRF) in

37. Gen. Ass. Off. Rec. 33rd session, Supp. No.15, A/33/15, Vol.I, part 2, annex I.

38. *UNCTAD, Trade and Development Report 1989* (UN 1989) page X. See also *UNCTAD, The Least Developed Countries, 1989 Report* (UN TD/B/1238) p.117. Note that ODA debts owed to OPEC countries and China are not covered by Res.165 (S-IX).

39. For this category, identified first in UNCTAD whose definition was used and adapted by the UNGA in Res.2768 (XXVI) in 1971, see W. Verwey, 'The UN and the Least Developed Countries: An Exploration in the Grey Zones of International Law'; in J. Makarczyk (ed.), *Essays in International Law in Honour of Judge Manfred Lachs* (Nijhoff, 1984), p.531. See also CERDS, Art.25, and the GATT Decision on Differential and More Favourable Treatment etc., the 'Enabling Clause' of 1979, BISD, 26th Supp. 1980.

August 1989 for IDA-only countries, a category which includes most of the least-developed States.[40] The scheme supports debt reduction operations on a grant basis, through cash purchases of commercial debt at substantial discounts. Support is on the familiar case-by-case basis so far insisted upon by developed creditor States, and a State applying under DRF should have 'an agreed medium-term adjustment programme and a strategy for debt management, including a programme for resolving its commercial debt problem'.[41] The UNCTAD Secretariat welcomed the creation of DRF but called for an integrated debt relief and aid strategy.[42] The UNCTAD Report urged comprehensive implementation of UNCTAD Resolution 165 (S-IX) which should result in writing off ODA debt and should involve all creditor countries; there should also be greater use of the Toronto options and a wider coverage of consolidation to cover 100% of Paris Club obligations. UNCTAD called for urgent study of ways in which debt service obligations to the multilateral institutions (which are not reschedulable) might be alleviated 'while safeguarding the institutions' credit worthiness'.[43]

G. And What of the Law?

A considered juridical assessment of this fast-moving area of practice is almost certainly premature. The following preliminary and tentative observations are offered. First, the hesitation of the ILA Monetary Law Committee in 1988 regarding the existence of a customary law obligation on creditor States to renegotiate official debt in face of 'certain magnitudes' of an external debt problem is well founded. As the Committee observe it would have to be shown that these negotiations were in fact based on the conviction of mutual obligations of both parties rather than a sense of practical convenience. It appears that this would be difficult if not impossible to establish.[44]

---

40.   IDA soft loans are reserved for member States with GNP per capita of $480 or less (in 1987 dollars), *World Bank Ann. Rep. 1989*, p.3. See further Chatterjee, chap.V infra.

41.   *UNCTAD, The Least Developed Countries, 1989 Report*, pp.119–120.

42.   As does the South Commission, see *Challenge*, pp.227–228.

43.   *UNCTAD*, loc. cit. n.41, p.121.

44.   *ILA, Report of 63rd Conference, Warsaw 1988*, p.424. Professor Bothe of Germany opined

In the practice of the Paris Club in the 1980s preconditions for the initiation of a renegotiation were that official creditors must be convinced that the debtor will be unable to meet its external payments obligations unless it receives debt relief, and that the debtor will take steps to eliminate the causes of payments difficulties and achieve lasting improvement in its payments position.[45] This hardly resembles recognition of a duty to renegotiate upon simple request. The operative legal principle remains consent, and if creditor governments insist on the case-by-case approach they are not acting unlawfully.

Second, as to the plea of necessity, an echo of this argument can be discerned in the first Paris Club precondition (above). In the Commentary to draft Article 33 in its articles on State responsibility the ILC refer to their formulation that 'necessity' means that the act not in conformity with the State's international obligation must be the only means of safeguarding 'an essential interest of the State'. The Commentary assumes that the maintenance of conditions in which essential services can function, the keeping of domestic peace, the survival of part of the State's population and the ecological preservation of all or part of its territory are circumstances which may trigger the lawful invocation of the principle of necessity.[46] If the principle is applicable in such circumstances to inter-State debt relations, it must apply also, according to the unimpeachable argument of the ILA Committee, where the creditor is a private foreign party, such as a bank. Such a creditor cannot enjoy greater protection *vis-à-vis* the debtor State than can a creditor State in an analogous situation. It will be interesting, and of significance for possible evidence of *opinio juris* on necessity in the debt-burden case, to see what observations governments may make to the ILC draft article.

A final practical comment by the Chairman of the ILA Monetary Committee was that the international financial institutions were equipped

---

that Paris Club practice had evolved into a rule of customary law that it would be illegal for creditor States not to accede to a debtor State's request to renegotiate in the Paris Club or comparable framework, idem, p.461.

45. Keller and Weerasinghe, op. cit. n.29 supra, at p.20.

46. YBILC 1980, Vol.II, Part Two, p.35, and ILA Report of International Monetary Law Committee in *ILA, Report of the 63rd Conference*, pp.426–433.

both to propose and apply a procedure surveying the use of the necessity plea:[47]

including measures designed to prevent excessive recourse to that device, notably by strengthening prudential surveillance of general purpose borrowing without hindering financial transactions incident to trade and services.

As for equitable burden sharing and the principle of solidarity, some may see signs of acceptance of these notions in recent State practice. Others may discern simple hard-headed pragmatism and negotiated compromises, or unilateral concessions *ex gratia* and 'without prejudice' to any legal rights or obligations in general international law. A court applying the sources of law in Article 38 of the ICJ Statute might be hard to convince that such notions had emerged from the realms of political claims and academic theorising to become principles of customary international law.

II. FOREIGN DIRECT INVESTMENT, THE NIEO AND PERMANENT SOVEREIGNTY

THESE aspects of claims for a NIEO have had more attention devoted to them by international lawyers than probably all the other issues in the 1974 resolutions put together. There is a huge and, on the whole, accessible literature dating from well before 1974 on international legal aspects of foreign direct investment and the principle of permanent sovereignty of States over their natural resources and, in some versions, over their wealth and 'all economic activities'.[48] For this reason, this section will be confined to a few brief comments on some of the remarkable recent trends in State practice.

For the record, the two relevant principles in the 1974 Declaration are:

(e) Full permanent sovereignty of every State over its natural resources and all economic activities. In order to safeguard these resources, each State is entitled to exercise effective control over them and their exploitation with means suitable to its own situation, including the right to nationalisation or transfer of ownership to its nationals, this right being an expression of the full permanent sovereignty of the State. No State may be subjected to

---

47. *ILA, Report of the 63rd Conference 1988*, p.834.
48. See principle (e) of the 1974 Declaration, quoted in the text.

economic, political or any other type of coercion to prevent the free and full exercise of this inalienable right;

(g) Regulation and supervision of the activities of transnational corporations by taking measures in the interest of the national economies of the countries where such transnational corporations operate on the basis of the full sovereignty of those countries;

Principle (p) on transfer of technology should also be borne in mind, but it is not possible to devote space to this aspect here.

It is also pertinent to be reminded of salient paragraphs of the earlier GA resolution of 1962 on Permanent Sovereignty:[49]

(1) The rights of peoples and nations to permanent sovereignty over their natural wealth and resources must be exercised in the interest of their national development and of the well-being of the people of the State concerned;

(2) The exploration, development and disposition of such resources, as well as the import of the foreign capital required for these purposes, should be in conformity with the rules and conditions which the peoples and nations freely consider to be necessary or desirable with regard to the authorisation, restriction or prohibition of such activities;

(3) In cases where authorisation is granted, the capital imported and the earnings on that capital shall be governed by the terms thereof, by the national legislation in force, and by international law. The profits derived must be shared in the proportions freely agreed upon, in each case, between the investors and the recipient State, due care being taken to ensure that there is no impairment, for any reason, of that State's sovereignty over its natural wealth and resources;

(4) Nationalisation, expropriation or requisitioning shall be based on grounds or reasons of public utility, security or the national interest which are recognised as overriding purely individual or private interests, both domestic and foreign. In such cases the owner shall be paid appropriate compensation, in accordance with the rules in force in the State taking such measures in the exercise of its sovereignty and in accordance with international law. In any case where the question of compensation gives rise to a controversy, the national jurisdiction of the State taking such measures shall be exhausted. However, upon agreement by sovereign States and other parties concerned, settlement of the dispute should be made through arbitration or international adjudication;

(7) Violation of the rights of peoples and nations to sovereignty over their natural wealth and resources is contrary to the spirit and principles of the Charter of the United Nations and hinders the development of international co-operation and the maintenance of peace;

(8) Foreign investment agreements freely entered into by, or between, sovereign States shall be observed in good faith; States and international organisations shall strictly and conscientiously respect the sovereignty of peoples and nations over their natural wealth

49. Res.1803 (XVII); Brownlie, *Basic Documents*, p.231.

and resources in accordance with the Charter and the principles set forth in the present resolution.

The controversial Article 2 of the CERDS perhaps completes 'the story so far' in terms of GA resolutions:

(1) Every State has and shall freely exercise full permanent sovereignty, including possession, use and disposal, over all its wealth, natural resources and economic activities.
(2) Each State has the right:
    (a)   To regulate and exercise authority over foreign investment within its national jurisdiction in accordance with its laws and regulations and in conformity with its national objectives and priorities. No State shall be compelled to grant preferential treatment to foreign investment;
    (b)   To regulate and supervise the activities of transnational corporations within its national jurisdiction and take measures to ensure that such activities comply with its laws, rules and regulations and conform with its economic and social policies. Transnational corporations shall not intervene in the internal affairs of a host State. Every State should, with full regard for its sovereign rights, co-operate with other States in the exercise of the right set forth in this subparagraph;
    (c)   To nationalise, expropriate or transfer ownership of foreign property, in which case appropriate compensation should be paid by the State adopting such measures, taking into account its relevant laws and regulations and all circumstances that the State considers pertinent. In any case where the question of compensation gives rise to a controversy, it shall be settled under the domestic law of the nationalising State and by its tribunals, unless it is freely and mutually agreed by all States concerned that other peaceful means be sought on the basis of the sovereign equality of States and in accordance with the principle of free choice of means.[50]

A. Economic Background to
Recent Trends

Recent assessments from both sides of the economic divide, the OECD and UNCTAD secretariats, speak of the change in attitude to foreign investment by many developing countries. A 1990 OECD study observes that such investment has won more appreciation by these countries as the costs of excessive borrowing for state enterprises have been recognised. Economic growth has been found to depend largely on private enterprise and invest-

---

50. Res.3281 (XXIX); Brownlie, op. cit. supra n.49, p.235.

ment,[51] the debt crisis has curtailed private bank lending, and ODA has not substantially 'taken up the slack'.[52] In these circumstances:[53]

> most developing countries have stepped up their efforts to attract foreign investment, not only for its contribution to their productive capital but also for its technology, training, management, and international marketing advantages.

The UNCTAD Secretariat's *Trade and Development Report, 1989* states:[54]

> Faced with a very limited savings capacity, a mounting debt-service burden, slow growth and even stagnation of export earnings and concessional flows, as well as the virtual collapse of commercial bank lending, LDCs have been turning towards foreign direct investment as a means of securing financial resources for their economic development and structural transformation.

The report points to reform of national investment laws and codes undertaken by many LDCs to encourage the establishment of foreign (or foreign-controlled) enterprises and to allow the employment of foreign manpower. Incentives offered by several LDCs include liberalisation of profit repatriation rules, tax holidays, and special foreign exchange and tax privileges to export-processing zones, set up on an 'enclave' basis separate from the domestic economy.

A more cautious note was struck by the South Commission who suggest that direct foreign investment 'may become increasingly important in meeting some of the capital requirements of developing the South'.[55] The thrust of their proposals, however, is the desirability of encouraging more South–South investment.[56]

With reference to manufactured exports, a recent study for the UN Centre on Transnational Corporations concludes that developing countries' need for viable export industries is generally agreed. Exports facilitate imports of

---

51. Cf. the detailed case studies by M. Shafer, 'Capturing the mineral multinationals: advantage or disadvantage?' (1983, Winter) 37 Int. Organisation, 91–119.
52. *Promoting Private Enterprise in Developing Countries* (OECD, Paris 1990).
53. Idem, p.36.
54. At p.157.
55. *Challenge*, p.233.
56. Idem, pp.183–184, 233.

necessary technology and products that the exporting country may be unable to produce, and are vital means of servicing external debt:[57]

> In this situation, there has been a major change in developing country attitudes towards transnational corporations. Many countries that were earlier hesitant regarding foreign direct investment are now welcoming foreign firms.

B. Bilateral Investment Treaties

There are now over 300 bilateral treaties on investment, sometimes referred to as BITs or IPPAs (for Investment Promotion and Protection Agreements). Their coverage in terms of developing States parties ranges from some of the least-developed countries in Asia and Africa to middle-income developing countries such as China, Malaysia, Morocco and Tunisia, and even to some Latin American States which for so long opposed any such commitments at the treaty level, including Bolivia, Panama, Paraguay and Uruguay. On the developed States' side, most of the OECD countries have concluded at least two or three BITs, and Germany has signed some 60. The United Kingdom's total to date is approximately 30, some 25 of which are in force.[58] The standards of treatment of investments by nationals or companies of one party in the territory of the other party stipulated for in these treaties reflect fairly closely the standards considered by Western States and many lawyers from those States to be required by customary international law. These treaty clauses stand in contrast to most formulations in the permanent sovereignty and NIEO resolutions.[59]

Economists and diplomats debate whether BITs have influenced investment decisions, a difficult methodological problem since how do we estimate what foreign investment might have taken place in a given developing country even absent a BIT with the actual investor's home State, in the case where a BIT between these two countries has been concluded? Investors' decisions

---

57.   M. Blomström, *Transnational Corporations and Manufacturing Exports from Developing Countries* (UN CTC 1990, p.56). *Accord Spero*, pp.252–254.

58.   See the OECD study cited in n.52 above, and the UN CTC study of 1988 on *Bilateral Investment Treaties*, ST/CTC/65.

59.   See Akinsanya in (1987) 36 ICLQ 58 and Warbrick in idem, p.929; Asante, 'International Law and Foreign Investment: A Reappraisal' (1988) 37 ICLQ 588 at 601–602, 606–608.

are based on many factors and perceptions of which the existence of a BIT is only one element.[60] It is plainly not the case that no foreign investment goes into developing countries that have either concluded no BITs, or have not concluded a BIT with a particular State from which investment might come. The jury is still out and perhaps can never reach a clear verdict on this one.

C. The Significance of the Bilateral Treaties

For the lawyer, there are two issues. One is the precise interpretation in practice of the sometimes complex and elaborate clauses found in BITs. The other, which bears upon the continuing vigour or possible decline of the provisions from the permanent sovereignty and NIEO resolutions, is the significance of this body of bilateral treaty practice for customary international law relating to the treatment of foreign investors, their property and contractual rights. Akehurst, Sohn and others have argued that where numerous bilateral treaties in the same subject area contain uniform or very similar clauses on a certain matter and the actions of States generally are consistent with these treaties, then the treaty provisions are likely to be accepted by courts or other decision-makers as evidence of a rule of customary law.[61] Baxter summarised the issue as follows:[62]

60. The International Chamber of Commerce Commission on Multinational Enterprises and International Investment declared in 1989 that 'the growing network of these treaties contributes to building an international framework of standards that will help increase the confidence of potential investors'. (Joint Statement of ICC and the International Organisation of Employers to 15th session of the UN Commission on TNCs, p.2.)

61. Akehurst, 'Custom as a source of international law', (1974–75) 47 BYIL at 42–44, 49–52; Sohn, 'Unratified Treaties as a Source of Customary International Law' in A. Bos and M. Siblesz (eds.), Realism in Law-Making op. cit. supra n.3. See also Thirlway, International Customary Law and Codification (Sijthoff, 1972) p.59; the extended jurisprudential treatment of the significance of lump-sum claims settlement agreements by Lillich and Weston, International Claims: Their Settlement by Lump Sum Agreements (Univ. Press of Virginia, 1975) pp.9–43 and the same authors' 'Lump sum agreements: their continuing contribution to the law of international claims' (1988) 82 AJIL 69.

62. Baxter, 'Treaties and Custom' (1970-I) 129 Hague Recueil at 89.

The weight to be given to any particular line of bilateral treaties varies according to the state of customary international law bearing on the subject-matter of the treaty, the number of treaties, the presence or absence of other inconsistent agreements or State practice, and like circumstances. At worst, the presence of a provision in a number of bilateral treaties can strengthen the rule of international law to which it gives expression. At best, the series of similar bilateral treaties can of itself establish the state of the law.

A decade ago, when far fewer BITs had been concluded and the number of contracting States involved was very limited compared to the present score, Mann wrote that the importance of such treaties 'lies in the contribution they make to the development of customary international law, in their being a source of law'.[63] His evaluation rested principally on three arguments: the large number of such treaties, whose scope was increased by operation of the mfn clause; the fact that many of the contracting States had been among the very States which had purported to reject the standards included in the treaties (e.g. on compensation for expropriated foreign property); and the fact that 'these treaties establish and accept and thus enlarge the force of traditional conceptions'.[64]

In the late 1980s two authors with actual or former UK Foreign Office service opined that BITs or IPPAs gave 'important support for those standards of customary international law which had seemed to be slipping away'.[65] They observed that not only IPPA contracting States now less readily afforded discriminatory treatment to foreign investment, but that other developing States had adopted a similar approach.[66] As might be expected from an international secretariat, the UN Centre on Transnational Corporations puts arguments pro and con the 'custom-forming effect' of BITs, finding that:[67]

it would be premature to conclude that an agreement is about to emerge in the international community on a comprehensive set of rules constituting the international law of investments.

---

63. Mann, 'British treaties for the promotion and protection of investment' (1981) 52 BYIL 241 at 249.

64. Ibid.

65. Denza and Brooks in (1987) 36 ICLQ 908 at 913.

66. For a contrary evaluation from the same period see Asante, loc. cit. supra n.59 at pp.607–608.

67. UN CTC study cited n.58 above, para.357, p.77.

No doubt, bilateral investment treaties are an important factor in the formation of custom, but the significant contrary positions and tendencies must be taken into account.

D. Lomé IV

The latest Lomé Convention[68] repeats provisions from its 1985 predecessor that 'fair and equitable treatment' shall be accorded to private investors who comply with ACP–EC development co-operation objectives and priorities and with appropriate home and host State laws,[69] and that the Parties:[70]

affirm the importance of concluding between States, in their mutual interest, investment promotion and protection agreements which could also provide the basis for insurance and guarantee schemes.

Lomé IV, however, goes further. In an annexed Joint Declaration on the Convention's investment articles the Parties agree to study the main clauses of a model protection agreement, drawing on existing BITs between the States Parties. They agree to give particular attention to legal guarantees to ensure fair and equitable treatment and protection of foreign investors; the most-favoured-investor clause; protection in the event of expropriation or nationalisation; transfer of capital and profits; and international arbitration in the event of disputes between investor and host State.[71] Granted, this Declaration is not formally part of the Convention, and the commitment is limited to the making of a joint study. Nevertheless, formulation of the matters highlighted for particular attention is not phrased in neutral language but leans to the side of concern for the legal protection of investors' rights and acknowledges the appropriateness of international arbitration of disputes between investors and developing host States.

68. Lomé IV 1990, see n.9 above.
69. Lomé III, Art.240, 24 ILM 571 (1985); Lomé IV, Art.258.
70. Lomé III, Art.243(1); Lomé IV, Art.260.
71. Annex LIII, (1990) 29 ILM 802.

E. Other State Practice

The strongest influence exerted by bilateral treaties occurs when their provisions are consistent with other forms of State practice on the subject. This multilateral Lomé Convention comprises one item of relevant practice. The MIGA Convention, in force from April 1988, is a weightier item in the corpus of practice relating to private foreign investment in developing countries.[72] This Convention is more than a multilateral guarantee scheme on insurance lines. The Agency is to engage in investment promotion activities including the conclusion of IPPAs among its member States,[73] and the encouraging of amicable settlement of disputes between investors and host countries.[74] It should also be emphasised that guarantees are restricted to investments where the Agency is satisfied as to, *inter alia*, compliance with host country laws and regulations, the investments, consistency with the country's declared development objectives and the investment conditions there including 'the availability of fair and equitable treatment and legal protection for the investment'.[75] The MIGA scheme is the subject of another contribution to the present volume.[76]

F. The Draft Code of Conduct on Transnational Corporations

Finally, mention must be made of the failure to resolve the deadlock in the protracted discussions on the draft UN Code of Conduct on Transnational Corporations. These efforts have proceeded intermittently since the mid-1970s and the latest text, prepared in 1988 by the Chairman of the Special Session of the UN Commission on TNCs,[77] reveals that consensus is still

---

72. Text in (1985) 24 ILM 1605 and (1986) 1 ICSID Rev. For. Investment L.J. 145. The Operational Regulations which are of considerable legal significance as well as practical importance are in (1988) 27 ILM 1227. See I. Shihata, 'Depoliticisation of investment disputes' (1986) 1 ICSID Rev. 1 at 13–25; S. Chatterjee in (1987) 36 ICLQ 76 and in the present volume at p.139, and J. Voss in (1987) 21 JWTL 5.
73. Now at least 45 developing and 10 or 12 developed industrialised States.
74. Art.23.
75. Art.12(d), and see Art.23(b)(ii).
76. See further Chatterjee, chap.V infra.
77. E/1988/39/Add.1; see ILA Int'l Committee on Legal Aspects of a NIEO, Report to

lacking on crucial clauses dealing with protection of property and contractual rights, compensation in case of taking of property, and the settlement of disputes. The Commission has agreed, however, on most other provisions in the draft, particularly those on standards of corporate conduct. This failure to agree on some of the core legal issues has to be set against the vigorous growth in the conclusion of BITs and the multilateral conventions discussed above.

The cumulation of all this practice, and relevant arbitration awards which it has not been possible to discuss,[78] must have some, perhaps considerable, modifying effect on whatever juridical significance the quoted principles of the 1974 Declaration and Article 2 of the CERDS may have possessed.

G. Trade-Related Investment Measures in the GATT Uruguay Round

As is well known, there is no comprehensive multilateral convention on international investment. Provisions of the Havana Charter negotiated in 1947 on treatment of foreign investment were unacceptable to influential groups in the US and were a major reason for the Charter's failure to secure the necessary ratifications. Some have advocated more recently the creation of a 'GATT for investment'.[79] On a less ambitious scale other options include amending present GATT Articles to include investment as well as trade, or pursuing investment issues that are seen as trade-related through the GATT dispute procedures, to try to obtain useful 'precedents'.[80]

In September 1986 the GATT Contracting Parties meeting in Punta del Este launched the present round of GATT negotiations, the Uruguay Round.[81] Trade-related investment measures (TRIMs) are on the agenda

Queensland Conference (1990) pp.6–13.

78. Including several important decisions of the US–Iran Claims Tribunal.
79. Eg P.M. Goldberg and C. Kindleberger in (1978) 2 Law and Policy in International Business 195–323.
80. See *Spero*, p.137.
81. Ministerial Declaration of Punta del Este, in GATT Focus, Oct. 1986, and (1986) 25 ILM 1624.

of the Round, a 'new' area for the GATT strongly advocated by the US with cooler support from the EC and Japan. TRIMs include:

local content requirements, demanding domestic sourcing of components;

licensing requirements, requiring an investor to license production locally in the host State and sometimes limiting royalties;

product mandating requirements, obliging an investor to supply certain markets with specified products;

trade-balancing requirements, which require the attainment of specified export or import levels;

export-performance requirements, obliging an investor to export a stated percentage of its production.

The TRIMs Negotiating Group adopted the following Negotiating Objective in January 1987:

Following an examination of the operation of GATT Articles related to the trade-restrictive and distorting effects of investment measures, negotiations should elaborate, as appropriate, further provisions that may be necessary to avoid such adverse effects on trade.

It is neither possible nor appropriate here to review the course of negotiations on TRIMs. If an agreement does emerge, in the form of proposed amendments to GATT Articles or a separate Code, it will be a further significant element in the overall pattern of norms, standards and practices on the international plane affecting legal relations between foreign investors and host States, including developed as well as developing host States. Apparently, the core political decision is whether certain TRIMs should be prohibited as inherently restrictive or distortive of trade, or whether the trade effects of all TRIMs should be determined on a case-by-case basis.[82]

The Ministerial meetings in February 1991, which restarted the Uruguay Round negotiations with some moves toward a compromise on agricultural subsidies, did not have a draft text of a TRIMs agreement. The Brussels document produced after the meetings enumerated points on which basic divergences of view existed, namely, coverage of any agreement; level of discipline and what could be a workable 'trade effects' test; extension of any

---

82. GATT Focus No.76, Nov. 1990, pp.2–3.

agreement to developing countries, and restrictive business practices.[83] It is a case of 'watch this space'.

III. DEVELOPMENT ASSISTANCE, INTERNAL REFORM AND HUMAN RIGHTS

THE 1974 Declaration combined in a single list a number of principles 'full respect' for which was stated to be the foundation for the NIEO. On closer examination and in the light of more recent policy formulations concerning economic development it can be seen that certain of those principles are uneasy bedfellows containing the seeds of incompatibility if fully respected. Economic and social sovereignty, enunciated in principle (d) and the extension of assistance to developing countries by the international community free of any political conditions, principle (k), might prove hard to reconcile with principle (r), the need for developing countries to concentrate all their resources for the cause of development, if the latter exhortation were seriously implemented.[84]

Economic sovereignty, in the sense of freedom from external intervention in policy formation and execution or from non-legitimate economic sanctions, is an accepted facet of a State's independence and overall legal sovereignty.[85] At this level of abstraction, the principle has an appealing clarity. When one descends to such concrete matters as World Bank structural adjustment loans and IMF financial resources available on a basis of conditionality, both the perception and the reality may be very different. For all the protestations by Bank and Fund officials that adjustment programmes are freely agreed and conditions voluntarily accepted, true statements in a formal sense, many commentators from developed and developing countries and some politicians from developing countries beg leave to differ. The members of the South Commission acted in their personal capacities, but they nearly all had personal experience of such transactions as senior officials or government

---

83. Idem, No.79, March 1991, pp.3–4.

84. Two other of the 1974 principles speak to economic, specifically financial, assistance for development, namely principles (l) and (o) quoted earlier, p.32 supra at n.16.

85. See ICJ in *Nicaragua v. United States of America*, ICJ Rep. 1986, p.133, paras.263, 264.

ministers.[86] Having recognised the need for structural reforms in developing countries, to improve the performance of the public sector and tax systems, to create a stable environment for the private sector, and to promote exports, the Commission submitted that:

> in the adjustment process of the 1980s, these needed reforms were frustrated by an unbalanced international approach towards structural adjustment and by the conditionality prescribed by the international financial institutions. The macro-economic policies – in particular fiscal and exchange rate policies – virtually forced upon developing countries as part of programmes for stabilisation and structural adjustment were geared to achieving a quick, short-term improvement in the balance of payments.

Moreover, the programmes 'pressed upon developing countries' did not provide sufficient external financial support to enable adjustment to occur and endure without choking their growth.[87]

So far as concerns the right of each State to adopt the social system that it deems most appropriate to its own development (principle (d)) there has emerged over the past five years or so a marked emphasis on human rights and democratic participation as key elements in the economic as well as the social development of national societies. This theme was notably absent from the 1974 GA resolutions on the NIEO and from resolutions on permanent sovereignty. Limitations of space again preclude comprehensive treatment of this change in approach, but some recent manifestations deserve attention.

A. *The Declaration on the Right to Development*

GA Resolution 41/28, the Declaration on the right to development, was adopted in December 1986 by overwhelming majority, with the US a sole opponent and eight other developed industrialised States abstaining. Its preamble recognises that the human person is the central subject of the development process and that development policy should make the human being the main participant and beneficiary of development – language echoed in Articles 5(1) and 13 of Lomé IV.[88]   Article 3(1) of the Declaration

---

86. See details of Commission membership in *Challenge*, pp.289–295.
87. Idem, p.67; see also pp.72, 240–241.
88. See reference in n.9 supra.

ascribes primary responsibility to States for the creation of national as well as international conditions favourable to the realisation of the right to development. Article 3(3) provides that States have the duty to co-operate in ensuring development and eliminating obstacles to it and continues:[89]

> States should realise their rights and fulfil their duties in such a manner as to promote a new international economic order based on sovereign equality, interdependence, mutual interest and co-operation among all States, as well as *to encourage the observance and realisation of human rights.*

Article 8(1) declares that States should undertake at national level all measures necessary for realisation of the right to development and should ensure equality of opportunity for all in access to basic resources including food, housing, education and health services 'and the fair distribution of income'. Effective measures to ensure that women have an active role in the development process were also required.[90]

Such is the emphasis on human rights in the economic and social fields that one might query whether one of the preambular paragraphs has been correctly drafted. It says:

> *Aware* that efforts at the international level to promote and protect human rights should be accompanied by efforts to establish a new international economic order.

Should it not read, rather:

> *Aware* that efforts at the international level to establish a new international economic order should be accompanied by efforts at the national level to promote and protect human rights?

B. The Declaration on International Economic Co-operation

The existence of a legal right to development is controversial and the issue cannot be pursued here, but the surfacing of individual human rights concerns in such a resolution is significant. In 1990 the GA held a Special Session on International Economic Co-operation and adopted a Declaration which, *inter*

---

89. Emphasis added.
90. Cf. Arts.4 and 150–155 of Lomé IV.

alia, emphasised the full utilisation of human resources and the recognition of human rights as stimulating creativity and initiative. The Declaration continues:

> A primary objective must be to respond to the needs of and maximise the potential of all members of society. Health, nutrition, housing, population policies and other social services are a key to both improving individual welfare and successful development ... The international community should support efforts to arrest the current escalation of extreme poverty and hunger.

C. IMF Practice

The IMF is paying more attention to social issues in members seeking financial support, but the Committee of the Whole emphasised in September 1988 that the Fund's central mandate is to help members maintain or restore policies conducive to growth, balance of payments and price stability, and that it is a State's prerogative to make social choices in implementing its policies. Questions of income distribution should not be part of Fund conditionality.[91] However, in all discussions on policy framework proposals with States entering on arrangements under the Structural Adjustment Facility and the Enhanced SAF the Fund's staff 'discussed poverty issues as a matter of course'.[92] Many such arrangements contain measures to lessen or compensate for the adverse impact of certain economic policies on specific vulnerable groups in the population.[93] The Fund Managing Director referred to these policies in a speech to the UN Economic and Social Council in July 1990, saying that the Fund 'encourages' governments to avoid raising taxes on basic staple foods, to protect critical expenditures on health, education and nutrition, and to compensate or retrain workers laid off. Such measures are not cost-free and M. Camdessus suggested that the two best ways of financing them are to increase national solidarity by increasing taxes paid by the richer

---

91. *IMF Ann. Rep. 1990*, p.41.
92. Idem, p.42.
93. Appendix V, idem, p.100, and see P.S. Heller and others, *The Implications of Fund-Supported Adjustment Programs and Poverty*, IMF Occasional Paper 58 (Washington DC, May 1988).

sections of the population; and by reducing military expenditure. When countries make these bold political moves, they must be supported.[94]

D. Lomé IV

Express recognition in a multilateral treaty of the importance of the promotion and protection of human rights for economic development came in Lomé IV. Article 5 provides that co-operation shall be directed towards human-centred development 'which thus entails respect for and promotion of all human rights', and that 'respect for human rights is recognised as a basic factor of real development'. The article goes on to record the Parties 'deep attachment to human dignity and human rights which are legitimate aspirations of individuals and peoples'. It further declares that the various categories of human rights are indivisible and inter-related:

> each having its own legitimacy: non-discriminatory treatment; fundamental human rights; civil and political rights; economic, social and cultural rights.

The ACP States may request financial and other help for specific schemes for the promotion of human rights in those States, including schemes in the legal sphere.[95]

The European Parliament resolved in September 1990 that a closer link should be created between development policy and respect for fundamental rights in the implementation of Lomé IV,[96] and in a specific resolution on violation of human rights in Kenya, the Parliament called on the EC Council and Commission to make representations to the Kenyan authorities pursuant

94. *IMF Survey*, 30th July 1990, p.237; *Challenge*, pp.117, 123–124, 275–277.
95. Art.5(3). For further discussion of Art.5 and its *travaux préparatoires* see G. White, 'Structural Adjustment with a Human Face' and 'Human Rights in Development: New Approaches in the Fourth Lomé Convention', to be published in *Manchester Discussion Papers on Development*, 1991 and in the forthcoming memorial volume for Judge Nagendra Singh, to be published by the Indian Society of International Law, edited by R.P. Dhokalia.
96. *The Courier*, No.124, Nov–Dec. 1990, p.II and see speech by Commissioner Marin, the EC Commissioner for Development, idem, p.III.

to Lomé IV, and to consider the possible suspension of the Convention's application to Kenya so long as Article 5 was not respected.[97]

In the framework of European political co-operation a Joint Statement by the EC and the Member States on Ethiopia following the fall of the government and the ending of the civil war recalled the commitments in Lomé IV, and declared that economic aid to Ethiopia would be more effective if democratic institutions were rapidly established.   The EC and the Member States:[98]

> look to the provisional administration to respect its commitments regarding human rights and the progressive democratisation of the country.

E. Other Expressions of View

A final illustration of these trends comes from the 'Overview' of the Chairman of the OECD Development Assistance Committee in the *1990 Report on Development Co-operation* who noted that:

> the signals being given are that allocation decisions henceforth will be more influenced than in the past by a country's record on human rights and democratic practice

and that we are hearing more about democratic processes from the developing countries themselves:[99]

> They have come to realise that development needs participation, transparency and the stability of the rule of law.

The same note was struck in the final paragraph of the South Commission's Report, also in 1990:[100]

> In the final analysis, the South's plea for justice, equity, and democracy in the global society cannot be dissociated from its pursuit of these goals within its own societies. Commitment to democratic values, respect for fundamental rights - particularly the right to dissent - fair

97.   Res. adopted April 1991, OJ 106, 22 Apr. 1991, and Bull. EC 3-1991, point 1.3.79.
98.   Bull. EC 5-1991, point 1.4.14.
99.   OECD, *1990 Report on Development Co-operation*, pp.12, 13.
100. *Challenge*, p.287.

treatment for minorities, concern for the poor and underprivileged, probity in public life, willingness to settle disputes without recourse to war – all these cannot but influence world opinion and increase the South's chances of securing a new world order.

F. Outlook

Of course, it is actions and not words alone which count, but these developments in opinion among policy leaders seem to reflect a genuine shift in emphasis when compared with the confrontational and unbalanced language of the 1974 resolutions. Perhaps the profound social and political changes in Central and Eastern Europe in the late 1980s which are transforming relations between those countries and the West have had some influence on thinking and policies elsewhere, with consequent changes in North–South economic relations and hence in legally relevant State practice to be anticipated.

Chapter III

EXTRATERRITORIAL JURISDICTION IN ECONOMIC TRANSACTIONS

Henry G. Darwin

Chapter III

EXTRATERRITORIAL JURISDICTION IN ECONOMIC TRANSACTIONS

Henry G. Darwin

I. INTRODUCTION

UNDER international law, a State is entitled primarily to exercise jurisdiction within its own territory, including territorial waters. Extraterritorial jurisdiction, i.e. the exercise of jurisdiction by a State in respect of conduct outside its territory, has often, particularly in connection with economic transactions, provoked objections from other States.[1]

Such disputes may be divided by subject-matter, e.g. those relating to restrictions on competition (antitrust), economic controls established in pursuit of objectives in the field of foreign policy, or action taken in connection with international transport. Equally, one may distinguish between substantive prohibitions on activities outside the territory of the State which has imposed them and procedural demands for documents held abroad. The course of disputes over recent decades has led to measures of co-operation, but also to measures of opposition by States resisting exorbitant claims to exercise jurisdiction. The whole debate has been marked by the interplay of provisions of internal law, often primarily designed for applica-

---

1.   A section giving some useful sources, with some abbreviated references used in footnotes, appears in the 'Further Reading and Selected Bibliography' at the end of this volume.

The views expressed in it are the personal views of the writer and do not express the position of any office or organisation with which he has been associated. It is based on a talk given to a Commonwealth Law Students' Conference at Cumberland Lodge, London, in June 1989.

61

tion within one State only, and principles derived from international law, such as act of state, state immunity and, above all, respect for sovereignty. This chapter reviews some important cases, disputes and actions of States and then comments on the underlying principles, so as to give a brief outline of this complex field.

Distinction is made, especially in US cases and writings, between personal jurisdiction, which is established by service, usually on a place of business in the country concerned, and subject-matter jurisdiction, which depends on the substance of the case, and between prescriptive jurisdiction, which imposes or prohibits certain conduct, and enforcement jurisdiction, which concerns whether a court will enforce the rule prescribed.

This chapter does not deal with certain other well recognised jurisdictions of a State in respect of activities outside its territory, e.g. over its own nationals and companies on the basis of their nationality, over crimes of universal jurisdiction, e.g. piracy, hijacking of aircraft, and certain grave war crimes, over ships and aircraft under its flag or on its registry, and over certain activities in offshore maritime areas outside its territorial sea.

II. ANTITRUST PROCEEDINGS

A. United States Cases

Anti-trust proceedings brought against restrictive trade practices or excessive economic concentrations have caused most international disputes over extraterritoriality.

The Sherman Act of 1890 of the United States made illegal 'every contract, combination in the form of trust or otherwise, or conspiracy in restraint of trade or commerce among the several States or with foreign nations'. It provided for criminal prosecutions and for civil suits, including suits in which parties injured by such a conspiracy could claim treble damages, i.e. three times the damage actually suffered.

Traditionally, US case law had, in general, followed a territorial line. Thus, in *American Banana*[2] (1909), the Supreme Court held that the

---

2.   *American Banana Co v. United Fruit Co* 213 US 347 (1909).

'character of an act as lawful or unlawful must be determined wholly by the law of the country where the act is done', and that the anti-trust laws of the United States did not apply elsewhere.

ALCOA[3] (1945) changed the trend of US case law. Aluminium Ltd was a Canadian company, which, with other companies outside the United States, managed aluminium production by limiting production quotas and reallocating unsold quotas. This agreement affected the sources and price for aluminium imported into the US. The US Court of Appeals exercised jurisdiction over the Canadian company, on the basis of what became known as the 'effects doctrine'. Judge Learned Hand said '... any state may impose liabilities, even upon persons not within its allegiance, for conduct outside its borders that has consequences within its borders which the state reprehends; ...'. The only precedents cited were two domestic US cases where all the facts lay within the US and one involving vessels in the high seas just outside the territorial sea to which an agreement with the flag State applied.

Swiss Watchmakers[4] (1963) concerned an agreement to protect the Swiss watch-making companies, reflecting the policy of the Swiss Government and strongly supported by them. These companies would not manufacture watches outside Switzerland or assist such manufacture; they would not export watch parts or watch-making machinery; they excluded non-Swiss citizens; they fixed the prices of watches and parts but only in Switzerland. The arrangements were initiated in Switzerland, but many of them were applied in the US by defendants there. The judgment was not limited to the consequences in America but, basing itself on the 'effects doctrine', the US court claimed to require changes even for the Swiss industries in Switzerland.

Zenith[5] (1969) concerned a Canadian agreement between radio manufacturers which made a pool of Canadian patents for supplies of goods to the Canadian market and declined to license them to outsiders. This arrangement was supported by the Canadian Government since the participants in the pool were willing to manufacture equipment in Canada for the Canadian

---

3. *US v. Aluminium Co of America (ALCOA)*, 148 F.2d 416 (2d Cir. 1945).
4. *US v. Watchmakers of Switzerland Information Center Inc.* 1965 Trade Cases (CCH) para.71352.
5. *Zenith Radio Corp v. Hazeltine Research Inc* 395 US 100 (1969).

market, which Zenith was not. The Supreme Court considered only the difficulties for non-participants as part of the US export market and not at all Canadian interests in their own market.

Westinghouse[6] concerned uranium. In 1973, a shortage developed, and Westinghouse, a US company, sued RTZ and other non-US producers for excluding it from the non-US production under an agreement between them. The dispute was exacerbated in that the US company was seeking to force itself into a market whose producers had been excluded by US law for many years from the US market. Also most foreign producers were obliged to resist the jurisdiction of the US court for fear that any judgment of the US courts could be enforced against them in their home courts, however unreasonable the basis of jurisdiction claimed.

These cases and others like them gave rise to intense international criticism. US concern about the trend of this case law appeared at first in academic circles, for example, in 1958, in a book by Professor Kingman Brewster, a distinguished American lawyer, who was also US Ambassador in London.

The Restatement (Second) of the Foreign Relations Law of the United States, published in 1965 by the American Law Institute, set out the 'effects doctrine' as applied in the case law; but it added an obligation, where two countries had concurrent jurisdiction, to 'minimise conflicts'. 'Each state should moderate the exercise of its enforcement jurisdiction', taking into account a number of factors. In brief, these were: the vital national interests of the two states, the potential hardship to the defendant, how far the required conduct is to take place in the other state, nationality of persons concerned, and the likelihood that enforcement action will lead to compliance. (See sections 18, 39 and 40.)

In *Timberlane*[7] (1977), this line of thinking was taken into American case law. Timberlane alleged that its competitors were trying to frustrate its purchase of a lumber business in Honduras. It began anti-trust proceedings against the Bank of America and other parties, alleging a conspiracy to

---

6.   *In re Westinghouse Electric Corp Uranium Contracts Litigation* 563 F.2d 882 (10th Cir. 1977); (Jan. 1978) 17 ILM 77.

7.   *Timberlane Lumber Co v. Bank of America*, 549 F.2d 597 (9th Cir. 1977).

prevent Timberlane from exporting lumber from Honduras to the US. Judge Choy in the Court of Appeals set out three requirements; first, some effect – actual or intended – on commerce, before the federal court may legitimately exercise subject-matter jurisdiction; second, a sufficiently large effect to present a cognisable injury to the plaintiffs; third, in international cases, an answer to the question whether the interests of, and links to, the US are sufficiently strong, vis-à-vis those of other nations, to justify an assertion of extraterritorial authority. The third element is 'the jurisdictional rule of reason' or 'the balancing test', whereby the court considers not only the interests of the forum state but also those of other states involved. His points follow but are not identical with those in the Restatement.

Mannington Mills[8] (1979) identified additional elements, namely, whether the conduct prescribed by the US court would be illegal in the country concerned, whether a similar order by another State would be acceptable, and whether a relevant treaty applied.

However much the balancing test appears to recognise competing claims to jurisdiction by other States, in practice the courts of the United States have almost never refused jurisdiction.

Writing in 1988, Neale and Stephens could find only a single case, *ONE Shipping*,[9] where the court had refused jurisdiction on civil anti-trust claims. Colombian shipowners had conformed to a Colombian law reserving shipping out of Colombia; the court said that Colombian interests outweighed 'whatever antitrust enforcement interests the United States may have in this case'. But, on appeal, the Court of Appeals affirmed this refusal more on grounds of Act of State than on a balancing of interests.

Action by the US authorities relating to mergers between companies outside the US, which had subsidiaries incorporated in the US, has varied. In 1969, the Swiss pharmaceutical companies, CIBA and Geigy,[10] sought to merge their worldwide interests. In the United States, the US Department of Justice limited its action to requiring the sale to a third party of substantial parts of the US businesses and other measures to maintain competition.

---

8. *Mannington Mills Inc v. Congoleum Corp* 595 F.2d 1287 (3d Cir. 1979).
9. *ONE Shipping Ltd v. Flota Mercante Grancolombiana* 830 F.2d 449 (2d Cir. 1987).
10. CIBA/Geigy, see Neale p.105.

In Consgold/Minorco,[11] an attempt in 1989 by Minorco, a Luxembourg company, to take over Consolidated Goldfields, a UK company, failed, though not opposed by the competition authorities either in the UK or in Luxembourg. Though the Securities and Exchange Commission discouraged this, the US court insisted that it must review the takeover by Minorco of Consgold as whole. The US had an economic interest in one aspect of the takeover, since among the assets which Minorco would acquire, through a chain of subsidiaries, was a substantial interest in Newmont Gold, the largest producer of gold in the US. The number of shares in Consgold itself owned by US residents, even through ADRs, was, however, only about 2.5%. This attitude contrasts unfavourably with the attitude of the German authorities in the *Philip Morris* case discussed in Section B immediately below.

The *Restatement (Third) of the Law of Foreign Relations of the United States*[12] of 1986 does not repudiate earlier case law; but it puts forward 'reasonableness' as the criterion restraining the jurisdiction to prescribe and sets out a number of criteria going beyond those in section 40 of the Second Restatement.

B. European Cases

In *Dyestuffs*[13] (1972), an arrangement for fixing the price of dyestuffs came before the European Court of Justice. One of the defendants was Imperial Chemical Industries, itself not trading in the EEC, but having subsidiaries trading there. The Court held that the parent company could properly be the object of the jurisdiction of the Commission and the Court, on the ground that the activities of the subsidiaries of ICI could properly be attributed to the parent outside the EEC since the Court found that the parent in fact controlled the action of the subsidiary. The Court said: 'Since a concerted practice is involved, it is first necessary to ascertain whether the conduct of

---

11. Consgold/Minorco, i.e., *Consolidated Goldfields plc v. Minorco SA*, 871 F.2d (2d Cir. 1989), see F.A. Mann 'The Extremism of American Extraterritorial Jurisdiction' (1990) 39 ICLQ 410; the proceedings were under the Clayton Act of 1914 which prohibits purchase of shares if it diminishes competition or leads to monopoly.

12. See especially Sec.403 of this Third Revision by the American Law Institute.

13. *Imperial Chemical Industries Ltd v. Commission*, Case 48/69 [1972] ECR 619.

the applicant has had effects within the Common Market. It appears from what has already been said that the increases at issue were put into effect within the Common Market and concerned competition between producers operating with it. Therefore the actions for which the fine at issue has been imposed constitute practices carried on directly within the Common Market'. But the greater part of the judgment is devoted to question whether the actions of the subsidiary were to be regarded as the actions of the parent, and that, by making use of its power to control its subsidiaries established in the Community, the parent 'was able to ensure that its decision was implemented on that market'. It found that the conduct was to be imputed to the parent company.

In *Woodpulp*[14] (1988) before the European Court of Justice, the Commission took action against companies outside the EEC, which had concerted marketing for the supply of woodpulp, the raw material of newsprint, to a number of countries including those of the EEC. This time, though the Advocate-General thought that the Court should formulate its decision in terms of 'the direct and immediate, reasonably foreseeable and substantial effect' of their action, the Court held that it had jurisdiction over almost all the participants in the arrangements, because, though they had concerted the arrangements outside, they had 'implemented' them within the territory of the EEC. The only exception which they made was for a company which had not played any independent role in the implementation of the pricing agreement.

In 1983, the *Philip Morris*[15] case arose out of the proposed merger of that well-known tobacco firm and Rembrandt, owners of the equally well-known 'Rothmans' brand. Considerations of competition in the tobacco industry in the Federal Republic were unfavourable to the merger; but the Kammergericht in Berlin did not object to the main merger between the parents. It prevented only the merger of the two German subsidiaries.

14. *Ahlström et al v. Commission*, Joined Cases 89, 104, 114, 116, 117 and 125–129 [1988] ECR 5193.
15. The facts are in Olmstead at pp.86–89.

III. EXPORT CONTROLS ON FOREIGN POLICY GROUNDS

EXPORT controls established for foreign policy reasons gave rise to a serious dispute between the US and its allies in an affair sometimes known as the 'Siberian Pipeline' dispute.[16] In June 1982, US export regulations were strengthened on goods and technical data for oil and gas transmission to hamper companies constructing a pipeline to carry natural gas from Siberia to Western Europe.

The amendments were expressed to apply not only to European subsidiaries of US companies but also European parent companies with US subsidiaries and not only to goods already exported from the US but also to goods already manufactured abroad using technical information under licences already granted to the European manufacturers, whose previous contracts and industrial projects were affected.

The European Community presented a strongly worded diplomatic Note in Washington objecting calling upon the United States to withdraw those measures. The Comments of the Community accompanying the Note[17] set out a detailed legal analysis of the reasons why the US measures were contrary to international law, saying, 'The United States measures as they apply in the present case are unacceptable under international law because of their extra-territorial aspects. They seek to regulate companies not of United States nationality in respect of their conduct outside the United States and particularly the handling of property and technical data of these companies not within the United States'.

The Community said, 'The territoriality principle (i.e. the notion that a State should restrict its rule-making in principle to persons and goods within its territory and that an organisation like the European Community should restrict the applicability of its rules to the territory to which the Treaty setting it up applies) is a fundamental notion of international law, in particular

---

16.   See Lowe, 'Public International Law and the Conflict of Laws: the European Response to the United States Export Administration Regulations' (1984) 33 ICLQ 515; also Lowe, 'International Law Issues in the "Pipelines" dispute: the British Position' in papers on the case in (1988) 27 Germ.YBIL 54.

17.   The Note of the EC, with accompanying Comments, and of the UK are in Lowe, p.197 and the Comments only in (Jul. 1982) 21 ILM 891.

insofar as it concerns the regulation of the social and economic activity in a state'.

The Community also objected, citing *Barcelona Traction*,[18] to the application of the new measures in that they purported to apply to companies incorporated in the countries of the EEC merely because they were linked through status as a subsidiary or shareholding or use of licences or purchase of goods. The US was not entitled to impose its corporate nationality on companies incorporated in Europe. 'Goods and technology do not have any nationality' and international law does not allow the use of 'goods or technology situated abroad as a basis of establishing jurisdiction over the persons controlling them'.

These Comments are of particular interest as they were prepared by the Commission of the Communities in consultation with experts from the Member States and were approved by the Committee of Permanent Representatives of the Member States (COREPER). The British Embassy sent a supporting Note setting out similar views.

The British and French governments as well as the German and Italian governments took various steps to encourage the companies to fulfil their contracts. The US authorities temporarily suspended the export privileges of the companies concerned but within six months from the tightening of the Regulations the US President had them rescinded.

In the *Libyan Arab Bank* case[19] (1989), the British Court refused to give effect, in relation to accounts in US banks in London, to an executive Order of the US freezing balances of Libyan banks.

IV. DISCOVERY OF DOCUMENTS ABROAD
IN SHIPPING AND OTHER CASES

INTERNATIONAL transport by sea and by air[20] has created special problems for regulation to protect competition.

---

18. The *Barcelona Traction* case [1970] ICJ Rep. 3 at 42.
19. *The Libyan Arab Bank v. Bankers Trust Co* [1989] 3 All ER 252.
20. The problems in the field of civil aviation cannot, for reasons of space, be discussed in this chapter, but on the Laker litigation in the US and UK, see Neale at p.117.

In cases against shipping companies in liner conferences established to co-ordinate shipping in a particular trade or region, the Department of Justice or civil plaintiffs have tried to obtain discovery of extensive documentation which was outside the US. This gave rise to strong objections and provoked the 'blocking statutes' which were enacted by other States to prevent the US courts and authorities from seeking access to documentation which was not in the US, on the grounds that the order of the US court infringed their sovereignty. These were discussed more generally in Part VII below.

In *RTZ v. Westinghouse*,[21] in order to get more evidence for its case in the US courts, Westinghouse obtained letters rogatory from the US court and then applied to the English court for an order under the Evidence (Proceedings in other Jurisdictions) Act 1975 to secure production of documents in the UK. The Attorney-General intervened to oppose the application. The House of Lords, citing *British Nylon Spinners*,[22] refused to give effect to the application on the ground, among others, that it involved an infringement of sovereignty and that UK policy was against recognition of US investigatory jurisdiction against UK companies.

Similarly, in *X AG v. A bank*,[23] the Commercial Court in London granted an injunction prohibiting the defendant bank, a US corporation, from producing, in response to a subpoena from a US court, documents held in London under a banking contract whose proper law was English; the main ground relied on by Legatt J was that it was a breach of confidentiality. But, referring to *RTZ v. Westinghouse* and the opposition of the UK government and the English courts to extraterritorial investigations by a foreign court, he said that this was one important factor which he should take into account as a matter of public interest in exercising his discretion.

V. OTHER JURISDICTIONAL DISPUTES

JURISDICTIONAL disputes, where US courts have sought to exercise jurisdiction in connection with property abroad, have occurred in fields other than

---

21. *Rio Tinto Zinc v. Westinghouse* [1978] 1 All ER 434.
22. *British Nylon Spinners v. Imperial Chemical Industries* [1952] 2 All ER 780.
23. *X AG v. A bank* [1983] 2 All ER 464.

those discussed above. For example, the US Securities and Exchange Commission in 1989 obtained from a New York court an order requiring the Chartered Bank, a UK bank, to pay into court sums originally deposited in its New York branch by alleged insider traders, though the sums had in fact, on the holders' instructions, been transmitted to its Hong Kong branch, despite the risk of actions against the Bank in Hong Kong.[24] This gave rise to diplomatic protests and the US proceedings were ended.

VI. MEASURES OF CO-OPERATION

MUTUAL Legal Assistance Schemes may help to reduce disputes concerning extraterritorial jurisdiction.

The Commonwealth Scheme relating to Mutual Assistance in Criminal Matters within the Commonwealth was launched by the meeting of Commonwealth Law Ministers in 1980. By 1990, legislation to give effect to the Commonwealth Scheme had been enacted or was in the course of preparation or enactment in many Commonwealth countries, such as Guyana, Kenya, Nigeria, Singapore, Trinidad and Tobago, Zimbabwe and the UK.

The arrangements may provide for the furnishing of assistance in criminal cases, e.g. identifying and locating persons, serving documents, examining witnesses, search and seizure, obtaining evidence, facilitating appearance of witnesses, transfer of prisoners as witnesses, obtaining judicial or official records, and tracing and forfeiting the proceeds of criminal activities.

These are, however, limited to criminal proceedings, while most of the disputes on extraterritoriality have concerned civil procedures. The Commonwealth Scheme naturally excludes various types of offences, such as political offences; but it also envisages that the requested State can refuse assistance where it would prejudice the security, international relations or other essential public interests of the requesting State. This obviously includes the interest that a State's sovereignty should not be infringed by unjustified acts of extraterritorial jurisdiction.

---

24. The Wang/Lee litigation in the US is outlined in an article in the *Wall Street Journal/Europe*, 30 May 1989.

The Hague Convention on the Taking of Evidence Abroad in Civil and Commercial Matters 1970[25] may encourage States to seek assistance from other States rather than attempting to exercise unjustified extraterritorial jurisdiction against their interests. It provides for the Court exercising jurisdiction to request the assistance of the Courts of another State to take and pass over evidence relevant to its case.

The main interest in the case has been where the dispute concerns discovery of documents outside the requesting State. In a series of cases, the US courts declined to excuse defendants from normal US practice on discovery merely because the Hague Convention could have been used. But in 1987 in *Aerospatiale*[26] the US Supreme Court held unanimously that a court should always consider the possibility of using the Hague Convention. The majority held, however, only that the court should use special vigilance to protect foreign litigants from being put at a disadvantage. The four judges who dissented said that there should be a presumption but not a rigid rule in favour of a first use of the Convention. The trend in case law is thus, at least to some extent, showing more respect for the Convention as a way of reducing disputes about extraterritoriality.

The Organisation for Economic Co-operation and Development (OECD) unanimously in 1964 adopted an Agreed Minute on the Exchange of Shipping Information, and later adopted wider Recommendations on Restrictive Practices affecting International Trade.[27] A number of bilateral agreements, especially with Australia and Canada, have been concluded by the US for similar purposes. These arrangements would have the effect that, where a government was considering action, it would at least give to the other States concerned an opportunity to comment. But they do not amount to a clear agreement on what the proper scope of jurisdiction of a State is and they offer no procedural assistance where extraterritorial jurisdiction is invoked by private parties as in civil suits for treble damages.

25.   The Hague Convention of 18 Mar. 1970 is published in UNTS No.1.12140, Vol.847 p.232 (1972) and in UKTS No.20 (1977).

26.   *Société Nationale Industrielle Aerospatiale v. Jones*, 482 US 302 (1982).

27.   Lowe, pp.240–254.

VII. MEASURES OF OPPOSITION

ATTEMPTS by States to exercise extraterritorial jurisdiction, especially by excessive demands for documents abroad, have, however, also often led to vigorous countermeasures.

A. Legislative and other Measures of Opposition

Legislative measures, sometimes known as 'blocking statutes', require that those to whom orders under them are directed should not comply with orders of foreign courts made in unjustified exercise of extraterritorial jurisdiction. They are directed not to furnish the documents held outside the United States or otherwise sought by the US court. The first measures were directed to shipping documents but they now extend to wider fields of litigation. Some statutes now go further and prohibit compliance with the substantive rather than evidential requirements of foreign court orders. Legislation in various forms has been enacted in Australia, Belgium, Canada, Denmark, Finland, France, Germany, Italy, the Netherlands, Norway, Philippines, South Africa, Sweden and the United Kingdom.[28]

Sometimes the provisions of ordinary law or administrative law can be used to block action. Thus, the Swiss authorities in *Société Internationale v. Rogers*[29] (1958) drew attention to Article 273 of the Swiss Penal Code which prohibits the making available of business secrets to foreign authorities, as well as Article 47 of the Swiss Bank Law. In *Fruehauf*[30] (1964), a US court sought to prevent sale of French cranes to China; under a general power arising when the controllers of a company act in a manner contrary to its interests, a judicial administrator was appointed, who completed the sale on behalf of the company.

---

28. Texts up to 1983 are given in Lowe at pp.78–186; the main UK Act is the Protection of Trading Interests 1980; UK orders made under it are listed in (1987) 58 BYIL 589.
29. 357 US 197 (1958).
30. *Fruehauf* case: (1966) 5 ILM 476: Lowe, p.xix.

B. Legislation against Treble Damages

Civil anti-trust suits for treble damages in extraterritorial cases under the
Sherman Act have led several countries to adopt legislation which expressly
refuses to enforce such judgments (e.g. the Foreign Anti-Trust Judgments
(Restriction of Enforcements) Act 1979 of Australia) or even authorises the
recovery by action in the State so legislating of sums paid in respect of treble
damage claims in the US courts (e.g. the Protection of Trading Interests Act
1980 of the UK).

The Communiqué of the Conference of Law Ministers of the Commonwealth in Barbados in 1980 said:

> Of particular concern was the question of the recognition and enforcement of multiple
> damage awards, a feature of anti-trust judgments under United States law. General support
> was expressed for the principle that arrangements for the recognition and enforcement of
> foreign judgments should contain a clear exclusion of multiple damages awards. Provisions
> for the recovery back of moneys paid under such judgments were also supported.

VIII. GENERAL COMMENTS

SOME general strands, running through the history of the actions and disputes
outlined above, can now be reviewed in this concluding section.

A. The Effects Doctrine and the
Balance of Interests

The first question which arose when reliance began to be placed on 'effects'
was how serious the effects on the US interests must be. But this problem
was overtaken by the claims of other countries and the 'balancing test', under
which the interests of the two States involved are supposed to be weighed by
the courts. Here the factors, as identified by the US courts, have varied, as
is seen in the successive Restatements. But the main objection to the
balancing test must be the lack of confidence in it and the subjective
character of the assessment as to the appropriate weighting, since it seems
that the US courts find in almost every case that the US interests predomi-
nate.

B. Sovereignty, Act of State, and Foreign Compulsion

Accordingly, the debate has sharpened and become a dispute between States. There has been increasing recourse to action both by diplomacy and by courts in order to assert the right of a sovereign State to respect for its sovereignty.

In some cases the US courts have declined to interfere with foreign arrangements, which result from specific, usually legislative, action of other States on the basis of the 'Act of State' doctrine recognised in the US case law, especially the *Sabbatino* case.[31] In *Dominicus Americana Bohio*,[32] the court accepted that, if the action by the US court would be an inquiry into the motivation of an act of a foreign government, the Act of State doctrine would prevent action, but held that this did not arise in the case.

In other cases, they have been prepared to take account of court or other action in the foreign country concerned, which has made compliance with the order of the US court or authorities illegal under the law of the foreign state concerned. Thus in *Société Internationale v. Rogers*[33] (1958), account was taken of Swiss criminal law preventing disclosure of bank records. The US courts take less account of civil liability; in *First National City Bank*[34] (1959), the US court relied on the fact that bank secrecy was not prescribed by a German statute and was not convinced that civil liability existed.

In addition to these instances of specific compulsion by the foreign law concerned, respect for sovereignty should, however, include respect for the sovereignty of a State which chooses not to impose statutory rules as to the particular conduct in its territory which has been made the subject of US action. Thus, in a Note of 25 August 1977,[35] about the US Export Administration Act, the UK government said that they 'do not accept any contention that if United Kingdom law is silent on a particular matter it is not an infringement of its jurisdiction if the United States legislate on that matter with regard to foreign subsidiaries of American companies'. The decision not

---

31. *Banco Nacional de Cuba v. Sabbatino*, 376 US 398 (1964).
32. *Dominicus Americana Bohio v. Gulf & Western* 595 F.2d 1287 (1979).
33. Supra n.29.
34. *First National City Bank v. IRS*, 271 F.2d 616 (2d Cir. 1959).
35. Lowe, p.147.

to legislate is also a decision of a sovereign State about its territory and its national companies.

All systems of law allow certain liberties to their economic entities to concert positions, as in Article 85(3) of the EEC Treaty. Even in the United States the Webb/Pomerene Act of 1918 and the Foreign Trade Antitrust Improvement Act 1982 allowed concerting of export activities, without regard to outside interests, provided US participants were not excluded. The courts of the US have certainly moved away from the more extreme position taken at an earlier stage but interstate disputes continue to show that objections to their practice remain.

One of the increasing problems is when States are forced to impose obligations on their companies in order to respond to unreasonable extraterritorial claims. But equally a State in such a situation cannot be expected to allow the State exercising excessive jurisdiction to infringe its sovereignty.

C. International Law and Comity

The main problem is one of sovereignty. As international economic activities intensify, the increasing conflicts between the views of States will lead to increasing disputes, putting in unfair jeopardy an increasing number of economic intermediaries. The only solution is an increasing respect for international law to reconcile the competing interests of States concerned. Though comity has been referred to and has played some part in moderating these conflicts, it is, except when understood as the same as international law, a weaker influence for avoiding conflicts.

D. The Correct Balance

It is accepted, under international law, that a State may exercise jurisdiction over crimes where some part of the ingredients of the offence take place abroad whereas others take place in the State exercising jurisdiction, as, for example, where a person writes and posts fraudulent claims from outside into that jurisdiction.[36] In the antitrust field, where a group is deliberately seeking to set up a cartel arrangement which is aimed at a State and is evidently illegal there, they should not be immune merely because they hold their meetings and concert their arrangements abroad.

On the other hand, sometimes a State decides, for its own internal reasons, to organise a particular industry in a particular way or to permit co-operative measures of the kind recognised as acceptable or desirable under the important grounds referred to national legislation or, e.g., in Article 85(3) of the Treaty of Rome. If so, it is an exorbitant exercise of jurisdiction for another State to claim to interfere with these on the grounds of its own economic policy, merely because the measures may have some incidental influence on its import trade in the goods concerned.

The intention of the measures which are under attack may be important. Is the intention deliberately to frustrate the competition policy of the State exercising extraterritorial jurisdiction, or do the arrangements give effect to the economic policy of some other country concerned? The resolution of the International Law Association at its meeting of 1972 required not only that there should be a substantial effects in the State exercising jurisdiction but also that the effect 'occurs as a direct and primarily intended result of the conduct outside the territory'.[37] Perhaps this aspect should enter more explicitly into the analysis of the respective rights of the State exercising jurisdiction and other States concerned.

E. The Future

The melancholy history of the claims and counter-measures, which is briefly outlined in this chapter, shows that the more extreme claims have not been accepted as legitimate under international law. But a larger measure of agreement is needed on what balance of interest justifies the exercise of extraterritorial jurisdiction if disputes are to be avoided.

The counter-measures taken by States in response to excessive extraterritorial action have led to some modification of positions. The best solution

---

36. E.g. *R. v. Baxter* [1971] 2 All ER 359.
37. ILA, *Report of the Fifty-fifth Conference 1972* p.xx; Lowe, p.57.

would be to reach international agreements on the points in issue. But, in the absence of satisfactory agreement or reasonable restraint, responses to abusive action, both in diplomatic dialogue and otherwise, may still in some cases be necessary as a way of manifesting and protecting territorial sovereignty.

Chapter IV

THE INTERNATIONAL MONETARY FUND

S.K. Chatterjee

Chapter IV

THE INTERNATIONAL MONETARY FUND

S.K. Chatterjee

I. INTRODUCTION

THE two principal financial institutions of international standing are the International Monetary Fund and the World Bank. This chapter concerns itself with the Fund and the next will cover the structure and operation of the World Bank.

The Articles of Agreement of the International Monetary Fund (IMF) were considered at a conference held in Bretton Woods, New Hampshire USA in July 1944, and on 27 December 1945 the Fund came into existence. The Fund's growth and development, its operational mechanism and practically all aspects of it are closely linked to historical factors and the economic exigencies of the time. Before going into various operational details of the Fund, it is necessary to trace briefly the factors that led to the setting up of the Fund. An identification of these factors should help to clarify the reasons for the Fund's changing its policies and operational mechanism over the years. This discussion is limited to the operational aspects of the Fund.

II. DEVELOPMENTS LEADING TO THE SETTING UP OF THE FUND

ON reflection, one could perhaps maintain that the path to the setting up of the Fund was concretely paved by the events occurring even prior to the conclusion of the Second World War. The Bretton Woods Conference of 1–22 July 1944 was part of a series of arrangements for the post-war period. The idea of the United Nations could not be conceived without certain related institutions such as the International Trade Organisation (although it did not materialise in the end), an international organisation that would regulate the liquidity of money together with an international organisation intended for the reconstruction of the economies devastated by the Second World War and for development work, especially for the newly-born countries whose independence was already a well-anticipated event.

At this juncture, one should also take into account the plans that were drawn up to combat the economic effect of the Great Depression of the 1930s. A dramatic collapse of commodity prices had occurred, disturbing the market across the world; industrialised countries suffered a series of deflationary pressures occasioned by the undercutting of prices of foreign products which required them to adopt flexible and/or multiple exchange rates. The gravity of the situation was reflected in the so-called 'beggar-my-neighbour' policy, that is, a policy on the basis of which countries attempted to export their unemployment to other countries. Efforts to resolve such problems individually or collectively proved short-lived. The Second World War served to bring these issues to a head.

In 1940, the then US Assistant to the Secretary of the Treasury, Harry Dexter White, developed a plan which in effect encompassed the nucleus of the functions of the future International Monetary Fund and the World Bank. In 1941, the distinguished English economist, John Maynard Keynes, called for an international currency union which would maintain accounts for the central banks in the world and which would be denominated in an international currency to be called 'bancor'. According to Keynes, bancor was to be defined in terms of gold, and the proposed international currency union, as a centralised organisation, would be allowed to alter its value. The key to the Keynes Plan was that the member countries would be allowed to exchange bancor for gold but not vice versa. Exchange rates which would be fixed in terms of bancor could not be changed without the prior permission of the Union.

The White Plan appeared to be much more elaborate than the Keynes Plan in that it included certain timely issues such as the question of facilitating and servicing of international debts, lessening the balance of payments difficulties, the possibilities of making subscriptions in both gold and national currencies, and the provision of purchase by a member of any other member's currency within certain limits. It emphasised the need for establishing fixed exchange rates for each currency which could only be determined with the consent of the proposed Fund and only altered in emergencies such as the necessity of correcting a fundamental disequilibrium in the balance of payments of a country. The White Plan also recommended that membership of this institution (the Fund) should be open to all members of the proposed United Nations.

Each of the Plans had its own merits and demerits, but despite certain basic differences between them, the need for international co-operation in respect of management of money and related matters, viz. investments and trade, was emphasised by both. Without going into the details of the Plans, it can be said that the International Monetary Fund was the outcome of the Keynes-White Plans, and the primary purposes of the Fund as set out in Article XX of the Articles of Association were decided to be:

i.   To promote international monetary co-operation through a permanent institution which provides the machinery for consultation and collaboration on international monetary problems.

ii. To facilitate the expansion and balanced growth of international trade, and to contribute thereby to the promotion and maintenance of high levels of employment and real income and to the development of the productive resources of all members as primary objectives of economic policy.

iii. To promote exchange stability, to maintain orderly exchange arrangements among members and to avoid competitive exchange depreciation.

iv. To assist in the establishment of a multilateral system of payments in respect of current transactions between members and in the elimination of foreign exchange restrictions which hamper the growth of world trade.

v.   To give confidence to members by making the general resources of the fund temporarily available to them under adequate safeguards, thus providing them with opportunity to correct maladjustments in their balance of payments without resorting to measures destructive of national or international prosperity.

vi. In accordance with the above, to shorten the duration and lessen the degree of disequilibrium in the international balances of payments of members.

The Fund was to be guided in all its policies and decisions by the purposes set forth in the above Article.

The establishment of the IMF had several implications – economic, political and even legal. For the first time, in disregard of their fiscal sovereignty, governments were required to agree to an exchange rate in conjunction with other governments, under the direction of the Fund authorities. Matters which in the past had been traditionally regarded as exclusively domestic matters, such as a decision to devalue or revalue a currency, now required approval of the Fund. Again, although depending upon the nature of the particular disequilibrium, financing through the Fund was made possible with a view to correcting balance of payments difficulties; governmental action to correct the situation by exchange restrictions or by raising barriers to imports could be used only with the Fund's approval. The Fund affirmed the need for international co-operation in respect of matters which formerly had been jealously guarded by States; in other words, Member States were required to formulate their domestic policies as to money and international trade in conformity with the Fund's broad policies. In respect of specified matters Member States became accountable to the Fund.

It is to be emphasised that at the time of setting up the Fund, the world economic situation was dominated by certain States; the reference currency for any international transaction, including the reference currency of the Fund, was the United States dollar. Over the years the world economic climate has changed for multifarious reasons; more industrialised States are now actors in the international financial market. On the other hand, the Fund cannot disregard the plight of the developing countries even though many of them are unable to contribute sufficiently to the Fund.

Over the years the Fund's operational activities and objectives have changed or enlarged; the Fund has also been called upon to accommodate the needs of the developing countries. Furthermore, the old monetary order has often been questioned by many. In part III below the most important changes that have occurred since the inception of the Fund are identified and briefly discussed.

This historical account of the Fund's development precedes sections describing the financial mechanisms employed by the Fund and its institutional aspects. A knowledge of all three is essential to a proper understanding of the Fund's operation and some readers may prefer to read first the later sections to ensure a fuller understanding of the historical section.

III. THE MAJOR CHANGES THAT OCCURRED BETWEEN 1945 AND 1990

IT is a daunting task to highlight all the major changes that occurred during these 45 years in a few paragraphs. The primary purpose is however to identify the principal reasons for which certain major changes in the Fund's operational mechanism became necessary and their profound impact upon the international economy.

A. Liberalisation of Exchange Restrictions
(1945-1969)

Exchange restrictions were a legacy of the 1930s compounded by the aftermath of the Second World War. Most of the countries in Europe, the Middle East and Asia imposed severe restrictions on imports, and planned to save their dollar reserves. In fact, in many cases, restrictions became discriminatory against US dollars. On the other hand, during the 1940s, even the pound sterling and most of the European currencies became inconvertible – that is, export earnings in these currencies could not be transformed into gold or US dollars. The Fund, during its initial period, advised its Member countries to adopt such domestic policies which, by virtue of improving their balance of payments positions, would eventually lead to a reduction of restrictions. This, in reality, was a difficult target to attain over a short period of time. By 1950, the economic effect of the Marshall Plan became evident in Europe, particularly in France and West Germany. To a large extent Western Europe was financially and economically reconstructed. By 1952, the time for implementing Article 14 of the Articles of Agreement was ripe.[1]

The consultation procedure between the Fund and its Members was activated in 1952: by then not only was exchange restrictions practice relaxed, but the policy of establishing convertibility of currencies was also progressively acknowledged. The actual implementation of this liberal policy became evident particularly in Western Europe in its intra-European trade, which was largely facilitated by the establishment of the European Payments Union.

---

1.   This Article dealt with transitional provisions.

Liberalisation of intra-European trade necessarily helped facilitate convertibility of European currencies.

By 1955, the Western States and Japan had established themselves as the world economic powers. Exchange restrictions both within Western Europe and in the rich countries outside Europe were relaxed. In 1956, the IMF reported that the effect of liberalisation of foreign exchange restrictions had become manifest in the flow of international trade for the first time since the outbreak of the Second World War.[2] Between 1961 and 1965, almost all OECD Member countries reduced exchange restrictions considerably. This process augmented the movement of capital and liberalisation of trade between States. Ironically, outflow of capital eventually became a contributory factor to an adverse balance of payments in many of the industrialised countries. On the other hand, a different scenario became manifest in the developing world between 1955 and 1965 – the period during which most of the former colonies attained their independence. Many of these countries not only followed an exchange restrictions policy but also tightened it as far as possible in order to deal with their balance of payments difficulties and to protect their own domestic industries.

The 1960s presented an interesting phenomenon. The industrialised countries, by virtue of allowing excessive outflow of capital, caused deficits in their balance of payments (by not having sufficient reserves), which necessitated their seeking the Fund's intervention to rescue them from their predicament – which eventually led them to impose exchange restrictions.[3] At the same time, in view of the chronic deficits in their balance of payments, developing countries sought the Fund's intervention, even though all along they had maintained a rigid restrictive exchange policy. In other words, the Fund's intervention became necessary for two different reasons, although the results were the same.

This unprecedented and unanticipated phenomenon led the Fund to create additional liquidity in the international monetary system, especially in view

---

2.   See the *Annual Report of the Executive Directors for the Fiscal Year Ended 30 April 1956,* (IMF, Washington D.C., 1956) at p.89.

3.   The British pound, e.g., was subject to severe strains in the world exchange markets, and the UK government had to seek the Fund's intervention.

of the fact that the industrialised countries, in the main, did not favour the idea of altering their exchange rates. This situation eventually led to the creation of the Special Drawing Rights (SDR).[4]

B. The Decline of Multiple Rates
(1947-1967)

'Multiple rates' is another name for multiple currency practices. Based on the 1930s experience, multiple exchange rates were viewed as a source of exchange rate instability.[5] One of the primary objectives of the Fund was to attain fixed rates and stabilisation of exchange rates. It is to be stressed however that multiple exchange rates in themselves may not affect exchange stability; it is the frequent changing of rates inherent in the system that may have a direct effect upon the par value of currencies. In an attempt to discourage the operation of multiple currency practices, in December 1947 the Fund issued to its Members a letter on Multiple Currency Practices advising them to consult the Fund prior to introducing such practices on an individual basis. It is believed that the vicious circle of high domestic inflation, which gave rise to balance of payments difficulties, in turn caused the use of multiple currency practices. As a means of controlling inflation Member countries would operate multiple exchange rates. The system was becoming ingrained in economies, so to speak, even in tax regimes and/or export subsidies, as its economic benefits became evident. Despite its unpopularity with the Fund authorities, it became apparent that the multiple exchange rates system was difficult to abandon, unless a substitute system could be formed.

As an initial modified step towards its goal, the Fund not only decided to consider the situations of countries requiring the use of the multiple exchange rates system, but also offered guidance to the Member States as to how the system could be avoided by improving the domestic economic situation. At the same time it urged them to abandon the practice of using 'mixed rates',

---

4.   See section IV.D. infra.
5.   See further Margaret G. de Vries, 'Multiple Exchange Rates: Expectations and Experiences', *Staff Papers* (IMF, Washington DC) Vol.12, pp.282–313.

compensation arrangements etc. However, the multiple exchange rates system was extensively used by many Members of the Fund, including some of the Western countries, until 1955. The newly-born developing countries had to use the multiple exchange rates system as a means of alleviating their persistent adverse balance of payments situation, a factor which contributed to the creation of 'hard' and 'soft' currencies based on the free convertibility of US and Canadian dollars.

However, by the 1950s, the Western European economies, as a consequence of their economic reconstruction programme with the aid of the Marshall Plan and heavy investments, dramatically improved their domestic economies and indeed became leading economies in the world. They gradually and steadily reduced or even abandoned the restrictions on trade and payments and established convertibility of their currencies. A number of developments occurred over a short period of time, which in effect augmented the Fund's programme of abolition of the multiple exchange rates system. The European Economic Community (EEC) was set up, a number of major European Powers also favouring a fixed or unitary exchange rates system. In fact, some of the developed States foresaw that countries operating the multiple exchange rates system would derive undue advantages in export trade over those operating a fixed or unitary exchange rates system. A number of countries beyond Western Europe – Argentina, Finland, Iran, Israel, Nicaragua and Turkey – also favoured this idea. Although not totally abolished, by 1967 the popularity and use of the multiple exchange rates system was significantly reduced.

C. The System of Par Values
(1946-1966)

Par Value stands for the exchange rate for a currency stated in terms of gold. At the time of setting up the Fund each Member was required to agree with the Fund an initial *par value*, as a prerequisite for use of the Fund's resources. A *par value* served as a firm base for a Member's exchange rate.[6]

---

6.   Each Member was required to maintain the spot exchange rate of its currency within a range of 1% of the *par*.

Par value could not be changed without the prior consent of the Fund, and the only ground for proposing a change in the *par value* was correcting the 'fundamental disequilibrium' in a Member's balance of payments. The *par value* system imported a fixed exchange rate of the gold standard and yet the Members had the advantage of changing it in legitimate circumstances. The most important aspect of the system was that unilateral action by a Member State was not permissible, although the Fund in practice could not withhold its consent for a change proposed for correcting a fundamental disequilibrium in the balance of payments of a Member State.

The *par value* system had its ups and downs. In 1948, France sought the IMF's permission to change *par value* and also for a provisional free market for certain currencies and transactions. As stated earlier, the Fund did not usually object to a proposal for change of *par value* on legitimate grounds, but the French proposal for a free market for certain currencies did not meet with the approval of the Fund, as it considered such an act might have an adverse effect on the economies of other Member States. Despite the Fund's disapproval of the French proposal, France changed her *par value*, which act prompted the Fund authorities to declare France ineligible for drawing resources from the Fund until 1954. In December 1958, a new *par value* for the French franc was established within the Fund. In November 1949, the Peruvian proposal for the abandonment of *par value* for a fluctuating exchange rate until a stable exchange rate level could be found was approved by the Fund authorities on a temporary basis; interestingly enough, Peru did not agree to another *par value*, although she had maintained a unitary fluctuating exchange rate system.

In 1950, the Canadian government permitted the Canadian dollar to fluctuate in response to market forces and suspended its fixed rate. Although this action was contrary to the provisions of the Articles of Agreement of the Fund, the Fund authorities, appreciating the circumstances which led the Canadian government to take such action, advised Canada to remain in close touch with the Fund and to set a new *par value* as soon as possible.[7] The *par value* system failed to attain popularity with many countries: Afghanistan,

---

7. Canada returned to the *par value* system in 1962.

Indonesia, Italy,[8] Korea, Thailand and Vietnam never set *par values* for their currencies. In other words, during the 1950s, a dual system came into operation: *par value* and fluctuating (multiple) exchange rates.

The Fund was bound by its Articles of Agreement which contained *par value* as an essential obligation for its Members. Some of the new Members maintained that without access to the resources of the Fund, no realistic *par value* could be established. This suggested that in order to develop an appropriate economic infrastructure which might contribute to strengthening the trading position of a country, resort to a fluctuating exchange rates system was essential; consequently, the question of their setting a correct *par value* would not arise. Indeed, by a resolution in 1964, the Board of Governors of the IMF permitted certain Members to draw on the Fund's resources even prior to their establishing an initial *par value*. Although the Fund adhered to the *par value* system, controversy as to the efficacy of the system outside the Fund was never-ending. But inherent in the system of flexible rates was the right of a government to take unilateral action, by-passing the Fund, even though one of its most important functions was to be involved in international consultation on exchange rate changes.

During this period another important development occurred in the international monetary world. A large number of countries, developed and developing alike, devalued their exchange rates considerably, as a measure to tackle high inflation. The gap between domestic consumer prices and export prices became significant, and indeed devaluation gained support as it helped boost the export trade of countries. The general price level in developed countries was ahead of exchange rates, and yet it did not affect their export position. In short, in developed and developing countries alike, with the rise in prices, there has been a more than corresponding rise in devaluation of currencies. The Fund's insistence on adhering to the *par value* system was primarily based on its Articles of Agreement; the opposition to the system was based on (practical) realities, although as stated above, certain non-adhering Member countries eventually joined the *par value* system.

---

8.   Italy agreed on initial *par value* in 1960.

During the same period another problem demonstrated the inadequacy of the monetary system enshrined in the Articles of Agreement of the Fund. With the increase in the volume of international trade and financial transactions the system could not provide adequate world reserves against the flow of liquidity. Consequently, the persistent reliance of countries on US dollars for use as their reserves, as an alternative subjected the US to continuous balance of payments deficits, which in turn affected the degree of confidence which the majority of Member countries had maintained in US dollars. The built-in inability of the international monetary system to introduce changes in exchange rates also contributed to the adjustment problem. It is to be stressed however that the demand for US dollars as reserves increased from both developed and developing countries for their own particular reasons. Perhaps the ethos of the Bretton Woods system was not wrong; nevertheless, the circumstances of the time occasioned by various factors, as explained above, required a review of certain aspects of the system.

A fixed exchange rates system presented difficulties for the principal currencies resulting in persistent adverse balance of payments in various Member countries. Fast growth in the industrial sector in the developed world, and the economic development programmes in the developing world particularly during the latter part of the 1960s, created extra demand for convertible currencies. The liquidity problem attained crisis proportions. In 1967, the pound sterling was devalued; and although it was not until 1971 that the US suspended convertibility of US dollars into gold, virtually occasioning the collapse of the *par value* system, the symptoms of such an eventual consequence had already become apparent in the late 1960s. In 1969, a novel reserve asset, designated as the Special Drawing Rights (SDR), to be allocated by the Fund, was created. The late 1960s witnessed a severe strain on the Bretton Woods system, and it can be maintained that the SDR was the outcome of a desperate attempt to save and reform the contemporary international monetary system.

D. The Period Between 1969 and 1978

This period witnessed some important developments: the creation of the SDR in 1969 by amending the Articles of Agreement for the first time in the history of the IMF;[9] the Arab-Israeli conflict of 1973 triggered an oil crisis requiring many Members of the Fund to draw on the Fund's resources. New drawing facilities had to be created; the maximum entitlement of a Member under its quota was increased under the compensatory financing facility; the Fund approved an increased number of extended stand-by arrangements. The Fund also established an extended facility to allow medium-term assistance to developing countries. New policy issues were considered to combat 'stagflation'. In April 1976, the Board of Governors submitted a proposal for amending the Articles of Agreement a second time, the effect of which would be, *inter alia*, to (a) introduce a new arrangement for exchange rates (a new Article IV); (b) allow Members to choose their exchange arrangements; (c) ensure a gradual reduction in the role of gold in the international monetary system; (d) to use SDR as the principal reserve asset; and (e) allow the Fund to review and consider changes, if necessary, in its functional policies, so as to meet the challenges presented to the existing international monetary system. After the entry into force of the Second Amendment on 1 April 1978, the Fund was given a new mandate in its operational mechanism, as fundamental changes had been made in the concepts enshrined in the original Articles of Agreement.

It is interesting to note that in 1974, the UN General Assembly Declaration entitled The New International Economic Order also contained a proposal for reforming the contemporary international monetary system.[10] Incidentally, the Committee of Twenty, created in 1972, allowed the participation of developing countries in the decision-making process, which prior to that date was the exclusive preserve of the industrialised countries, and by 1974 increasingly greater attention was being paid to the economic problems of developing countries.

Between 1972 and 1978, the Fund's membership from the non-capitalist countries was enlarged. Hungary and Romania joined the Fund, followed by the Socialist Republic of Vietnam (replacing the Republic of South Vietnam

9.   The First Amendment took effect on 28 July 1969.
10.   UNGA Res.No.A/Res/3201 (S-VI) of 9 May 1974; see also *Resolution on Monetary Reform*, UNGA Res. A/Res/2565 (XXIV) of 13 Dec. 1969; 'Group of Ten Report on the Functioning of the Monetary System' (1985) 24 ILM 1687; and the 'Group of Twenty-Four Report on Changes in the Monetary System' idem, p.1699.

in 1976).[11] The Fund was therefore required to address the problems of socialist and/or centrally planned economies more extensively than ever before.

This period also required the Fund to confront novel and yet perhaps predictable phenomena. It found it necessary to keep the international monetary system under constant review, particularly the floating exchange rates. In April 1977, the Executive Board adopted procedures for the guidance of Members' exchange rates policies and implementation of the surveillance system through which the new Article IV was to be implemented. As a result of the Second Amendment, Fund Members became free to use the exchange rates of their own choice, although their practices and policies in relation to the exchange rates regimes were subject to the surveillance of the Fund. The Group of 24 also regarded the surveillance function of the Fund as crucial for an orderly international monetary and financial system.

The period between 1969 and 1978 must be regarded as one of the most memorable periods in the history of the Fund to date. It struggled to retain the Bretton Woods system and yet found itself unable to accommodate world economic forces and events; it was made to appreciate that the basis and scope of the Fund's activities and operations must be broadened with the exigencies of unforeseen situations. This period also signalled the economic and financial vicissitudes that the Fund and the international community might encounter in subsequent decades in the area of international monetary co-operation.

E. The Period Between 1979 and 1990

The effect of the world economic recession of the mid-1970s was bitterly felt in 1979. The year 1979 was born with the 'world debt crisis'. The causes of the debt crisis were multifarious; the high oil price of the 1970s compounded by high inflation; low output in the industrialised world culminating in high unemployment with a corresponding increase in domestic prices. The plight of the developing countries in managing their economies became immeasurable – their borrowing from commercial banks rose to a record high.

---

11. In 1980, the People's Republic of China assumed the place of China in the Fund.

Interestingly enough, due to the availability of large amounts of petrodollar based finance, borrowing from commercial sources became much easier during the early 1980s. Many of the non-oil-producing developing countries did not take sufficient macroeconomic measures to adjust their balance of payments deficits, resulting in a high accumulation of external debts and reduced rates of growth. The question of their paying back debts did not arise; the situation was one of 'we can't pay' rather than 'we won't pay'. Most of the debtor debt-service ratios, that is, the amount in percentage terms that debt-service payments represents of export earnings, rose so significantly that to advance any more loans to these countries became a unprofitable proposition for both lenders and borrowers. The classic example was represented by the statement made by the Mexican government in 1982 to its creditors that it could no longer meet its debt-service payments, even though Mexico has always been an oil-exporting country. This situation alarmed the lenders, pointing to remote prospects for recovery of bad debts and signalling the reduction in world trade in the future, with its attendant consequences, economic or otherwise. As for the lending banks themselves, an urgent review of their lending policies was called for.

The Fund's response to the Mexican crisis was based on the study made by itself of the various causes, including the governmental fiscal policy, deepening public sector deficit etc. The Fund approved Mexico's use of SDR 3.6 billion, with the package of an economic recovery programme in conjunction with borrowing from commercial banks. In fact, the Fund's approval of the availability of its resources was made conditional upon finance being secured from commercial banks. Although this approach signified a departure from the Fund's usual practice, it represented two very important developments: first, that the Fund alone should not be exclusively involved in development and reconstruction programmes, as the case may be, for its Member countries, and second, that the commercial world, in general, should be allowed to participate on a co-operative basis in such programmes, in conformity with general international policies. Of course, an additional source of finance and expertise would also lessen the demands traditionally made on the Fund. The second most important example was the case of Brazil. The Fund, upon being approached by the Brazilian government, adopted a similar approach to the Brazilian proposal for a loan from the Fund.

The Fund advocates and adopts a country-by-country approach, which contains both structural adjustment and financing aspects, which should eventually lead to high productivity, high employment, high savings and consequently more investment and a higher flow of export trade.

Such is the magnitude of the current debt crisis that there does not seem to exist any miraculous way of remedying it. However, ironically, it has made both the borrowers and lenders aware of how not to borrow and lend. Commercial banks were required to play an important role in dealing with the management of the debt problem in order to ensure that loans were advanced not only for the borrower's economic development purposes, but also that their balance of payments position would be improved. During this period, the Fund's approach to international monetary policy, including the debt crisis, became more direct and realistic than ever before. The following are some of the essentials of this new approach: surveillance over the external debt policies of its Member countries; monitoring of the external borrowings of its Members through a technical assistance programme; publication and dissemination of information and statistics on debts; a broader use of its consultation procedure.

The Baker Plan refers to essential factors of sustained growth. However, its achievement requires the successful completion of two stages: management of existing debts, and the adoption of a policy particularly at the domestic level to ensure that debts are accumulated in a controlled manner only for essential reasons. This may not be achieved over a short period of time. Such is the basic crisis with which the whole international monetary policy and the IMF are now most concerned.

This brief account of the growth and development of the IMF since its inception is highly relevant to an understanding of the functions of the IMF past, present and future. The current system of functioning of the Fund has also provoked some controversy. The Group of 10 and the Group of 24 have put forward various recommendations suggesting how the system may be modified.[12]

12. For the full texts of these recommendations, see (1985) 24 ILM 1685–1736.

IV. SOME BASIC CONCEPTS ESSENTIAL FOR AN UNDERSTANDING
OF THE OPERATIONAL ASPECTS OF THE IMF

IN this Section an attempt is made to explain the operational aspects of the
Fund especially with reference to the mechanics of the financial assistance it
offers to its Members. This takes various forms, the most important of which
are:

(a)   Credit Tranche Policy;
(b)   Stand-by Arrangements including Extended Stand-by;
(c)   Compensatory Financing Facility;
(d)   Buffer-stock Financing Facility:
(e)   Floating Facility;
(f)   Extended Facility; and
(g)   Supplementary Financing Facility.

It is not possible here to discuss in detail each of these facilities. It has
therefore been decided to explain the basic mechanics of the Fund's extension
of financial assistance and also to give a brief account of some of the most
important facilities.

A. The Mechanics of Financial Assistance

All transactions of the Fund are carried out through its General Department
and the Special Drawing Rights Department. The principal sources of the
Fund's general resources are subscriptions and borrowings. Financial
assistance in the form of loans is made available by the Fund to its Members
by selling currencies or SDRs in exchange for their own currencies.
Assistance is granted to those applicants who maintain an acceptable balance
of payments system. Each Member is required to pay a subscription equal to
the quota allocated to it. Usually, payment is made mostly in a Member's
own currency, unless otherwise stated. Under its Articles of Agreement, the
Fund can borrow from entities such as treasuries, central banks and even
from private sources, including commercial banks. Finance in a Member's
currency cannot be raised by the Fund from a source other than the Member
itself, without the consent of the Member concerned; it must be emphasised

however that a Member is under no legal obligation to lend to or approve borrowings by the Fund of its currency whether from itself or from another source. One of the sources of loans to the Fund is the General Arrangements to Borrow (GAB), which arrangement is made periodically.[13] Under this arrangement the Fund borrows in the currencies of industrialised countries, namely, Belgium, Canada, France, Italy, Japan, the Netherlands, the United Kingdom and the United States, and also from the central banks of Germany and Sweden. The Fund has a special arrangement with the Swiss Government (which is not a Member of the Fund) whereby the said government may grant loans to participants who make purchases that are financed by borrowings made by the Fund under GAB, provided that there exists a relevant bilateral agreement between the Government of Switzerland and the participant. The Fund has the authority to raise supplementary finance from any other recognised sources. It borrowed a significantly large amount from the Saudi Arabian Agency, the Austrian National Bank, the Central Bank of Kuwait, Banco de Guatemala, the Swiss National Bank and the Central Bank of Venezuela. The Fund borrows with a view to providing finance to its deserving Members, and in 1982, it adopted guidelines for borrowing, which are subject to review as and when deemed necessary by the Fund authorities. It must however be emphasised in this connection that the Fund's borrowing is only a supplementary source of finance, quota subscriptions remaining the primary source of the Fund's financing.

B. Purchase and Repurchase as Mechanism of Financial Assistance

The purchase and re-purchase mechanism is fundamental to the operation of the Fund's financial assistance scheme. It provides finance primarily for assisting a Member in correcting an adverse balance of payments. Assistance is given by selling currencies of other Members or SDRs to the borrowing State in exchange for its own currency. When a Member borrows from the Fund, it is said to be purchasing (or drawing) from the Fund as, in effect, the

---

13. Information on the borrowing arrangement under GAB may be found in the Reports of the Executive Board.

Fund sells the currencies or SDRs to the purchasing Member concerned. When a Member purchases the currency of another Member, the Fund instructs the depository that holds the Fund's deposit of a designated currency (which is usually the central bank of the Member country) to debit the Fund's account and credit the account designated by the Member country with that amount. The purchasing Member also credits the Fund's account with its own currency equivalent to the amount it purchased. Each borrowing (purchasing-drawing) Member has the obligation to buy back its currency from the Fund with other currencies or SDRs. When a Member does so, it is said to be 're-purchasing' its currency.

C. Types of Financial Assistance Offered by the Fund

The Fund operates various policies and facilities in offering financial assistance to its Members. Depending upon the basis for seeking financial assistance from the Fund by a Member, the Fund applies the relevant facility and conditionality.[14] However, in all cases the grounds for seeking financial assistance from the Fund must be the correction of balance of payments. As stated earlier, over the years, the Fund has extended financial assistance to its Members under various new facilities according to the exigencies of time and circumstance. In other words, in modification of its original rigid polices, the Fund has gradually adopted a flexible lending policy. Most of the facilities are linked to the quota, originally allocated or otherwise, and based on tranche drawings. The liberalisation policy of the Fund has been made possible by raising the quota limits of its Members, particularly the developing Members, and extending currency holdings under the reserve and credit tranche policies, which is known as 'floating the specific facility'. As from May 1981, stand-by or extended arrangements were also allowed to float.

A Member's reserve tranche represents the excess of its quota over the Fund's holdings of its currency in the General Resources Account which however excludes holding occasioned by purchases made under the Fund's

---

14.   Infra section F.1.

other policies and facilities. The mechanics of the reserve credit tranche drawings have been explained by the Fund in the following passage:[15]

> ... suppose that the member has a quota equivalent to SDR 100 million, that the Fund's holdings of its currency are equivalent to SDR 340 million, and the member has outstanding purchases of SDR 100 million under the compensatory facility, SDR 25 million under the credit tranche policies, and SDR 140 million under the extended Fund facility. Since these outstanding purchases are excluded for the purpose of calculating the reserve tranche, the latter in this case would be SDR 25 million.

In this way a Member can have a favourable/positive reserve tranche position even if the Fund's holdings of its currency substantially exceeds its quota, and drawings can still be allowed under these facilities without reducing its reserve assets.

D. The Special Drawing Rights (SDRs)

The opposite of 'general' is 'special'. These are 'special rights' that are granted to the Members of the IMF in order to allow them to supplement their existing reserve assets by drawing resources from the Fund.[16] These are allocated by the Fund to the Members participating in the scheme.[17] SDRs can be used for a wide range of transactions, including the obtaining of foreign exchange. Neither the allocation nor the use of SDRs is subject to conditionality. SDRs are determined on a daily basis as the weighted average value of a basket of the currencies of those Members who have the largest share in export of goods and services. The currencies included in the basket are converted into US dollar equivalents at the exchange rates prevailing in the London foreign exchange market. The US dollar value of the SDR is obtained by adding together the US dollar equivalents. The market rate between a currency and the US dollar and the rate between the US dollar and the SDR are used to determine the SDR rate for any other

---

15. A.W. Hooke, *The International Monetary Fund: its Evolution, Organization and Activities*, IMF, Washington D.C., Pamphlet No.37, p.41.

16. J. Gold, *Special Drawing Rights: Character and Use*, (IMF, Washington DC 1970), p.1.

17. By June 1982, all Members of the Fund became participants in the Special Drawing Rights Department.

currency. The currencies determining the value of the SDR are reviewed every five years to ensure that they represent the currencies of the Members with the largest export of goods and services over the past five years.

The Fund has the authority to cancel SDRs, as it can also create liquidity by allocating them to participants in the Special Drawing Rights Department under Article XV, Section 1 of the Articles of Agreement. Decisions on allocation of SDRs are made for basic periods, normally five years, although variation in the length of the basic periods has occurred.

The following procedure is usually followed in creating additional liquidity by SDRs. A proposal for allocation of SDRs is made by the Managing Director of the Fund at least six months before the commencement of the next basic period or within six months of a request for a proposal from the Executive Board of the Board of Governors. A proposal for an allocation must be consistent with the objectives of the Fund. The Board of Governors has the power to modify a proposal submitted by the Managing Director. All proposals for SDR allocation must receive the broad support of participants, and the concurrence of the Executive Board. Allocation of SDRs is based on the size of the quota of a Member immediately preceding such allocation.

A participant may receive SDRs from other participant(s) by mutual agreement between themselves. The Fund may also designate participants to receive specified amounts of SDR from other participants and in that event the latter are allowed equivalent amounts of freely usable currencies in exchange. The Fund operates a quarterly designation scheme, designations being made on condition that the Member's balance of payments position is not unduly adverse and that its gross reserve position is strong.

There is no obligation for a participant to maintain a minimum holding of SDRs. This system enables a Member in a credit position to sell its holdings of SDR if it so chooses. SDR holders are paid interest by the Fund on their holdings and the Fund levies charges[18] on participants on their cumulative allocations. Although a fixed rate of interest is usually operated in connection with SDRs, the Fund has the authority to change the rate of interest.[19]

---

18.   The rate of interest is the same as the rate of charge.
19.   Art.XXVI, s.3; see also Rules and Regulations.

In order to accommodate the Special Drawing Rights facility, a Special Drawing Account was set up, in addition to the General Account, which is the principal and original Account of the Fund. Participation in the Special Account is discretionary, and without participation in the General Account, participation in the Special Drawing Account is not possible. SDRs are intended to satisfy not only 'global needs' but also 'long term' needs. In taking decisions on creating SDRs, the Fund is not concerned with the short-term management of international liquidity.[20] Decisions to allocate or cancel SDRs must be taken in such a manner as will help fulfil the purposes of the Fund and avoid economic stagnation, inflation and deflation in the world.[21] No decisions are taken by mathematical or mechanical tests but by rational judgment reached in the light of the prevailing international monetary situation and world economic conditions.

The objective of SDRs is to supplement existing reserve assets, and not to replace them. SDRs have an international character in that, although they are transferred bilaterally, by virtue of the obligations due to the Fund the effect that their transfer produces is international.

A participant is allowed to use its SDRs until it has exhausted its limit. The fact that the Fund is informed of a transfer by the transferor operates as a deterrent to the abuse of SDRs. The Fund cannot obstruct a transfer even if it becomes evident that there was no need for the transfer. In the event of a participant wishing to use its SDRs by transferring them to a designated participant, it has an obligation to inform the Fund of its intention in order to enable the latter to give instructions to the participant(s) that it will designate the currency as convertible in fact. Similarly if a transferor of SDRs wishes to receive a particular currency convertible in fact, it must notify the Fund accordingly. The following principles are fundamentally important in relation to currencies provided for SDRs:[22]

---

20.   J. Gold, *Special Drawing Rights*, op. cit. supra n.16, pp.16–17.
21.   Art.XXIV, s.1(a); see also *A Report to the Board of Governors of the International Monetary Fund containing the Managing Director's Proposal on the Allocation of Special Drawing Rights for the First Basic Period*, (IMF, Washington DC 1969) pp.4–5.
22.   J. Gold, *Special Drawing Rights*, op. cit. supra n.16, p.45.

1. The first is that the transferor of special drawing rights is entitled to receive the currency convertible in fact (of the first category) which it requests in return for the transfer to a designated participant.
2. The second is that the designated participant may provide any convertible currency, whether of the first or second category, which it sees fit.
3. The third principle is that if the currency convertible in fact provided by the transferee is not the currency convertible in fact requested by the transferor, the issuer of the currency provided must convert it.

A participant has the right to give notice of termination of its participation in the facility at any time, and notice becomes effective as soon as the Fund receives it.[23] The Fund has an obligation to redeem all SDRs held by an ex-participant who must return to the Fund an amount equal to its net cumulative allocation. In the event of the Fund's liquidating the Special Drawing Rights Account, a participant will be required to pay the Fund an amount equal to its net cumulative allocation, and the Fund will redeem the SDRs held by the participant.

E. Credit Tranche Drawing and Stand-by Arrangements

The Fund's basic lending policy is based on credit tranche drawings. Credit is made available in four tranches, each tranche being the equivalent to 25% of the quota allocated to a Member. Drawings from the second tranche are known as upper tranche drawings. Credit tranche drawings must be repaid as soon as the balance of payments position and the reserve position improve so as to include the borrowing country's currency in the Fund's quarterly budget, but no later than five years from the date of borrowing. Normally, repayments must commence three years and three months after a drawing has been made.

Whereas a credit tranche drawing (purchase) may be made by a Member on the strength of availability of credit under its allocated quota, credit under a stand-by arrangement requires the approval of the Fund; but once approved, the Member is assured of the availability of credits over a specified period of time,[24] provided that it satisfies the performance criteria and other terms of

---

23. Art.XXVI, s.1.
24. The maximum period of a stand-by arrangement may be for three years, but traditionally

the stand-by arrangements. Under this arrangement, the Fund stands by, so to say, the borrower, in order to enable it to complete the purpose for which the arrangement is made.[25]

F. Extended Facility

The title of this facility is significant. It is a facility which is an extension of the normal facility for which a Member may be eligible. This facility was established in 1974; its objective is to allow a Member to receive financial assistance/support from the Fund over a period longer than the usual in order to enable it to implement appropriate corrective policies. This facility is not restricted only to structural correctional programmes; it may be extended to a Member which is actively engaged in a development programme, but owing to its adverse balance of payments position, unable to pursue it successfully. Extended facility is usually granted for a period of three years on condition that the borrowing country achieves adequate growth by increasing her export trade and limiting the need for imports. In other words, in seeking financial assistance under this facility the Member concerned is required to establish that its plan is likely to achieve sustainable growth over a period of time.

The maximum limit for drawing under the extended facility is 140 per cent of the quota which a Member is allocated provided that the Fund's holdings of its currency do not exceed 165% of quota. Repurchases must be made in 12 equal half-yearly instalments as early as possible but no later than ten years after the drawings. They commence four and half years after the drawings made by the Member.

1. Conditionality

The Fund has no authority to challenge a request for drawings by its Members under their reserve tranches. Use of the Fund's general resources must be in accordance with the general policies advocated and followed by the Fund, the principal aim of which is to resolve difficulties associated with an

---

it is granted for one year.
25. For a discussion of certain aspects of the stand-by arrangement, see Section F.2 infra.

adverse balance of payments, however caused, by pursuing the relevant provisions of the Articles of Agreement. 'Conditionality' stands for the policies that a Member is expected to follow when using Fund resources in an effort to deal with balance of payments problems. The term 'conditionality' apparently connotes certain 'legal restrictions'. Members are expected to abide by certain policies/conditions in borrowing resources from the Fund.[26] Although short of strict legal obligations, in practice, a failure to observe these policies/conditions by a Member may jeopardise its prospect of obtaining financial assistance from the Fund. From this standpoint, any controversy as to the legal status of 'conditionality' seems to be unnecessary.

The original Articles of Agreement of the Fund did not contain any provisions for conditionality; the system of attaching conditions to lending resources and ensuring the ability to repurchase the currency by the Member concerned is an 'afterthought' based on practicality. By interpretation, however, the Fund possesses the capacity to impose conditionality in that the Articles of Agreement provide that the Fund's resources must be of a revolving character.

Conditionality is not attached as a means of recovering the debt from a borrower, but to ensure that the borrower by virtue of improving its general economic conditions is able to repay, although this distinction may be difficult to sustain in law. The condition of satisfying performance under a stand-by arrangement[27] has therefore been devised. These latter arrangements entail higher risks even for the borrower; the Fund attempts to ensure that the obligations of borrowing are fulfilled and that the need for such large borrowings may not arise again soon.

It may be maintained that conditionality is not a rigid and static concept; indeed, since its inception in 1952, the original terms of conditionality have been revised in 1968 and again in 1979. The following are some of the most important guidelines on conditionality agreed by the Executive Board in 1979:

---

26. See however Group of 24 Communiqués on 'Lending: Reform and Debt Problems', in which Ministers opposed an excessive emphasis on policy-based lending, conditionality: (1985) 24 ILM 897–900.

27. Section F.2 infra.

(a)   In order to minimise demands on the Fund's resources, Members should introduce policies whereby such resources, where appropriate, may be sought at an early stage of their balance of payments difficulties rather than at a later stage. Thus an unduly long period requiring a greater effort for correction of balance of payments with a more rigorous form of conditionality attached to borrowings may be averted.

(b)   Where adjustment programmes cannot be completed within the traditional one-year period associated with stand-by arrangements, upon justification this period may be extended to three years. This guideline, in reality, favours a borrowing Member, but implied in it is the suggestion that a borrowing Member may not automatically seek an extension of time.

(c)   By virtue of their composition and mechanics, stand-by arrangements are to be treated differently from international agreements. Breach of obligation under these arrangements does not amount to violating an international obligation.

(d)   In the event of the Fund's helping a Member to formulate a pro-gramme to correct its balance of payments difficulties, the Fund must pay due regard to the domestic, social and economic objectives and priorities of the Member, and the circumstances responsible for causing the adverse balance of payments situation. This directly indicates that the sole objective of conditionality is not to subject a borrowing Member to rigid conditions of borrowing, but within its framework to allow it to improve its overall economic position.

(e)   Consultation between the Fund and a borrowing Member is a cornerstone of conditionality, in relation to stand-by or extended stand-by arrangements. The consultation clause is to be activated when a borrowing Member has failed to satisfy its performance criteria. The primary objective of consultation is to assist a Member in difficulty to meet its performance criteria so as to restore its right to draw or make purchases from the Fund.

(f)   Only upper tranches under a stand-by arrangement are subject to performance criteria and phasing-out conditions.

(g) As a means of safeguarding the objectives of the Fund, stand-by arrangements may be subject to fulfilment of certain conditions by the Member seeking funds under such arrangements.

(h) Conditionality must be non-discriminatory, that is, in similar cases, the conditions of granting resources must be the same. This obviously entails a degree of value judgment.

(i) Performance criteria represent an aspect of conditionality. They stand for the level of performance a borrowing Member is required to attain during the stipulated period of borrowing resources. Performance criteria involve macroeconomic variables, which include ceilings on the expansion of bank credits and a ceiling on bank credit to the government, limits on the contracting of new external short-term and medium term debts, and avoidance of introduction or intensification of current international payments.[28]

(j) In the event of a Member's failing to establish advance performance criteria, a review is required in order for an understanding to be reached for a succeeding period. This is a precautionary measure against any future failures by the borrowing Member to satisfy the performance criteria. In practice, however, the Fund appreciates the difficulties a Member may experience in fulfilling its performance criteria.

(k) The IMF may analyse and assess the performance of the programmes financed by the Fund's general resources in order to carry out a proper consultation procedure and consider further requests for the use of the Fund's resources.

(l) The Executive Committee has the right to undertake periodic reviews of programmes supported by stand-by arrangements in order to evaluate the policy measures adopted by a borrowing Member and the extent to which performance criteria have been satisfied.

'Conditionality' has been devised not so much to impose conditions on the use of the Fund's resources by a borrowing Member, but more to ensure that the borrowing Member utilises the resources in the most appropriate way so

28. A.W. Hooke, op. cit. supra n.15, at p.40.

as to be able to improve its balance of payments position and macroeconomic conditions, which might reduce the need for such borrowing in the near future. The consultation procedure clearly indicates that any rigidity of conditionality may be 'mellowed' by activating it. It entails consideration not only of the reasons for failure to achieve the performance criteria, but also the circumstances that might oblige a borrowing Member to depart from conditionality. The foundation of conditionality is based on mutual benefit and understanding between the Fund and its borrowing Members.

2. Stand-by arrangements

Under a stand-by arrangement, the Fund provides assurance, in advance, to a Member that it can make drawings on the Fund's General Resources Account, as determined, over a specified period of time, which is usually between one and three years, provided the conditions of drawings are met. This facility was first extended by the Fund in 1952.

In 1974, in order to alleviate the financial difficulties of Members, principally caused by the unprecedented oil crisis, the Executive Board offered an 'extended arrangement'.[29] Extended arrangements may be described as a special category of stand-by arrangements, save for the fact that on the basis of such arrangements a Member is allowed to draw a larger amount from the Fund. The primary purpose of offering a stand-by or an extended stand-by is the same as to allow a Member to achieve an improved balance of payments position sustainable over a period of time. In other words, on the strength of the improved balance of payments position, and associated economic benefits, the Member may not be required to borrow under such an arrangement in the near future.

3. The legal character of stand-by and extended stand-by arrangements

Both stand-by and extended stand-by are negotiated arrangements. Under such an arrangement, the Member concerned works out a viable borrowing

---

29.   See the Executive Board's Decision No.4377 (74/114) as amended by its Decisions 6339 (79/119) and 6830 (81/85).

strategy which is examined by the Fund authorities in order to ensure not only that the Member concerned has the capacity to handle and implement it, but also that it will contribute to sustainable economic growth. The negotiated terms are embodied in a Letter of Intent, which contains a unilateral statement made by the Member concerned demonstrating how it would propose to attain the projected targets. This may be described as a self-imposed burden based on realistic aspirations. The Fund does not dictate to the Member what should be included in a Letter of Intent. The terms and conditions of the extended arrangement are determined on the basis of the information supplied by the Member in its Letter of Intent. The following represents some of the information that a Member is expected to supply: balance of payments adjustment strategy; total investment in both public and private sectors; public sector programmes; agricultural development programme(s); public sector policies; the extent of government revenues and subsidies; incentives for private sector savings; the extent of government spending; general monetary and fiscal policies; export promotion policy; ceilings on domestic credit; extent of borrowings from both internal and external sources; exchange rates policy; industrial development policy; import liberalisation policy etc. In the event of the Fund's being satisfied with the contents of the letter of intent, it assures the Member of the stand-by or extended stand-by facility. The unilateral character of the letter of intent may provoke controversy as to its legally binding nature. The legal character of a stand-by arrangement, including a letter of intent, was clarified by Gold when he stated that:

> ... a stand-by arrangement is not an agreement between the Fund and the Member, and the Member undertakes no contractual commitment to pursue the policies for the support of which stand-by arrangement is approved. On the contrary, the provisions of stand-by arrangement do create certain obligations for a member, for example, it is bound to consult and to repurchase in accordance with the terms of the stand-by arrangement.[30]

30.   J. Gold, *The Stand-by Arrangements of the International Monetary Fund: A Commentary on their Formal Legal and Financial Aspects* (IMF, Washington DC, 1970), p.50.

3. Some of the important clauses usually included in a stand-by or extended stand-by arrangement

(i)   The *period* for which the arrangement has been granted.

(ii)   The *amount* for which the arrangement has been made. As from 1984, a Member's right to draw under a stand-by or an extended stand-by may be interrupted in the event of its bearing any overdue financial obligation to the Fund.

(iii)   *Performance criteria clause.* Performance criteria are chosen by the borrowing Members; again, they represent unilateral statements. Failure to meet performance criteria would interrupt a Member's right to make drawings under the arrangement. The Fund does not specify any criteria, and yet legal obligations emanate from the Letter of Intent and the stand-by arrangement. It is for the borrowing Member to determine how it might be able to perform within the stipulated period and with the available Fund resources. Should a borrowing Member fail to perform accordingly, it becomes answerable to the Fund. Such a situation certainly jeopardises the Member's prospects of borrowing in the future. To reiterate, this is one of the most important aspects of the Letter of Intent. Failure to implement the 'intent' makes the Member accountable to the Fund, although apparently it represents a unilateral statement of intent.

(iv)   *Purchase clause.* Under this clause the Member undertakes an obligation to make purchases in the currencies of other Members selected in accordance with the policies and procedures of the Fund. Purchases may be made in SDRs.

(v)   *Payment of charge clause.* A borrowing Member undertakes to pay a charge for the stand-by or extended stand-by arrangement in accordance with the scale of charges determined by the Fund. Charges are levied in consideration of the commitment made by the Fund to make SDRs and currencies available on call.

(vi) *Repurchase clause.* Under this clause a Member is required to repurchase the equivalent of the borrowed amount in its own currency in accordance with the decision of the Fund.

(vii) *Consultation clause.* Consultation clauses are applicable to purchases made beyond the first credit tranche. Such clauses are implemented as and when necessary during the entire period in which a Member has outstanding purchases in the upper credit tranches and until all repurchases are effected.

(viii) *Rate of exchange clause.* This clause states the rate of exchange for the Member's currency at which transactions will be conducted during the period of the arrangement.

4. The general obligation of Members

Article VIII of the Articles of Agreement details the general obligations of Members of the IMF. In addition to these general obligations a Member may be required to undertake and perform certain 'special' obligations that may be attached to certain specific acts of a Member. Article VIII enumerates the following general obligations:

(i)   avoidance of restrictions on current payments;
(ii)   avoidance of discriminatory currency practices;
(iii) convertibility of foreign-held balances;
(iv)   furnishing of information;
(v)   consultation between Members regarding existing international agreements; and
(vi)   obligations to collaborate regarding policies on reserve assets.

In summary, no Member shall, without the approval of the Fund, impose any restrictions on the making of payments and transfers of current international transactions. This provision will not apply where imposition of limitations on the freedom of exchange operations in a scarce currency, on a temporary basis, has been approved of by the Fund, and when exchange restrictions, as a transitional arrangement, have been permitted by the Fund.

One of the most important obligations of the Members is to furnish to the IMF such information as the latter deems necessary for its activities, and in particular, information on international investment, national income, price indices, exchange control system in effect, and import and export of merchandise in terms of local currency values. According to Article VIII (5)(b), 'Members shall be under no obligation to furnish information in such detail that the positions of individuals or corporations is disclosed'. Otherwise, all information must be as accurate and detailed as possible. By agreement with Members, the Fund may obtain further information on any other relevant matter.

The Fund acts as a centre for the collection and exchange of information on monetary and financial problems. This aspect of the obligations is in fact beneficial to Members themselves in that the Fund can alert a Member in sufficient time as to the deteriorating effect of its current fiscal and economic policies, and offer guidance for improvement, if necessary, and can also use such information in arranging a loan to a Member from itself or through commercial banks.

Under Section 7 of Article VIII each Member undertakes to:

... collaborate with the Fund and with other members in order to ensure that the policies of the member with respect to reserve assets shall be consistent with the objectives of promoting better international surveillance of international liquidity and making the special drawing right the principal reserve asset in the international monetary system.

In 1985, the Deputies of the Group of 10 issued a Report on the Functioning of the Monetary System, which recommended, *inter alia*, that:[31]

... While the present institutional framework for surveillance is considered adequate, the Deputies agree that the existing channels need to be used more effectively and co-ordinated better. They also agree that the central role of the IMF in surveillance should be preserved. At the same time, they underline that other institutions, consultative bodies, and groups of more limited membership should continue to play their role in the surveillance process. In this regard, they have noted the important role played by the OECD in the surveillance of the economic policies of the industrial countries. In considering ways of strengthening surveillance, a distinction has been made between surveillance in the form of country-specific

31.   See further 'Group of Ten Report on the Functioning of the Monetary System' (1985) 24 ILM 1685 at 1690.

consultations with an international institution (e.g. bilateral surveillance), and surveillance which focuses on the international adjustment process and the interaction of national policies (e.g. multilateral surveillance).

V. ORGANISATIONAL ASPECTS

A. Membership

Membership in the Fund is open to every sovereign State which is able and prepared to fulfil the obligations of membership contained in the Articles of Agreement of the Fund. At present almost all sovereign States except Switzerland and the component States of the Soviet Union are Members of the Fund, although in view of current political developments in the Soviet Union, the membership structure must change soon.

B. Primary organs

The following are the primary organs of the Fund: the Board of Governors, the Executive Board and a Managing Director.

1. The Board of Governors

The highest decision-making body in the Fund is the Board of Governors which consists of one Governor and one Alternate Governor appointed by each Member of the Fund. Governors are chosen by respective Members, although, in practice, they are usually the Minister of Finance or the Governor of the country's central bank.

In addition to certain general powers, the Board of Governors deals specifically with matters such as admission of members, the determination of quotas, and the allocation of SDRs. Most of its other powers have been delegated to the Executive Board.

The Board usually meets at an Annual Meeting which is held in conjunction with the Annual Meeting of the Board of Governors of the World Bank. However, it shall meet whenever called upon to do so by at least 15 Members or by Members having at least one quarter of the Board's total voting power. The presence of a majority of the Governors with at least two-thirds of the total voting power of the Fund's membership is required for a quorum for a meeting.

2. *The Executive Board*

The Executive Board consists of the Executive Directors and the Managing Director. Each Executive Director appoints an Alternate who may participate in meetings but can vote only when the Executive Director is absent. The Members with the six largest quotas in the Fund[32] appoint an Executive Director each. An Executive Director remains in his office until a successor is appointed by his government. The other 16 Executive Directors are elected by groups of those Members not entitled to appoint an Executive Director. Elections for these Executive Directors are held every two years, although by-elections are held, when needed. In the event of the currencies of the Members with the largest quotas not having been used in the outstanding transactions of the Fund in the preceding two years, then the Member whose currency has been so used may appoint an Executive Director.[33] In such a situation, the number of elected Executive Directors may be correspondingly reduced, unless the Board of Governors decides otherwise in order to maintain the balance in the Board's composition or to ensure the smooth working of the Executive Board.

The Executive Board functions in continuous session. Its meetings are held as and when necessary. The presence of a majority of the Executive Directors having not less than one half of the total voting power is required for a quorum. The Managing Director of the Fund is the Chairman of the Executive Board. The Executive Board conducts the day-to-day business of the Fund. It reports to the Board of Governors. The scope of functions of the Executive Board is as broad and varied as the provisions and objectives contained in the Articles of Agreement.

32. The People's Republic of China, France, Germany, Japan, the UK and the US.
33. Since 1978, Saudi Arabia has appointed an Executive Director.

3. The Managing Director

The Executive Board selects the Managing Director of the Fund for a period of five years. Traditionally, this position has been earmarked for a national of a European Member of the Fund, while the position of the Deputy Managing Director has again traditionally been taken by the United States. The Managing Director is the Chairman of the Executive Board, the Chief of the Fund's operating staff, and participates in meetings of the Board of Governors, the Interim Committee and the Development Committee etc. Subject to the general control of the Executive Board, he is responsible for the ordinary business of the Fund, and appointment and dismissal of staff.

In addition to these principal organs, the Fund consists of various committees and departments. Support services are primarily provided by the Administration and Secretary's Department and the Bureau of Language Services.

C. Voting

The Fund operates a weighted voting system. Each Member has a basic allotment of 250 votes, in addition to one vote for each part of its quota that is equivalent to SDR 100,000. Elected Executive Directors cast all the votes of their countries as a unit, although they are entitled to indicate the votes of individual Members in the group.

Decisions, whether by the Board of Governors or the Executive Board, are usually adopted by a simple majority of the votes cast. In respect of important matters, however, a larger majority is required. Basically, a 70% majority of the total voting power is required to resolve such matters. A very 'high' majority (about 85%) is required to decide more important matters, such as those related to the structure of the Fund, the allocation of SDRs and changes in quotas. Although the largest Members together, or a large Member in conjunction with a group of countries, or a group of countries can in theory veto proposals, in practice, most decisions in the Executive Board are arrived at by consensus, and formal votes are rarely taken. This point is very important in the understanding of the Fund's operational activities.

The 1984 Group of 24's Revised Programme however made the following recommendations on the decision-making process in the international financial institutions:[34]

> The role of developing countries in the decision-making process in the international financial institutions needs to be substantially increased. The system of weighted voting has led to a situation where, after the Eight Quota Review, developing countries as a group have no more than 38% of total votes. While the principle of weighted voting may be unavoidable in financial institutions, a better balance in the voting pattern is needed for a more equitable and effective functioning of these institutions.
>
> The share of developing countries in the total votes in the multilateral financial institutions should be increased to 50%. For this purpose, consideration might be given to, *inter alia*, an increase in basic votes. The present geographical representation of developing country regions in the Boards of the Bank and the Fund should be preserved.

VI. CONCLUSIONS

THIS discussion, which has concentrated on the important operational aspects of the IMF, attempts to establish the changes that have occurred in relation to them. It is therefore necessary to interpret the Articles of Agreement in the light of changing world economic exigencies. From this standpoint, the IMF seems to have kept pace with new situations, which has been reflected in practice by the opening of various new accounts and a Trust Fund.

There are two points, however that deserve a particular mention. First, the position of the developing countries in the IMF *vis-à-vis* the larger contributing Members. As stated earlier, although in theory, the latter category of Members do have the right to exercise their weighted voting in order to veto an application for finance made by a developing country, in practice, consensus has been the basis for decision-making. It is to be appreciated that by virtue of contributing more than the others, such countries may assert their right to secure appropriate investments for their contributions. However, such an attitude on their part has as yet not been pronounced. Second is the question of whether the IMF authorities encroach upon the sovereignty, fiscal or otherwise, of a loan-seeking Member. In order to answer this question, one may draw an analogy with the practice of

34.   (1985) 24 ILM 1712.

domestic commercial banks in granting an overdraft to their customers. Such banks ensure the viability of their customers by assessing their incomes and expenditures and their policy of earning and spending. Additionally, they have the right to conduct what is known as 'surveillance' over their customers' accounts.[35] At the macroeconomic level in a country, the procedure is more elaborate; otherwise, the basis for granting loans remains very similar. From a legal standpoint, it may be maintained that a loan granted by the IMF represents a decision of its Members; the IMF remains accountable to its members, and hence it has an obligation to ensure that loans are granted only in appropriate cases, and that they are realised according to schedules so as to enable other deserving Members to derive benefits from the Fund's available resources.

Finally, in view of the world economic situation, particularly since the 1980s, the IMF has adopted a more lenient attitude towards repayment of debts, and this has been reflected in its policy of rescheduling of loans.[36] As in the case of other international organisations, the mandate for the IMF's activities was given by the international community; it is for the international community to alter that if they should so decide. The changes that the IMF has gone through since its inception in the 1940s manifest its readiness to respond to the exigencies of the time.[37]

---

35. 'The Group of Twenty-Four Report on Changes in the Monetary System' (1985) however maintained that the Fund surveillance has to date been largely ineffective over the major industrial countries where Members have substantial effects on the world economy. See (1985) 24 ILM 1699 at 1707.

36. See the following chapter on the World Bank.

37. See former 'Group of Ten Report on the Functioning of the International Monetary System', op. cit. supra n.31, at p.1695.

Chapter V

THE WORLD BANK

S.K. Chatterjee

Chapter V

THE WORLD BANK

S.K. Chatterjee

I. INTRODUCTION

THE International Bank for Reconstruction and Development (IBRD), popularly known as The World Bank, was conceived at the UN Monetary and Financial Conference held in Bretton Woods, New Hampshire, USA in July 1944. The headquarters of the Bank are located in Washington, DC, USA. The International Monetary Fund and the Bank are complementary institutions in that whereas the former was set up in order to promote international currency stability principally by helping its Member States to correct their balance of payments deficits and making them subject to certain standards of international monetary conduct, the IBRD was established in order to finance the reconstruction and development of the economies of its Member States. The Bank came into operation on 25 June 1946. Like the IMF, the Bank is also governed by its Articles of Agreement.

The World Bank Group consists of the IBRD, the International Development Association (IDA)[1] and the International Finance Corporation (IFC).[2] The International Development Association is an integral part of the Bank. Whereas the aims of the IBRD and IDA are to promote economic and social progress primarily in developing countries, the International Finance Corporation works closely with private investors in its Member States and

---

1. The IDA was established in 1960.
2. The IFC was established in 1965.

119

invests in commercial enterprises in them. IBRD, IDA and IFC work as a family unit. Whereas IBRD and IDA share the same staff, IFC has its own staff, although the latter shares certain administrative and related services with the Bank. These three institutions are led by one President.

The principal functions of the Bank are:

- to lend funds in appropriate cases;
- to provide advice and technical assistance to its Member States, in appropriate cases; and
- to serve as a catalyst to stimulate investment.

Each Member of the Bank has a basic vote in addition to one vote for each share it holds.

II. A BRIEF DISCUSSION OF THE ORGANISATION AND STRUCTURE OF THE BANK

THE World Bank consists of the following organs:

- a Board of Governors;
- the Executive Directors;
- a President, and
- various staff, such as financial, operations, economics and research, personnel and administration, external relations, legal and the secretary's department.

In addition to these staff, there also exist operations evaluation staff, who evaluate results of operations after loans have been disbursed. They report to the Executive Directors and the President of the Bank. The President serves as Chairman of the Executive Directors, and as the Chief Executive of the Bank and the International Finance Corporation.

The Board of Governors being the highest organ, it gives directions to the Bank. This Board consists of one Governor from each Member State. It meets once a year to review the Bank's operations and policies. The Board of Governors delegates most of its functions to the Executive Director. Five of the Executive Directors are appointed by the largest stockholders,[3] and the remaining are elected by the Governors representing the other Members. Each Executive Director has an alternate. The Executive Directors are responsible for all policy matters. The President of the Bank is selected by the Executive Directors, and is responsible for the operation of the Bank's business, its organisation and staff members, under the direction of the Executive Directors.

The titles of the staff are self-explanatory, the role of the financial and operations staff needs some elaboration. The financial staff are responsible for the financial operations of the Bank and advise on its financial policies. They raise funds for the Bank in the capital markets and from other sources and invest its resources. In addition to coordinating the Bank's plans and budgets, they operate its accounting and financial reporting systems. They also conduct independent audits and approve financial functions. It is to be noted that the Bank's Tokyo office and the internal audit department come under their jurisdiction. IDA replenishment negotiations are done by the financial staff of the Bank.

The Bank's development-assistance programmes, including feasibility studies of the Member States seeking assistance, whether in the form of IBRD loans or IDA credits, are carried out by its operations staff. These staff are allocated to specific regional areas, namely, Eastern and Southern Africa, Western Africa, East Asia and Pacific, South Asia, Europe, Middle East and North Africa, and Latin America and the Caribbean. Each region is led by a vice-president. In addition to these vice-presidents, there are three more functional vice-presidents: one of them is responsible for providing general policy and functional guidance for regional operational activities; another one is in charge of technical staff in the energy and industry sectors; co-financing is the responsibility of the third vice-president.

The scope of functions of the operational staff is wide and varied in that the evaluation of each project entails a number of complex stages, including negotiations, and the question of whether the assistance may be utilised to its optimal level. A further aspect of the responsibilities of the operations staff relates to the 'project cycle', which will be discussed in section VII below.

---

3.   The United States, the United Kingdom, France, Germany and Japan.

III. MEMBERSHIP

ONLY States that are Members of the International Monetary Fund may be considered for membership of the IBRD. Each Member's quota in the IMF determines the subscription that a Member of the IBRD may contribute to its capital stock. The 'tying membership' is also useful for ascertaining a Member's economic condition at the time of its seeking assistance from the Bank. Most of the States that are Members of the IBRD are also Members of the IFC and IDA. Indeed, membership of the IDA is open to all Members of the IBRD. Like all other UN specialised agencies, the usual conditions of expulsion, and withdrawal of membership, apply to the World Bank Group.

IV. SOURCES OF FINANCE

THE primary sources of finance for the Bank are the following:

(a)   subscriptions by Members to the Bank's capital stock;
(b)   the Bank's paid-in capital from its retained earnings;
(c)   repayments on its loans; and
(d)   medium-term and long-term borrowing in the capital markets of Europe, Japan, the Middle East and the United States.

In view of its status coupled with its record of prudent financial management, the IBRD gains access to financial markets in many countries and raises funds. It places its debt obligations directly with central banks or governments or government agencies. Commercial banks and investment banks have also traditionally provided the IBRD with funds. It usually raises funds on the basis of a system of periodically adjustable interest rates, which are adjusted every six months according to the average cost of a pool of IBRD borrowings. By virtue of the interest rates being flexible, this system is less costly, and a loan is not attached to any fixed rate of interest until it matures. Furthermore, the Bank, in practice, borrows more than its current requirements at times when the rate of interest is favourable to itself, in anticipation of its future needs. The benefit of this practice ultimately accrues to IBRD borrowers.

In addition to its own capital subscribed by its member governments, the International Finance Corporation raises funds through borrowings, including borrowings from the IBRD. Over the years, local investors and financial institutions have provided a significant amount of finance for ventures assisted by the IFC. The IFC follows a strict policy of raising finance for its ventures on reasonable terms, from other sources. The question of the IFC's raising finance does not arise unless the government of the host country approves the investment, and it will invest only if arrangements for repatriating its investments and earnings exist. Syndications are another method of attracting private financing for projects in which the IFC may be involved.

The IDA receives grants from governments, and its main sources of funds are grants from the OECD countries and certain OPEC countries. Some developing countries also contribute to the IDA. Furthermore, a part of the net earnings of IBRD is transferred to the IDA.

V. LENDING CRITERIA

UNDER its Articles of Agreement, the political character of a Member State has no relevance to determining its eligibility for a loan or credit or assistance, as the case may be. The Bank's lending criteria are based only on economic considerations; the Bank has no authority to lend money to promote or achieve the military or political ends of a Member State. Both the IBRD and the IDA lend finance and/or technical assistance mostly for specific projects in the public and private sectors to promote development in almost any area, including agriculture, education, transportation, energy, rural development,industry, health, population, nutrition and water supply, in addition to non-project lending, including lending for structural and sectoral adjustment.

Whereas the IBRD assists developing countries other than the very poor, the IDA primarily grants credits to its poorest Member States, which are determined by referring to their annual per capita income, as they are not eligible for IBRD loans. However, in certain circumstances, it may be possible for a Member State to borrow both IBRD loans and IDA credits.

The objective of the IFC, on the other hand, is to promote economic development in developing countries by helping to mobilise domestic and foreign capital with a view to promoting growth in the private sector.

Irrespective of her economic strength, any developing country may seek assistance from the IFC for the purpose of stimulating growth e.g. in agriculture, manufacturing and mining industries, tourism and service industries and even for developing and/or strengthening capital market institutions.

The average maturity periods for loans respectively for the IBRD, IDA and IFC are: 15–20 years; 50 years and 7–12 years, with grace periods usually of 3–5 years, 10 years and 3 years. Whereas the recipients of IBRD loans are governments, government agencies, and private enterprises supported by government agencies, only governments receive IDA credits, although the recipient governments may, in turn, re-lend credits to governmental or private organisations. IFC loans are granted to private enterprises and governmental organisations that assist the private sector. Loans and credits are granted by the IBRD and IDA on the strength of government guarantees; no guarantees are required for loans from the IFC.

The lending criteria of the three institutions may appear to share many common elements, yet it is possible to identify distinctive characteristics of these criteria in relation to each of them. The Bank's financing and assistance are primarily meant for helping recipient countries to meet their foreign exchange costs. The Bank will not be involved in any project unless the national government participate in it and the projects are designed and implemented with its collaboration.

It has now become a practice to involve commercial banks in financing projects. It may be maintained that the Bank's role as a lender of assistance, in any form, is not as important as its role in ensuring that the specific project, when completed, will promote the infrastructural development of the country. The Bank's involvement in any way is very significantly based on the trust it has developed in the borrower and *vice versa*. The primary objective of the Bank's involvement is to ensure that the recipient country can eventually lessen its reliance upon it and meet its future development needs and financial needs from conventional sources of capital.

The IFC, on the other hand, takes a market-oriented approach towards development, that is, it attempts to mobilise resources, both domestic and foreign, on commercial terms, for business enterprises and financial institutions in a country. In this sense, the IFC undertakes a much more onerous task than the IBRD, especially when it pays attention to smaller and poorer developing countries. The IFC is required to identify and promote ventures, find sponsors for them and persuade them to invest capital and expertise in them. Its primary goal is not only to create an investment climate but also to maintain and promote it. If requested by a Member State, it provides technical assistance on diverse matters, including the development of a specific market or sector, and the design of laws and regulations to promote private investment. The IFC invests with other investors, and its investments are united. The IFC's finance can only be invested in its Member States and Switzerland. It does not take part in the management of a venture in which it has equity interest. Periodic visits and consultations are its basic means of maintaining interest in the project. However, only in very exceptional circumstances will the IFC exercise its voting rights as a shareholder in a venture. It is to be emphasised that it is prepared to assist all kinds of useful ventures; priority is given to those countries in which the private sector is still underdeveloped. The IFC's investments specifically aim at development of skills, promotion of scientific knowledge, increase in employment, and development of a country's natural resources on fair terms. As its loans must be made in conjunction with a venture, it must ensure that the venture itself is financially sound and otherwise viable.

The following criteria must be satisfied in order to receive IDA credits:

- the creditworthiness of the prospective borrower;
- the level of poverty in the prospective borrower's country;
- the economic performance of the country over the past few years; and
- the quality of the project.

The IDA lends only to governments, to ensure that infrastructural development is achieved through governmental participation and according to the priorities they have set.

The Bank can grant non-project lending only in special circumstances, such as when the reconstruction and rehabilitation of an economy is urgently necessitated by natural disasters, or in the event of a sudden fall in export earnings of a country which is dependent on a single commodity export, or a sharp deterioration in terms of trade owing to a rapid rise in import prices or where imports seem to be essential for fuller utilisation of production capacity. In recent years, however, the Bank has extended non-project lending to include structural and sector-adjustment loans in order to assist developing countries to correct current account deficits over a short period of time (3-5 years). In fact, by interpretation of their objectives, such lendings may be designated as lendings for restructuring the economies of developing countries.

VI. INTERRELATIONSHIP BETWEEN IBRD, IDA AND IFC

As stated earlier, organisationally these three institutions are interrelated, although from a legal standpoint, each of them is a separate legal entity. Exigencies of circumstance in the economic world led to the establishment of the IDA and IFC. Their creation clearly signifies that the Bank's lending criteria and funds would not meet the needs of economic development to which the Bank has been devoted.

Functionally, the IBRD advances loans only to creditworthy borrowers on projects the materialisation of which, in the view of the Bank, would bring a high economic return tot he Member State concerned. In order to serve the interest of developing countries more fully, the IDA provides assistance to the very poor developing countries on more lenient terms and conditions than those adopted by the IBRD, so that its credits do not become too burdensome on the balance of payments position of these countries. Financially, the IDA is to a certain extent supported by the IBRD.

Whereas the IBRD and IDA primarily lend assistance to governments or government agencies, IFC loans are made available to eligible private enterprises in a Member State. The combined assistance programmes of these institutions therefore cater not only for countries of different economic structures and requirements, but also for both the public and private sectors of an economy. By virtue of the level of economic development achieved, a Member State can move from being an IDA Member to being an IBRD Member. The IFC can offer assistance in the form of equity, convertible debentures and, in the main, offers the kind of financial assistance that may not be made available by the IBRD. It is possible for the Bank and the IFC jointly to finance a project. Again, in view of the infrastructural development achieved through IBRD loans, assistance provided by the IFC often proves an extremely useful complement.

Since its inception, the IFC has been extremely active in assisting investors by raising funds, often in conjunction with governments. Special attention is paid to smaller and poorer developing countries' needs. In order to increase the flow of foreign direct investment, in October 1985,under the auspices of the IBRD, the Multilateral Investment Guarantee Agency (MIGA) was set up, which came into operation on 13 April 1989.[4] This Agency offers guarantees against various non-commercial risks for encouraging direct foreign investment in developing countries, one of the conditions of which is that the investment programme must have been chosen by the developing country concerned and not by the investor. Another important aim of the Agency is to provide technical assistance to attract foreign investment. Whereas assistance to large-scale industrial projects is provided by the Bank, medium and small-sized industries are now assisted through development finance companies. The IFC's investment in such companies complements the Bank's participation, in that the IFC invests in equity to allow development finance companies to borrow from the IBRD funds.

In summary therefore, lending and assistance from the World Bank Group are directed to governments including government-sponsored institutions, and to private enterprises. The objectives are primarily two: infrastructural development, and development in the private sector. These two aspects of lending and assistance are complementary, and have the same ends: increase of productivity, economic self-sufficiency, increase in employment, acquisition of technical skill, appropriate and rational utilisation of resources, both natural and human, improvement of conditions of health and promotion of education. Only the strategies and certain criteria of extending assistance of these institutions are different, by virtue of the different reasons for which they were established.

VII. THE PROJECT CYCLE

BOTH the IBRD and IDA provide financial and technical assistance to their Member States on a project basis. The stages through which a proposed project must pass for the determination of its viability and appropriateness

---

4.   The text of the Convention establishing MIGA has been published in (1985) 24 ILM 1605.

are described as a 'project cycle'. Although the criteria of the IBRD and IDA for granting loans and credits are different, the project cycle they adopt is identical. The IFC's project cycle is different from that of the IBRD and IDA. It is a misnomer in that the decision whether a project will receive IBRD or IDA financing or assistance depends on the economic condition of the Member State concerned and not on the characteristics of the proposed project only.

The following are the stages that a project cycle entails: identification, preparation, appraisal, negotiation and approval, implementation and supervision, and post-evaluation.

These stages are preceded by a stage which may be called the 'studying the economy of the country' stage. The Bank and IDA require detailed information about the economy of the country concerned, and the specific needs of the sectors in relation to which borrowing is sought. Such information is provided by 'country economic missions' conducted by experts who collect basic details about the economy by paying a visit to the country. The reports prepared by such missions include, *inter alia*, the purposes of borrowing, the sectors and areas to which borrowing will be directed, level of employment, trade policies, success or failure of other projects, and such other information that the Bank may require for formulating a strategy for assistance.

There follows a discussion of the stages involved in a project cycle.

A. Identification of Projects

Identification of projects is primarily the task of the country applying for borrowing, although the Bank can give assistance in identifying the projects that might be most suitable for the country. In assisting a country in this regard, the Bank's 'identification mission' contacts the mission, if any, that supervised a project in the past in the same country, or it may gather information as to the basic characteristics of the country from the projects already completed by other UN agencies. All draft projects must contain not only details about the projects, including available and projected financial and manpower and technological resources, but also basic infrastructural and societal information. In other words, an appropriate feasibility study must be prepared so as to enable the Bank to ascertain the viability of the project and any actual operational difficulties. Many countries do however identify their projects without seeking any assistance from the Bank's project identification mission. The Bank does not take the initiative to identify projects; the request for identification of projects must be received by the Bank from the country concerned.

B. Preparation

Preparation stands for 'designing' a project, which entails considering the technical, managerial, economic and financial dimensions of the project. This is perhaps the most difficult and time-consuming stage. Depending upon the nature of the project, all infrastructural details must be considered: the available natural resources, use of alternative resources where available, training needs, economic, social, environmental aspects, opportunities for marketing and capability to maintain the project. Care is taken to ensure that no unmanageable project is imposed on the country, nor any project that would have an adverse effect on the social fibre of the country.

In the absence of sophisticated information systems, a long time (sometimes several years) may be necessary for completing this stage. The Bank often finances, usually partly, project preparation work.

It is to be emphasised that not only the financial aspects, but also the nonfinancial aspects of a project, such as the level of relevant training available or the time and money required for training local people, are paramount concerns of the Bank. The Bank is primarily guided by the borrower's idea of the project.

C. Appraisal

The work that this stage entails is self-explanatory. However, certain important issues deserve brief discussion. Appraisal is solely the Bank's responsibility. At this stage, evaluation of the proposed project is carried out by reflecting on its features and prospects. Given the resources available within the borrower's country and the external resources that may be made available to her, the Bank examines the economic and socio-economic needs that the project might meet, the nature of difficulties that might be encountered in implementing it, and whether a successful implementation might operate as a springboard for further economic development programmes in the country.

This is another lengthy process. An appraisal mission usually pays a visit to the country, assessing the project from economic, financial, managerial and institutional standpoints. Reviewing a proposal is an integral part of appraisal, covering the technological and technical aspects of a project, costing, stages of implementation and its suitability to the country. This can be explained by means of an example. If the project relates to building a hospital, in addition to reviewing the engineering and architectural aspects of it, other related aspects, such as the nature of diseases, the training of doctors and health personnel and even the quality of access roads, are considered. Of course, the aspects of the economic and social benefits that may be derived from the project are of paramount importance. To this end, the Bank is required to examine a cost-benefit analysis of the project, the income and employment-generation capacity of the project, the effect of the project on the country's balance of payments and also whether the project will require high expenditure in essential supplies, whether machinery or otherwise, for its operation. For example, in relation to a proposal for setting up a secondary school for girls in a rural area, not only must the question of supply of teachers, books and other requirements be considered, but also the question of whether parents would permit their daughters to attend such a school to follow modern curricula which might be contrary to the ethos of their culture. Availability of resources, manpower or otherwise, the capability of the people to handle it, its cost-effectiveness, and its capacity to create employment and perhaps make the country self-sufficient in the agricultural sector must all have been considerations in installing for example, an irrigation system in a country.

The final considerations, namely, whether a project may be unduly burdensome for a government, and its spill-over effect, that is, whether a project may complement another one already in existence or a new project, are very important issues that receive the attention of the Bank at this stage.

The institutional aspect of the appraisal consists of examining the management and operational policies of the central bank of the borrowing country. The World Bank authorities may be required to direct the national authorities to change certain aspects of their management style and policy in order to facilitate the implementation of the project. Although this aspect of the

Bank's direction to the borrowing country might provoke controversy in many quarters, in reality, the Bank has a responsibility to ensure that the funds accumulated by its Member States are appropriately and beneficially utilised and that the borrowing country is able to repay the fund by the stipulated date. The Bank may recommend special training programmes for employees and people involved in the operation and implementation of the programme.

It is to be emphasised that environmental issues are considered seriously in appraising projects and, in certain cases, Bank lending may become conditional upon environmental safeguards, and these issues, whether lending is conditional upon them or not, are monitored during the life of the project.

D. *Negotiation and Approval*

In the absence of any appraisal of a project, of course no negotiation can commence between the borrower and the Bank. At this stage, negotiators are primarily concerned with the terms and conditions of loans. The appraisal assists negotiators in determining the economic and financial capabilities of the borrowing country. There exist standard loan agreements, according to which negotiations are conducted, but each country's special circumstances are taken into consideration. After the negotiations are completed, a report on the proposed loan is submitted to the executive directors along with the 'appraisal report' and other necessary documents, for their approval.

E. *Implementation and Supervision*

Implementation of the project is the responsibility of the borrower. The Bank continuously monitors the programme effected by the country. The borrower is also required to submit periodic reports to the Bank. In order to ensure an effective implementation of the project, the Bank's 'supervision mission' visits the country periodically. Funding is disbursed by the Bank periodically, upon receipt of satisfactory evidence as to the progress made by the borrower. The advantages of sending 'supervision missions' to the recipient country are many: they can on behalf of the Bank witness the progress made by the country, assist the country to solve any problem relating to the project, and ascertain whether the project may be allowed to proceed according to the original plan or whether it requires modification. In the latter event, the recipient country and the Bank agree to new terms and conditions of the loan, upon discussion. During or even at the beginning of the implementation stage, the recipient country is often advised to acquire resources, financial or otherwise (technical, technological, etc.) from other sources, and to arrange machinery, plant, equipment etc. through international competitive bidding open to suppliers and contractors in all Member States and in Switzerland.[5]

Implementation and supervision must go hand in hand. As implementation of a project progresses, closer supervision becomes necessary in order to ensure that in the event of a problem arising it may be treated jointly. It may be described as a two-way learning and correcting process.

F. Evaluation of Projects

This stage comes into effect after the total fund has been disbursed by the Bank, and the Bank itself evaluates the project not only to determine whether disbursement of the loan in a particular case was justifiable and indeed proved its effectiveness, but also to add to the wealth of experience which may be utilised in other similar cases.[6]

VIII. WITHDRAWAL OF PROCEEDS OF IBRD LOANS AND IDA CREDITS

WITHDRAWAL of proceeds of IBRD loans and IDA certificates is governed by the loan documents and the constitutional guidelines of the Bank relating to withdrawal of loans and credits. Funds can be withdrawn only to finance the goods and services suitable for a project which has been approved and also to meet project expenses as they are incurred. Although disbursements are usually made by the Bank headquarters, in some cases the Bank may advise the borrower to submit the papers to the Regional Mission/Resident for partial processing in an attempt to hasten the process. Missions are often

---

5.   See section X infra.

6.   The publication entitled *Annual Review of Project Performance Audit Results* has been published since 1977 by the Operations Evaluation Department.

authorised to do the full review of a project and of the utilisation of finds disbursed. At the time of negotiating a schedule entitled 'Withdrawal of Proceeds of Loans' is drawn up by agreement between the two parties, and amendments to this schedule may be made in accordance with the provisions of the main loan documents. There are General Conditions of Withdrawal and Disbursements of Loans from the IBRD and IDA.

IX. APPLICATION AND PROCEDURE FOR WITHDRAWAL

APPLICATIONS for withdrawal can be made either for direct payment to a third party or for reimbursement of the expenditure already incurred. Reimbursements are normally made for US$20,000 equivalent.

The two most important Application Forms used for these purposes are: Form 1903 (Application for Withdrawal) and Form 1931 (Application for Special Commitment). The latter is used to request the Bank to issue a special commitment guarantee covering a commercial bank under a letter of credit. The items of information required to be supplied are basically the same under both these procedures, and include the following:

(a)   the reasons for withdrawal or seeking reimbursement;
(b)   justification for withdrawal and reimbursement under the loan agreement;
(c)   whether sufficient funds are available to cover payment or commitment;
(d)   documentary evidence in support of withdrawal and reimbursement (e.g. commercial bank's report on payment(s); evidence of shipment; bill(s) of lading etc.); and
(e)   the application to be signed by duly authorised person(s).

Where necessary, a borrower is allowed to use separate sheets detailing all expenditures and justifications thereto. Separate applications must be made for each currency requested. In the event of the Bank's rejecting an application for withdrawal or commitment, it notifies the borrower promptly giving the reason for the rejection.

A borrower is required to submit Form 1903 to the Bank in triplicate. Payment instructions must be clearly stated showing the full name and address of the payee's bank, the account number and name as they appear on the account. In the event of the payee's bank not being located in the country of the currency claimed, the name and address of the commercial bank's correspondent in that country must be provided.

The procedure for making an application for a special commitment (Form 1931) is somewhat different from that under Form 1903. When the commercial bank in the supplier's country refuses to open or confirm the credit in the absence of a guarantee or security, the Bank, at the request of the borrower, may provide the commercial bank the guarantee or security it requires under its Special Commitment procedure. This procedure requires the borrower to ask the Bank to issue to the commercial bank, usually in the supplier's country, its special irrevocable commitment agreeing to reimburse the bank for payments made or to be made under the relevant letter of credit. Such commitment remains effective even if the loan is subsequently suspended or revoked. A borrower wishing to avail itself of this facility must send the Bank Form 1931, in duplicate, supported by (i) a copy of the contract or purchase order relating to the payment to be made; and (ii) two copies of the letter of credit proposed to be issued by the commercial bank. If approved, the Bank will issue its Special Commitment on Form 2018 together with a copy of the letter of credit to the negotiating bank. In the event of any amendments being made to the letter of credit, the negotiating bank must submit all such amendments to the IBRD for its approval, which will include: the name of the beneficiary, the value of the letter of credit, whether the expiry date of the credit is required to be extended, and the description and quantity of goods.

The commercial bank concerned undertakes an obligation to notify the Bank after each payment made or documents negotiated. The commercial bank also sends a 'Request for Payment' on Form 2015 to the Bank. Notifications made by cable or telex, or by any other rapid means of communication, are also regarded as valid notifications and constitute request for payment.

The Bank's Special Commitment Limitation Clause usually includes, *inter alia*, that:

> Since such financing is limited, we shall not be obligated to make payments to the extent that they would in the aggregate exceed the equivalent, as determined by us when payments are made. It is our policy to retain sufficient funds in the Loan/Credit to fully cover outstanding Special Commitments. Our borrower has agreed that if, because of this limitation clause, we

cannot disburse the full amount needed to pay you, any uncommitted portion of the account may be disbursed to cover the deficiency, and in the event the uncommitted portion of the account is insufficient to cover the deficiency, our borrower will arrange to make such payment promptly to you after receiving our notification.

Whereas a Bank loan is usually expressed in US dollars, IDA credits are issued in SDRs. When issuing a Special Commitment, the Bank limits its liability by including a clause which provides that it cannot disburse amounts in any currency that would exceed the dollar equivalent or SDR equivalent in the case of IDA credits. Conversion is done by using the current exchange rate for the currency concerned, leaving a margin to cover normal currency fluctuations. The Applicable Exchange Rate (AER) is established by the Bank for each currency for the valuation of all transactions on a particular date.

Under the borrowing arrangement, the Bank is required to notify the borrower and the implementing agencies of the amount withdrawn from the loan account, along with the necessary details, namely, the currency in which disbursements have been made, exchange rate, and the category charged, US dollar or SDR equivalent. Withdrawals from the loan account are normally made in the currencies of expenditures, but withdrawals for expenditures (which have been made in the currency of the borrower) are usually made in another currency or currencies selected by the Bank.

X. PROCUREMENT OF GOODS AND WORKS UNDER IBRD LOANS AND IDA CREDITS

'GOODS and works' in this context includes 'related services' such as insurance, transportation, training and installation, but not consultants' services. Legal obligations as to procurement emanate from the relevant Agreement, the General Obligations by virtue of being a Member of the Bank, the bidding (tender) documents, and the contracts signed by the borrower with the supplier(s) of goods and services. It is to be emphasised that procurement of goods and works is related to the principal loan agreement; in other words, procurement is to be made with a view to fulfilling the objectives of the loan. For the procurement of goods, works and services, the Bank is required to be satisfied that:

(a)   it would promote the achievement of the purposes for which the loan has been sought;

(b)   it would have the effect of minimising the costs of operating the project, and increasing efficiency in the execution of the project;

(c)   all probable and eligible bidders have been offered an opportunity to compete in providing goods, works and services financed by the Bank. Participation is open to bidders from both developed and developing countries, and Switzerland;

(d)   local contractors and manufacturers in the borrowing country are encouraged to participate.

Where, however, international competitive bidding would not appear to be the most economic and efficient method of procurement, other methods for it are prescribed in the Loan Agreement. The particular methods prescribed for primary goods and works in relation to a project are indicated in the Loan Agreement; however, the Bank has issued Guidelines as to Procurement under IBRD loans and IDA credits. This discussion is based on these Guidelines.

The procedures outlined in the Guidelines apply to all procurements financed wholly or in part by the loan granted by the IBRD. In the event of a borrower procuring goods, works and services from sources other than the Bank-granted loan, the Bank must be satisfied that the procedure to be used would fulfil the borrower's obligations as to the implementation of the project under the Loan Agreement. The Bank would generally like to ensure that the goods and works to be procured:

(a)   are of satisfactory quality for the project;

(b)   would be delivered according to the time scheduled for completion of the project; and

(c)   are so priced as not adversely to affect the financial viability of the project.[7]

---

7.   See further the *Guidelines on Procurement under IBRD Loans and IDA Credits*, issued by the Bank (1985).

Goods, works and services must be provided by nationals of and producers and suppliers from the Bank Member States and Switzerland.

Finance will not be made available by the Bank for transportation of goods if the services are rendered by enterprises from ineligible sources, except 'where pooling arrangements in shipping conferences in which shipping lines from ineligible sources hold the major share make the nationality of the carrier immaterial or where other means of transportation are not available or would cause excessive costs or delays.'[8]

Signing of a procurement contract in advance by a borrower, that is, prior to its signing the principal Loan Agreement with the Bank, may be acceptable provided the borrower establishes that such act was performed in the interest of a more rapid and efficient execution of the project, although the fact remains that the borrower does so at its own risk. Any finance that may be reimbursed by the Bank in relation to such advance contracting, if accepted, is referred to as 'retroactive financing'. However, even in such cases, the Bank's review procedure becomes applicable. A borrower is required to follow the Bank Guidelines in relation to advance contracting for purposes of procurement. Paragraph 1.9 of the Guidelines provides that:

> Manufacturers and contractors in the Borrower's country are encouraged to participate in the procurement process since the Bank seeks, through its procurement procedures, to encourage the development of local industry. Manufacturers and contractors in the Borrower's country may bid independently or in joint venture with foreign manufacturers or contractors, but the Bank does not approve conditions of bidding which require mandatory joint ventures or other forms of association between local and foreign firms.

The Bank does not finance any procurement which may be considered as 'misprocurement'. In that event, the Bank cancels that portion of the loan allocated to procurement, and retains the right to exercise other remedies available under the Loan Agreement.

---

8. Para.1.6, *Guidelines*, op. cit. supra n.7.

XI. INTERNATIONAL BIDDING

INTERNATIONAL bidding (tender) is employed for procuring goods, services and works on competitive terms. In view of constraints of length, no detailed discussion of the bidding techniques and the nature of the legal documents required for effecting them can be held here; the reader is strongly recommended to consult the Guidelines on Procurement issued by the World Bank which also contain a comprehensive account of bidding procedures. Although international bidding is open to all Members of the IBRD and Switzerland, domestic manufacturers and contractors are given preference, so as to allow the host country to utilise available local resources through its own enterprises in order to minimise the degree of their dependence upon foreign enterprises.

International bidding is usually subject to performance bonds (normally 2% of the total estimated expenditure) to be given by the enterprise that intends to undertake the work. Performance bonds signify a degree of commitment on the part of the enterprise to the proposed work. Arrangements for finance, whether entirely through the IBRD or in conjunction with a regional development bank or with other sources, such as the bidder itself, is a pre-condition of bidding. The host country must detail, accordingly, the specifications of every aspect of the project, including the machines required, in addition to supplying all other relevant information, namely, purposes of the project, availability of local resources, natural or otherwise, market conditions, general economic condition of the country, export earnings, expenditures on imports, current population and its growth rate, health conditions, and the country's general infrastructure.

The host country is required to conclude contracts with various parties: with the providers of finance, such as the IBRD, a regional development bank or any other institution that may have offered finance, and with the suppliers of goods, works and services. Although certain standard clauses are incorporated into such contracts, depending upon the nature of the project, variations in the standard clauses often become necessary. Notices inviting international tenders for such projects are often published in reputable newspapers of international standing.

XII. IBRD AND INVESTMENT PROTECTION

THE title of the Bank is significant. It was set up for two distinct purposes: reconstruction of the economies devastated by the Second World War, and economic development of those Member States that suffer from economic backwardness or of the Member States that would like to bolster their economies and, in particular, sectoral programmes in those countries. Any Member State of the Bank may avail itself of these facilities, although, undeniably, developing countries have become the major applicants for IBRD loans. Of course, as stated earlier, IDA credits are made available only to the very poor countries. The involvement of the World Bank Group in strengthening the economies of developing countries has a reasonably long history. Although developing countries have had the benefit of bilateral investment, albeit to a limited extent in many cases, especially in view of their lacking infrastructure or resources, the World Bank has consistently advocated the promotion of private foreign investment in these countries on a multilateral basis. To this effect, in 1985, under its initiative and auspices, the Convention Establishing the Multilateral Investment Guarantee Agency (MIGA) was set up. It came into effect on 13 April 1989, with a view to promoting investment in developing countries by investors from developed countries under the protection of insurance policies. Under this Convention, the choice of investment must be made by the host country, and the Convention seeks to provide cover for the following types of risk:

(a) Risks relating to currency transfer in a freely usable currency or another currency acceptable to the holder of the guarantee.

(b) Expropriation and similar measures (including legislative or administrative action) which will have the effect of depriving the holder of a guarantee of his ownership or control or a substantial benefit from his investment, but not non-discriminatory measures of general application which governments normally take for the purpose of regulating economic activity in their territories.[9]

---

9. Art.11(a)(ii) of the Convention.

(c) Breach of contract by the host government concerned and, when the investor will not have recourse to a judicial or arbitral body to determine the claim due to repudiation or breach, when a decision by such bodies will not be rendered within a reasonable period of time or when their decision may not be enforced.

(d) Loss of or damage to an investment due to war and civil disturbance occurring in the host country.

As stated earlier, MIGA does not offer protection against risks representing 'non-discriminatory measures of general application which governments normally take for the purpose of regulating economic activity in their territories.'

It is unfortunate, however, that since the coming into operation of the MIGA not many private foreign investors have taken advantage of the insurance scheme provided by this Convention. This provokes the question whether investment flow in developing countries may be increased only by offering guarantee of protection or whether certain perceptions of investors and beneficiaries need to be changed.

XIII. BASIC FEATURES OF IBRD LOANS AND IDA CREDIT AGREEMENTS

ALL IBRD Loan and IDA Credit Agreements are governed by the General Conditions Applicable to Loan and Guarantee Agreements issued by the IBRD (hereinafter referred to as the General Conditions). These General Conditions also apply to guarantee agreements that may be concluded between the Bank and its Members. In addition to the Section on Definition of various Terms, the following headings are included in the General Conditions:

Loan Account   (Interest and other charges; repayment, place of payment);

Currency Provisions   (currencies in which with-drawals are to be made and in which the principal and premium are payable);

Withdrawal of Proceeds of Loans	(the conditions of withdrawal and the commitments by the Bank; documentation on expenditures actually incurred etc.);
Cancellation and Suspension of Loans	(specific grounds are indicated);
Acceleration of Maturity	(generally in the case of default by the borrower);
Bonds	(the terms and conditions of executing and delivering bonds to the Bank with an endorsement of guarantee of the guarantor thereon);
Enforceability of Loan Agreements and Guarantee Agreements	(delay or omission to exercise any right, power or remedy accruing to any party under the loan or guarantee agreement upon any default shall impair any such right)

Miscellaneous Provisions; and

Executive Date and Termination

These General Conditions are followed by Schedules in relation to Bonds and Guarantees.

A Loan Agreement clearly provides that parties shall accept all the provisions of the General Conditions. Depending upon the subject matter of the Loan Agreement, the conditions will vary: however, a general pattern of such Agreements has emerged, and it is possible to identify certain common elements in all loan agreements. After identifying the amount of the loan agreed to be advanced by the Bank, the agreement provides for the following: use of proceeds of loan, bonds, execution of the project, consultation, information and inspection, particular covenants (that the parties must perform their projects with due diligence and efficiency, including the obligations as to repayment, payment of interest etc.), remedies to the Bank in the event of a default, effective date and the date of termination and a miscellaneous clause followed by schedules (relating to allocation of proceeds of loan, amortisation schedule, description of project, procurement etc.). A loan agreement provides, *inter alia*, that the borrower and the Bank shall fully co-operate to assure that the purpose of the loan is accomplished and that they will from time to time exchange views through their representatives with regard to the project for which the loan has been granted. It is clearly stated that on the basis of the mutual intention of the borrower and the Bank no other external debt shall enjoy any priority over the loan by way of a lien on governmental assets. The loan agreement, the bonds and the project agreement are free from any taxes that may be imposed under the laws of the borrower or 'laws in effect in its territories on or in connection with the execution, issue, delivery or registration thereof and the borrower shall pay all such taxes, if any, imposed under the laws of the country or countries in whose currency the loan and the bonds are payable or laws in effect in the territories of such country or countries.'

IDA Credit Agreements are drafted in similar fashion. It is interesting to note in relation to disputes arising from such loan and credit agreements that the parties agree, in advance, to refer any dispute to arbitration.

XIV. SETTLEMENT OF DISPUTES

IN conformity with the provisions of the Convention on the Settlement of Investment Disputes between States and Nationals of Other States, 1965, the IBRD and IDA loan agreements provide for settlement of investment disputes by conciliation and arbitration rather than by court procedures.

Article 42 of the Convention may now be regarded as representing the standard choice of law clause in investment agreements to which the IBRD and/or IDA is a party or even in respect of other bilateral investment agreements between other parties. It provides that:

(1) The Tribunal shall decide a dispute in accordance with such rules of law as may be agreed by the parties. In the absence of such agreement, the Tribunal shall apply the law of the Contracting State Party to the dispute (including its rules on the conflict of laws) and such rules of international law as may be applicable.

(2) The Tribunal may not bring in a finding of *non liquet* on the ground of silence or obscurity of the law.

(3) The provisions of paragraphs (1) and (2) shall not prejudice the power of the Tribunal to decide a dispute *ex aequo et bono* if the parties agree thereto.

Incidentally, the MIGA Convention also provides for a similar choice of law clause. Facilities for settling investment disputes are offered by the International Centre for Settlement of Investment Disputes (ICSID) which was set up under the Convention on the Settlement of Investment Disputes. The following are some of the arbitrations in which awards were rendered by ICSID Tribunals: *AGIP and the People's Republic of the Congo*, 1979;[10] *Benvenuti et Bonfant srl. and the People's Republic of the Congo*, 1980;[11] *Amco Asia Corporation and Others and the Republic of Indonesia*, 1983, 1984 and 1988;[12] *The Liberian Eastern Timber Corporation and the Government of the Republic of Liberia*, 1986;[13] *Asian Agricultural Products Limited and Republic of Sri Lanka*, 1990.[14]

The ICSID method of settling investment disputes allows investment agreements to be de-localised with a view to enabling parties to dissociate themselves from any national or local jurisdiction and gain confidence in the settlement machinery, one of the principal attributes of which is neutrality. The conciliators and arbitrators, as the case may be, are chosen from panels

10. (1982) 21 ILM 726.
11. Idem, p.740.
12. (1985) 24 ILM 1023.
13. (1987) 26 ILM 647.
14. (1991) 30 ILM 580.

consisting of eminent conciliators and arbitrators, maintained by the Centre. The Centre allows transnational corporations access to conciliation and arbitration. One of the most important advantages of ICSID arbitrations is that the parties accept in advance the obligation to enforce awards, and consent once given by the parties as to the assumption of jurisdiction by a Tribunal cannot be withdrawn unilaterally.

XV. CONCLUSIONS

THE World Bank Group provides for development assistance to both public and private sectors in its Member States. The contractual arrangements made for development assistance particularly between the IBRD or IDA and the recipient country may best be described as 'development agreements', which in view of their inherent characteristics as determined by their purposes and objectives, may not be designated as commercial contracts *stricto sensu*, nor may they be designated as commercial treaties. The profit element, if any, for the IBRD or IDA, is represented by the very low rate of interest it earns on loans and credits. Development agreements are *sui generis* in character: they may be described as 'quasi-international agreements'.[15] They predominantly contain public international law elements, such as *pacta sunt servanda*, principles of State responsibility and international minimum standards. Even the contracts concluded with third parties, e.g. bidding contracts or procurement contracts, need not be governed by any municipal law.

The tying membership between the World Bank Group and the IMF reduces the incidence of breach of agreements by beneficiary countries. By virtue of not being motivated by profits, as is the case with ordinary commercial contracts, the review procedure enforced by the Bank where necessary, operates in the interest of both the Bank and the beneficiaries. Accountability pertaining to development agreements operates for both parties: the Bank must ensure that the funds raised on behalf of its Members are not misused; beneficiaries, on the other hand, must also ensure that in order to protect their standing with the Bank in the future, breach of

---

15. See A. Vedross, 'Quasi-International Agreements and International Economic Transactions' (1964) 18 Year Book of World Affairs 230-247.

agreements does not occur, unless such breach may be regarded as being *force majeure*. Re-scheduling of loans is available, but a discussion of that is beyond the scope of this chapter.[16] Generally speaking, the overall purpose of assistance by the World Bank Group is not only to help beneficiary countries to build their economies but also to allow them to found the basis for market economies where the borrower so desires.

16.   See Chapter VIII infra, 'The Sovereign Debt Crisis: A Lawyer's Perspective'.

Chapter VI

STRUCTURE AND OPERATION OF THE GATT

Ioannis Alex. Tzionas

Chapter VI

STRUCTURE AND OPERATION
OF THE GATT

Ioannis Alex. Tzionas

THE General Agreement on Tariffs and Trade – the GATT – is the main international institution governing the bulk of the world's trade. It serves as a basis of 'law and order'[1] upon which international trade relations are conducted, thereby providing the institutional underpinnings of the international trading system.

In this chapter selected salient features of the fundamental structure and operation of the GATT will be presented in a concise manner, though the topic is enormously wide. The first part begins with the origins and objectives of the GATT and proceeds to the sources of GATT law and the institutional framework. The second part provides the substantive legal foundations upon which GATT law is based and the limitations thereto. The supervisory mechanism for overseeing the GATT system and resolving disputes deriving therefrom are dealt with in the third part. The multilateral negotiations conducted within the context of the GATT are looked at in the last part with particular emphasis placed on the Uruguay Round.

---

1.   Panel Report on *New Zealand – Imports of Electrical Transformers from Finland*, BISD 32S/55, para.4:4.

I. CONSTITUTIONAL FRAMEWORK

A. Genesis of the GATT

Amid a climate of growing internationalism, the advent of the post-World War II era brought together statesmen from various countries throughout the world with a view to restoring the international trading system. Mindful of the disastrous economic policies of the interwar period which were held partly responsible for World War II, national delegations engaged, in 1946, in a series of conferences under the aegis of the United Nations, resolved to lay down legal disciplines governing the conduct of international trade relations.[2]

Two events preceded these meetings: first, the Bretton Woods Conference, held in 1944, resulted in the establishment of the International Monetary Fund (IMF) and the International Bank for Reconstruction and Development (IBRD), now the World Bank.   This conference was concerned with international monetary and financial matters, but, acknowledging the complementary character of monetary and trade issues, it called for co-operation in international commercial relations.[3] Second, in 1945 the United States issued a document entitled 'Proposals for Consideration by an International Conference on Trade and Employment' reflecting the earlier US–British discussions and calling for an 'International Trade Organisation' (ITO).   Shortly thereafter it invited other countries to participate in multilateral negotiations on the reduction of tariffs.

In 1946 the United Nations Economic and Social Council adopted a resolution put forward by the US and called for a Conference on Trade and Employment. To this end, a Preparatory Committee was established to draft a charter for the International Trade Organisation (ITO). It convened in London in 1946 and in Geneva in 1947. Its preparatory work culminated in the plenary 'United Nations Conference on Trade and Employment' held in Havana (21 November 1947 to 24 March 1948) where the text of the charter

2.   For the GATT negotiating history see generally John H. Jackson, *World Trade and the Law of GATT*, (Michie, 1969) chap.2.

3.   United Nations Monetary and Financial Conference (Bretton Woods, N.H. 1–22 July 1944) Proceedings and Documents 941, cited in Jackson, idem, p.40.

– the so-called 'Havana Charter' – for the International Trade Organisation was signed by 53 countries.

In parallel to the drafting work for the Havana Charter, multilateral negotiations aimed at the lowering of tariffs were carried on as a result of the US initiative. These two strands proceeded separately but they were related to each other. The latter constituted the gestative process of the GATT. On 30 October 1947, 23 countries signed the Final Act authenticating the GATT; eight of them signed the Protocol of Provisional Application by which the GATT entered into force on 1 January 1948,[4] while the remaining fifteen did so shortly thereafter. Nonetheless, the GATT was neither designed to stand alone nor indefinitely. It was intended to be applied provisionally, pending the coming into force of the ITO Charter. Ironically, history reversed their fortunes. The ITO never came into existence by reason of the US Congressional failure to adopt it. Conversely, the GATT survived and has continued to apply for 45 years, though still on a 'provisional' basis!

B. GATT Objectives

The GATT inherited a legacy of high tariffs coupled with discriminatory quantitative restrictions. Its rationale for international trade regulation was the reduction of tariffs and the outright elimination of quantitative restrictions subject to specified exceptions. It is therefore hardly surprising that, from its inception, the GATT was primarily concerned with the reduction of tariffs. Yet tariffs are no longer at the top of the negotiating agenda. Non-tariff barriers, services and other trade-related subjects figure in their place instead.

On the other hand, the original group of 23 countries has been remarkably expanded. 103 governments currently (December 1991) subscribe to the GATT and another 29 informally apply it on a *de facto* basis so that it now regulates approximately 90% of the estimated total $3.5 trillion of the world's merchandise trade.[5]

---

4.   55 UNTS 194. The text of the GATT in its current form is contained in Vol.IV of GATT Basic Instruments and Selected Documents (BISD) (GATT) Focus No.86 Nov./Dec.1991, p.8.
5.   GATT Press Release No.1504, 19 Mar. 1991; GATT Focus No.86, Nov./Dec. 1991, p.8.

It seems most unlikely that the GATT architects had contemplated, let alone made allowance for, this expansion of membership and broadening of competence of the GATT. Nonetheless its cardinal objective, deriving from the grandiose preamble of the General Agreement, is 'to liberalise international trade and place it on a secure basis, thereby contributing to the economic growth, development and welfare of the world's peoples'.[6] This objective should be attained by means of:

- substantial reduction of tariffs and other barriers to trade, and
- elimination of discriminatory treatment in international commerce

by entering into reciprocal and mutually advantageous arrangements.

C. Sources of GATT Law

The establishment and evolution of the GATT system is founded on a network of more than 180 agreements[7] as well as other legal instruments which serve as sources of GATT law. These can be classified as follows:[8]

- the text of the General Agreement with its annexes and schedules of concessions and the Protocol of Provisional Application
- accession agreements by which new contracting parties accede to the GATT
- agreements amending the text of the General Agreement
- agreements replacing, changing or rectifying individual schedules to the GATT
- agreements containing new schedules of concessions normally as a result of multilateral negotiations
- the Tokyo Round Agreements
- the Multifibre Arrangement.

6.   GATT Activities 1989, p.11.
7.   See GATT Document GATT/LEG/1 and supplements; see also GATT Analytical Index; GATT, Status of Legal Instruments, 1989.
8.   See E. McGovern, *International Trade Regulation. GATT, the United States and the European Community* (Globefield, 1986), pp.4–8 for a summarised classification, which is adopted here.

Decisions, interpretations and recommendations by GATT competent bodies can as often as not be regarded as legislative in character, thereby creating a body of secondary legislation alongside the above primary sources.[9] In arriving at interpretation and application of GATT law the CONTRACTING PARTIES[10] resort to certain interpretative sources and principles. The GATT preparatory work and the Havana Charter constitute valuable interpretative sources to which reference is frequently made by interpreting bodies.[11]

D. Membership of the GATT

A government obtains the status of contracting party to the GATT either by being an original signatory thereto, or by subsequently acceding to the GATT, or through sponsorship upon obtaining independence from a government that is already a contracting party.[12] The first method has obviously only historical interest. The most commonly used method of accession is that provided for by Article XXXIII. Under this, negotiations between the CONTRACTING PARTIES and the candidate contracting party commence with a view to determining the tariff and other trade concessions to be granted by the latter in return for the trade benefits of its accession. The acceding country is normally required to reduce tariffs and bring its trade policies into conformity with the GATT. The CONTRACTING PARTIES decide on the accession by a two-thirds majority. Full membership is usually completed in three stages: 'observer status',[13] 'provisional accession' and 'protocol of accession'. Finally, under Article XXVI paragraph 5(c), as soon as a customs territory has acquired full autonomy in the conduct of external relations it may become a contracting party upon the declaration of its

9.   Idem, p.5.
10.   See infra section E, 'Institutions'.
11.   Panel Report on *Canada - Import Restrictions on Ice Cream and Yoghurt*, BISD 36S/68; Panel Report on *European Economic Community - Restriction on Imports of Dessert Apples - Complaint by Chile*, BISD 36S/93 paras.12.12 and 12.16 to 12.18.
12.   See Jackson, op. cit. supra n.2, pp.89–95.
13.   The former USSR, for instance, possessed this status: GATT Focus No.71, May–June 1990.

sponsoring contracting party.[14] Upon the accession a Protocol is signed and a schedule of the agreed tariffs is usually drawn up. Withdrawal from the GATT is open to any contracting party after a six-month period of written notice which is shortened to 60 days for the Protocol of Provisional Application.

When referring to contracting parties the General Agreement speaks of governments and territories, not countries. Likewise, the status of membership is not firmly attached to countries in the traditional sense of statehood. Customs unions may well participate in the GATT in their own right. The EC has never formally acceded to the GATT, yet it is one of the protagonists thereto, though being accommodated on a pragmatic basis. The Community took part in GATT negotiations for the first time during the Dillon Round (1960–61), which resulted in a schedule being drawn up to replace the earlier schedules of concessions of the Member States. In the ECJ's view, the Community assumed the powers previously exercised by Member States in the area governed by the GATT on 1 July 1968, following the introduction of the Common Customs Tariff.[15]

Underlying the GATT is the neo-liberal philosophy imbued with the economic ideologies of free trade, open market and undistorted competition. Thus, special provisions (Article XVII) are laid down for regulating state trading enterprises.

---

14.   Hong Kong followed this path in April 1986: previously the UK was 'responsible' for it. This resulted in an awkward situation in a dispute, in 1981, between Hong Kong and the EC over quantitative restrictions in which the UK was both complainant and respondent! (Panel Report on *EEC – Quantitative Restrictions against Imports of Certain Products from Hong Kong*, BISD 30S/129).

15.   Joined Cases 21 to 24/72 *International Fruit Company v. Produktschap voor Groenten en Fruit* [1972] ECR 1219, Case 9/73 *Schlüter v. Hauptzollamt Lörrach* [1973] ECR 1135; for a detailed analysis of the EC's status in the GATT and the GATT's status in EC law see Joined Cases 267 to 269/81 *Amministrazione delle Finanze dello Stato v. SPI and SAMI* [1983] ECR 801. Useful comments on this point by Professor J. Usher are most gratefully acknowledged.

E. Institutions

The GATT was originally designed as a multilateral agreement, not as an international organisation. This, in part, explains the absence of sufficient institutional infrastructure. However, in the light of the changing international economic environment and under the force of practical necessities, the GATT has evolved in such a way that today it clearly possesses all the attributes of an international organisation.[16] In operating and carrying out its objectives the GATT is assisted by a number of institutional bodies.

When the contracting parties act jointly they constitute the principal institutional body, the 'CONTRACTING PARTIES' (in capital letters).[17] They possess a wide range of powers classified under four categories of competence: regulatory, deliberative, legislative and external.[18]   Each contracting party is entitled to have one vote and most decisions are taken by majority.   Amendment of the GATT is extremely hard to achieve since Articles I, II and XXIX require unanimity and the remaining Articles require a two-thirds majority (Article XXX Amendments).   Except in the case of waivers, accession of new contracting parties and approval of regional agreements under Article XXIV:10, very few issues are put to a vote.   In practice the GATT operates very much by consensus.   This is one of the manifestations of pragmatism, a distinctive feature of the GATT.

Whereas the CONTRACTING PARTIES is the highest organ of the GATT, it is the Council which essentially carries out most of the day-to-day work, and in practice administers the GATT.   The Council was established by a decision of the CONTRACTING PARTIES in 1960 with a view to dealing with routine and urgent matters.[19]   Not all the contracting parties participate in the Council: it consists of representatives of the contracting parties willing to do so.   Unlike the body of CONTRACTING PARTIES which convenes once a year, the Council meets on average nine times a year and the scope of its power, albeit delegated, is almost as wide as that of the

---

16.   See O. Long, *Law and its Limitations in the GATT Multilateral Trade System* (Graham & Trotman/Martinus Nijhoff, 1987) p.45.

17.   Art.XXV:1.

18.   See F. Roessler, 'The Competence of GATT' (1987) 21(3) JWTL 73 at 77–81.

19.   BISD 9S/8.

CONTRACTING PARTIES: except for the granting of waivers and decisions on certain major policy issues.

In addition to these institutions, a Committee is established by each Tokyo Round Agreement, which together with the Consultative Group of Eighteen and a number of other committees and bodies with sector-specific competence completes the GATT institutional organs. A significant contribution to the operation of the GATT is made by its Secretariat which provides it with valuable legal and administrative services.

In recognition of and as a response to the systemic shortcomings of the GATT, it has been boldly suggested that a global umbrella institution accommodating international commerce be established, a World Trade Organisation (WTO) laying down the institutional and procedural framework for international trade relations encompassing also the GATT which would then deal only with substantive obligations.[20]

II. NORMATIVE STRUCTURE

A. Substantive Rules and Principles

The GATT is founded on a number of basic rules and fundamental principles which together articulate the substantive law governing trade relations between the contracting parties. These constitute the foundations of GATT law, the most significant of which are dealt with below.

1. Non-discrimination

The rule of 'non-discrimination' is the cardinal and most sanctioned rule in the GATT and provides for non-discriminatory treatment of like products irrespective of their origin. It comprises the 'most-favoured nation' (MFN) principle and the 'national treatment' principle.

The MFN principle lies at the heart of the GATT. It is enshrined basically in Article I of the General Agreement. In accordance with this principle each contracting party is under obligation to grant to all contracting parties

---

20.   J.H. Jackson, *Restructuring the GATT System*, The Royal Institute of International Affairs (Pinter, 1990), pp.91–103.

treatment as favourable as it gives to any other country with respect to terms and conditions of importation and exportation of products. If contracting party A reduces the tariff rate on imports of widgets originating in country B, A is likewise under obligation to reduce unconditionally the tariff rate on imports of like widgets originating in contracting party C. A negotiated the tariff reduction with B and, as is usually the case, the latter reciprocated (namely, granted other concessions in return). Under the unconditional MFN treatment, as opposed to conditional MFN, C is entitled to be granted this tariff reduction without having to 'pay for it'. It must be apparent that the MFN principle is concerned with discrimination between products of supplying countries, though it is brought about by the importing country.

The benefits attached to imports under the MFN treatment might well be negated if, through domestic tax or regulatory measures, they were discriminated against, subsequent to their having crossed the borders, in the internal commerce of the importing country. The national treatment, expressed in Article III, is aimed at preventing precisely this type of discrimination. Every contracting party is free to pursue any regulatory and tax policy provided that imported and domestic products are treated on an equal footing. Obviously this principle is intended to prevent discrimination with reference to domestic and imported products. The MFN and national treatment principles are complementary. Immensely intractable conceptual and practical problems arise in relation to defining the term 'like product' whose scope is not the same in every context.

2. Tariffs and their protection

Reduction of tariffs has been, since the inception of the GATT, the linch-pin in the course of liberalisation of trade. Reduction has been achieved in the past through tariff negotiation procedures, either on a major multilateral level ('rounds') or by the individual entry of new contracting parties. Of these procedures, only the former will be dealt with here. In the course of negotiations, concessions on tariffs were exchanged initially between interested parties on a 'product-by-product' basis. The agreed tariff was then multilateralised. Apart from being cumbersome in practical terms, this method also gave rise to intractable legal problems. It was replaced in the Kennedy Round by the 'linear cut' method – applied ever since – whereby agreement on tariff reduction 'across the board' is sought. The level of treatment agreed upon to be accorded to a product is termed 'binding' and the product concerned 'bound'. That binding forms the maximum level or 'ceiling', which may be set at any level but is normally below the rate previously applied, since this is precisely the rationale of tariff negotiations.[21] Safeguarding these tariff concessions is a key element in the GATT. The total bindings make up the 'Schedule' of each contracting party. The Schedules are incorporated into the GATT and constitute an integral part thereof. They can be modified only through negotiations. Each contracting party is required to observe its tariff bindings and not to impose a custom duty in excess of that listed for each product on its Schedule. Of course, they are in no way prevented from imposing lower duties. An undeniable success for which the GATT prides itself is the achievement of substantial reduction of tariffs throughout its history.[22]

3.   Elimination of quantitative restrictions

The most glaring and direct interference with the flow of international trade occurs through the imposition of quantitative restrictions or 'quotas' whereby only a specified amount or value of certain product can be imported or exported in a given period.[23] Import restrictions are by far the most common. The basic GATT approach is, subject to specific exceptions, to eliminate quantitative restrictions irrespective of whether they are effected through quotas, import licences or other measures. It involves a precise, unconditional and comprehensive prohibition.[24] The use of quotas, in the view of economists, are the measures most likely to distort markets, prices and efficiency. These effects run counter to the GATT economic philosophy and, partly because of this, in the GATT there is an unqualified preference

---

21.   See K. Dam, *The GATT: Law and International Economic Organisation* (University of Chicago Press 1970) p.17.

22.   Since World War II there has been a lowering of customs duties from an average of 40% to the current average of 4.7% on industrial goods in developed countries.

23.   See Jackson, op. cit. supra n.2, p.305.

24.   See Panel Report on *Japan - Trade in Semi-Conductors*, BISD 35S/116 para.104; E.-U. Petersmann, 'Grey Area Trade Policy and the Rule of Law' (1988) 22(2) JWT 23 at 30.

for tariffs to quotas as trade policy instruments. Prohibition of quantitative restrictions is probably the principle with the most exceptions and the one which gives rise to most disputes.

4. General principles of GATT law

Alongside the positive rules provided for by the General Agreement, jurisprudentially developed general principles are now well established, the most pre-eminent of which are briefly explored below.[25]

i. Reciprocity

An overarching principle broadly expressed in the preamble of the General Agreement is reciprocity whereby 'reciprocal and mutually advantageous agreements' are to serve as a vehicle for the attainment of GATT objectives. More specific manifestations of this principle are found in Articles XXVIII:2 (Modification of Schedules) and XXVIII bis paragraph 1 (Tariff Negotiations). Although this was a guiding principle during the early tariff negotiation rounds, its legal value and status have been severely challenged particularly after the introduction of the 'linear-cut' method. Reciprocity has been seen as a departure from the MFN principle;[26] nonetheless, it is departed from in the 'linear-cut' tariff negotiations.[27] Difficulties arise in relation to ascertaining and measuring reciprocity as well as in its actual application.[28] Reciprocity is a nebulous concept in GATT law frequently misunderstood and misapplied by certain contracting parties.

25.   For an analytical examination of the basic principles of GATT law see E.-U. Petersmann, *Constitutional Functions and Constitutional Problems of International Economic Law* (University Press Fribourg, 1991), pp.221–244.

26.   See R.E. Hudec, 'Tiger, Tiger in the House: A Critical Appraisal of the Case Against Discriminatory Trade Measures' in E.-U. Petersmann and M. Hilf (eds.), *The New GATT Round of Multilateral Negotiations: Legal and Economic Problems* (2nd edn, Kluwer, 1991), p.175.

27.   See Jackson op. cit. supra n.2, p.243.

28.   It has been argued that 'the GATT does not require reciprocity but the practice ... among the major negotiating parties was always to seek reciprocity, whatever that means', J. Jackson, *The World Trading System. Law and Policy of International Economic Relations* (MIT Press, 1989). p.123.

ii.   Legal certainty

The principle of 'legal certainty' or 'legal security' is known in most national legal systems and also in EC law.[29]   Its content and scope are hard to define precisely but it manifests itself through the concepts of 'reasonable expectations', 'stability and predictability' and 'non-retroactivity'. Contracting parties trade on the assumption that the competitive conditions of the market will not be distorted by any trade measure, whether consistent with the GATT or not, and also their balance of concessions and obligations will not be upset by the introduction of any measure capable of having such effects. Furthermore, it is essential for any transnational trade transaction to be carried out in a secure trading environment.   Businessmen and their lawyers are notoriously concerned about stability and predictability in their transnational contractual relations.   It has been held that 'one of the basic aims of the General Agreement was security and predictability in the trade relations among contracting parties'.[30]   In this respect, Articles III (National Treatment) and XI (General Elimination of Quantitative Restrictions) 'are not only to protect current trade law but also to create the predictability needed to plan future trade'[31] and 'the existence of a quantitative restriction should be presumed to cause nullification or impairment not only because of any effect ... on the volume of trade but also for other reasons e.g. it would lead to increased transaction costs and would create uncertainties which could affect investment plans'.[32] Moreover two Panels examining a Community system for granting refunds on sugar exports found that the system constituted a 'permanent source of uncertainty' in the world export markets and, therefore, its application constituted a threat of serious prejudice in terms of

---

29.   See J.A. Usher, *The Influence of National Concepts on Decisions of the European Court* (1976) 1 E.L.Rev. 359, 363–367.

30.   Panel Report on *Manufacturing Clause,* BISD 32S/74 para.39.

31.   Panel Report on *United States – Taxes on Petroleum and Certain Imported Substances,* BISD 34S/136 para.5.2.2.

32.   Panel Report on *Japanese Measures on Imports of Leather,* BISD 31S/94 para.55.

Article XVI:1.[33] The non-retroactivity concept is based on Article XIII:3(b) (Non-discriminatory Administration of Quantitative Restrictions) of the General Agreement and was developed through the panel reports.[34]

iii. Proportionality

The GATT does not oblige contracting parties to pursue any particular economic or social policy;[35] they are utterly free to do so. What the GATT does, however, is to suggest that, in pursuit of these policies, fewer trade-distorting and more transparent trade policy instruments are to be preferred.[36] Moreover, when a contracting party invokes one clause of the general exceptions (Art. XX), the measure taken has to be 'necessary' to the achievement of the objective for which it is invoked and, among all those reasonably available, that one which 'entails the least degree of inconsistency with the GATT provisions'.[37]

iv. Transparency

The principle of transparency is best expressed in the GATT through a clear and unequivocal preference of tariffs over other trade policy instruments, as well as through the obligation imposed on the contracting parties

33. Panel Report on *European Communities – Refunds on Exports of Sugar*, BISD 26S/290 at 319; Panel Report on *European Communities – Refunds on Exports of Sugar – Complaint by Brazil*, BISD 27S/69 at 97.

34. See Panel Report on *EEC Restrictions on Imports of Apples from Chile*, BISD 27S/98 para.4.20; Panel Report on *European Economic Community – Restrictions on Imports of Dessert Apples – Complaint by Chile*, BISD 36S/93 para.12.27.

35. Cf. F. Roessler, 'The Scope, Limits and Function of the GATT Legal System' (1985) 8(3) World Economy 287, 291–295.

36. E.-U. Petersmann, 'Strengthening the Domestic Legal Framework on the GATT Multilateral Trade System: Possibilities and Problems of Making GATT Rules Effective in Domestic Legal Systems' in E.-U Petersmann and M. Hilf, op. cit. supra n.26, pp.90–91.

37. Panel Report on *United States – Section 337 of the Tariff Act of 1930*, BISD 36S/345 para.5.26; on the interpretation of the requirement 'necessary to the enforcement' in the context of Art.XI:2(c)(i) see Panel Reports on *Japan – Restrictions on Imports of Certain Agricultural Products*, BISD 35S/163 paras.5.1.3.5 and 5.1.3.6 and on *Canada – Import Restrictions on Ice Cream and Yoghurt*, BISD 36S/68 paras.80 and 81.

to publish promptly and, if possible in advance of their implementation, all trade regulations irrespective of their conformity with the GATT 'in such a manner as to enable governments and traders to become acquainted with them' (Art. X:1). The issue of notification of regulations granting subsidies appeared several times in GATT disputes. Perhaps the most blatant disregard of this principle is seen in export-restraint arrangements.

B. Exceptions

Like any other legal system, the GATT contains a number of exception clauses so as to render the basic normative structure operational. They introduce a dimension of flexibility into the system, vital for the GATT to pursue its objectives. Obviously an international trade agreement is likely to provide more safety valves than a domestic legal system: depending, of course, on the list of the membership, the diversity of interests, and the degree of the homogeneity of the legal and economic systems of the members thereto. But GATT is generous with 'exceptions' in that these often limit the substantive rules and principles to their very core. And this gives a distinctive character to the GATT system. Given that the GATT substantive rules are frequently departed from, significant doctrinal and policy issues are involved in determining whether and to what extent these exceptions can be legitimised under the GATT decision making processes. For example the CONTRACTING PARTIES may find themselves between the Scylla of granting a waiver or laying down special rules for the developing countries and the Charybdis of the proliferation of the exceptions and the attendant erosion of multilateralism. Here the conceptual term will be taken at its widest. The method selected is not so much concerned with the identification of the link between a rule and its exception as with the presentation of the exceptions according to a systematic classification.

1.   'Grandfather rights'

By signing the Protocol of Provisional Application (PPA), the contracting parties committed themselves to apply Parts I and III of the General Agreement provisionally, and Part II (namely Articles II to XXIII which contain most of the substantive obligations) 'to the fullest extent not inconsistent with existing legislation'.[38] Such clauses are invariably inserted into subsequent protocols of accession of new contracting parties. The effect of these clauses is to permit the contracting parties to maintain mandatory legislation inconsistent with Part II of the General Agreement in force on 30 October 1947 or on the date of each accession. Grandfather legislation can be subsequently modified without losing its status of 'existing legislation' provided the degree of inconsistency with the General Agreement is not increased.[39] This was confirmed by a Panel Report which examined whether extension of the expiry date of a grandfather clause could be justified under paragraph 1(b) of the PPA. The Panel held that bringing national legislation into conformity with the GATT is a 'one-way street' only permitting movements towards liberalisation.[40] Evidently, the policy is to minimise the degree of inconsistency of existing national legislations with the GATT and gradually bring them into line with GATT law. Laws promulgated after 30 October 1947 or the date of each accession in no way can qualify for this right. Few laws currently benefit from grandfather rights.[41]

2. *Differential and more favourable treatment for developing countries*[42]

The majority of the GATT contracting parties are developing countries. Their economic development and integration into international trading system is a central issue in the GATT. There is, however, a long-standing debate surrounding the position of developing countries in the world trading system. This focuses on two points representing respectively the arguments of the two sides.[43] Developing countries contend that their products do not enjoy fair access to developed country markets nor do they have a balanced share of the

38. Para.1, Protocol of Provisional Application.

39. Working Party Report on *Brazilian Internal Taxes*, BISD Vol. II/181 at 187.

40. Panel Report on *United States Manufacturing Clause*, BISD 31S/74 para.38.

41. See generally M. Hansen & E. Vermulst, 'The GATT Protocol of Provisional Application: A Dying Grandfather?' (1989) 27 Columbia J. Transnat'l L. 263; P.F. Knobl, 'GATT Application: The Grandfather is Still Alive' (1991) 25(4) JWT 101.

42. For an analytical examination of the issue, see R.E. Hudec, *Developing Countries in the GATT Legal System*, Thames Essay No.50 (Gower/Trade Policy Research Centre, 1987).

43. See generally Jackson, op. cit. supra n.28, pp.276 et seq.

expansion of world trade. Moreover they are not satisfied with the GATT rules in relation to the accommodation of their interests and, in any event, they claim that 'equality' in international trade requires differential treatment between 'unequals'.[44] Developed countries, on the other hand, acknowledge that developing countries should be treated differentially and more favourably but also assert that the privileges granted to developing countries are intended to assist them by promoting their capacity to participate more fully in the GATT legal disciplines and not to perpetuate discriminatory policies. Furthermore, the more advanced developing countries should be prepared to bring their policies into line with the GATT rules (the 'graduation issue'). Irrespective of the plausibility of each side's arguments, the GATT grants a special freedom to developing countries to pursue their economic policies and recognises their less favourable economic status in special provisions distributed throughout the General Agreement and the Tokyo Round Agreements but concentrated principally in Article XVIII and Part IV of the General Agreement. In so far as these provisions deviate from certain GATT disciplines technically they constitute exceptions thereto. Nonetheless, this remains a major doctrinal and policy issue concerning both developing and developed countries alike. Under the general rubric of 'differential and more favourable treatment of developing countries' there are four legal fronts to be explored.

First, Article XVIII, the original relevant GATT provision, permits developing countries to raise tariffs in order to protect infant industries or to introduce quantitative restrictions for balance of payments reasons (to be distinguished from the general balance of payments clause), to take any measure to promote a particular industry or to apply for permission to deviate from GATT rules so as to establish a particular industry. Second, Part IV – namely Articles XXXVI to XXXVIII – 'on trade and development' was added to the General Agreement in 1965 and came into force on 27 June 1966, whereby developed countries committed themselves to assist the

---

44. In a symbolic expression of this dissatisfaction, Uruguay launched a massive complaint in 1962 under Art.XXIII against 15 developed countries for 562 alleged trade restrictions. This was not so much to pursue settlement of a dispute as to voice concern for more favourable treatment, BISD 11S/95 and BISD 13S/45. (See R.E. Hudec, *The GATT Legal System and World Trade Diplomacy* (2nd edn, Butterworths, 1990), pp.240–242.)

developing countries 'as a matter of conscious and purposeful effort' and not to expect reciprocity of concessions by the latter. Third, following initiatives in the context of the United Nations Conference on Trade and Development (UNCTAD), an ambitious programme to promote trade with developing countries was launched under the Generalised System of Preferences (GSP) whereby products originating in developing countries would enjoy preferential treatment in their access to industrial countries. The scheme had to be implemented through the GATT. Indeed, in 1971 the CONTRACTING PARTIES approved a waiver to the MFN principle under Article XXV:5 which virtually 'legitimised' the GSP for a period of ten years. It was, however, left to individual countries to implement the schemes. Finally, in November 1979, before the expiry date of the GSP the CONTRACTING PARTIES adopted, in the context of the Tokyo Round, a decision entitled 'Differential and More Favourable Treatment, Reciprocity and Fuller Participation of Developing Countries',[45] known as the 'enabling clause', which institutionalised the preferential treatment in favour of or among developing countries in the world trading system. It also affirmed the principle, first introduced in Part IV, that developed countries would not expect developing countries, in the course of trade negotiations, to make concessions which were inconsistent with their individual development, financial and trade needs.

3. Regional arrangements

Economic goals of individual countries may well be pursued through the formation of economic associations between two or more countries. In fact, this is a growing trend increasingly appealing to many countries, particularly in recent years, and it is basically expressed in the form of customs unions and free-trade areas usually – but not necessarily[46] – between adjacent or neighbouring countries.[47] The GATT recognises the benefits for the parties involved in economic integration and does not prevent the formation of

45. See infra pp.184–185.
46. Israel–United States Free Trade Agreement of 12 April 1985, (1985) 24 ILM 653; see also the Report of the Working Party on this agreement, BISD 34S/58.
47. See J.J. Schott, 'More Free Trade Areas?' in J.J. Schott (ed.), *Free Trade Areas and US Trade Policy* (Institute for International Economics, 1989), p.1.

customs unions and free-trade areas provided that they meet certain criteria intended to ensure, above all, that they do not raise new trade barriers and that substantially all trade within the grouping is free. A free-trade area comprises a group of two or more customs territories in which duties and other trade barriers are eliminated on substantially all the trade in products originating in such territories.[48] A customs union is a higher stage of economic integration in that it provides for elimination of duties and trade restrictions at least in products originating in the union and possibly with respect to substantially all the trade between the constituent territories. More importantly, it establishes a common external customs tariff towards third countries.[49] Since economic integration is a long process, the GATT also provides for the establishment of interim agreements leading to the formation of customs unions and free-trade areas. All three types of agreement are inherently discriminatory to the extent that their members grant trade benefits to one another without extending them to third countries. The provisions of Article XXIV are problematic and the language vague. Indeed, several nebulous concepts lurk therein. These, coupled with the fact that no prior authorisation for their establishment is required if the conditions provided in paragraphs 5 to 9 are satisfied, give rise to questions relating to the conformity of such agreements with the criteria of Article XXIV, the most striking being that of the Treaty of Rome. Although the EC is one of the protagonists in the GATT, its conformity with the provisions of Article XXIV is in theory still an open question.[50] It is submitted, however, that in the light of the language of Article XXIV and, despite initial scepticism, legally the EC more than qualifies as a customs union under the GATT provisions.[51] *Quaere*, however, whether the EC is really still an 'exception' in

48.   Representative types are the European Free Trade Association (EFTA) and the US–Canada Free Trade Agreement.

49.   An example is the European Economic Community (EEC).

50.   See the report of a Committee appointed to examine the conformity of the EEC Treaty as well as the EURATOM Treaty with the provisions of the General Agreement, BISD 7S/70; see also the Working Party Report adopted 9 Mar. 1983 on the accession of Greece to the EEC, BISD 30S/174.

51.   Cf. Jackson, op. cit. supra n.2, p.606; Leutwiler Report in A. Dunkel, *Trade Policies for a Better Future. The 'Leutwiler Report', the GATT and the Uruguay Round* (Nijhoff, 1987), p.67.

terms of a customs union under Article XXIV, given the current degree of its integration.

4. Waivers

When one or more contracting parties need, in exceptional circumstances not provided elsewhere in the GATT, to derogate from a GATT rule, they may apply for a waiver. In such case, the CONTRACTING PARTIES have the power under Article XXV:5 to waive an obligation imposed upon a contracting party by the GATT. The decision is taken by a two-thirds majority of votes cast by at least half of all the contracting parties. The overwhelming majority of the waivers concern individual contracting parties or small groups of them who are seeking 'temporary' formal 'legitimisation' of trade laws or practices which would otherwise be inconsistent with the GATT. There are, however, very few waivers of general application.[52] Periodical review of the waivers is normally standard. Four illustrative waivers are presented here. First, the waiver to the European Coal and Steel Community.[53] Second, the waiver to the US regarding Section 22 of the Agricultural Adjustment Act of 1933 – as amended – whereby the US in 1955 was granted permission to apply certain restrictions on imports of agricultural products.[54] This waiver was unsuccessfully challenged by the EC under the GATT dispute settlement procedures. The Panel, in the first ever case examining the scope and meaning of a waiver, affirmed the validity of the waiver and held the US measures consistent with the terms of the waiver.[55] Third, the waiver granted to the US for its participation in the US–Imports of Automotive Products Agreement.[56] Finally, the waiver granted to the EC concerning EC transitional measures (from 3 October 1990 to 31 December 1992) related to the unification of Germany. Under this, the MFN principle was waived to permit the EC to grant duty free treatment to certain imports from the former Eastern European countries as a result of trade relations already

---

52. See Generalised System of Preferences.
53. BISD 1S/86.
54. L/339, BISD 3S/141.
55. BISD 37S/228.
56. BISD 14S/37.

established between the former German Democratic Republic (GDR) and those countries before German unification.[57]

5. Agriculture

The long-standing concerns and governmental regulation of agriculture existed well before the establishment of the GATT. Likewise, the inherent peculiarities of the agricultural sector are acknowledged by the GATT and realised through the differential treatment of agricultural products in deviation from the basic rules. Of these exceptions the two most notable will be mentioned. First, contracting parties are allowed to impose quantitative restrictions on imports of agricultural products necessary to the enforcement of certain price and quantity regulatory schemes governing the production and marketing or disposal of agricultural products.[58] Second, unlike manufactures, the granting of subsidies on certain primary products is permissible, subject to specifically provided conditions.[59] Both these exceptions are frequently resorted to in such a way that a very large segment of the agricultural sector is regulated by these provisions. This, coupled with the US waiver of 1955, entails that the bulk of trade in agricultural products circumvents the basic GATT provisions and is effectively denied free access to markets. Three observations are worth mentioning in relation to this phenomenon: first, there is an apparent lack of political will to subject agriculture to GATT legal disciplines. Farm supports, as is well known, were the cause of the December 1990 impasse of the Uruguay Round and are still the main stumbling block. Second, and correlatively, the language of the GATT provisions in this respect is so vague as not effectively to regulate agricultural products. Finally, the peculiar nature of agriculture needs elaborate substantive rules.

---

57. BISD 37S/296.
58. Art.XI para.2(c).
59. Arts.9 and 10 of the Subsidies Code.

6.   General and security exceptions

Article XX of the GATT contains a list of general exceptions, while Article XXI specifically provides for exceptions for the protection of essential national security interests. The range of general exceptions is broad enough to cover measures necessary to protect: public morals; human, animal or plant life or health; importation or exportation of gold and silver; products of prison labour; national treasures of artistic, historic or archaeological value; conservation of exhaustible natural resources; obligations under any international commodity agreement; price control and export restrictions; and acquisition or distribution of products in general or local supply. But the provision by far the most commonly invoked is one which allows measures necessary to secure compliance with national laws or regulations which are not inconsistent with the provisions of the GATT, including those relating to customs enforcement, enforcement of monopolies, the protection of patents, trade marks and copyrights and the prevention of deceptive practices. Unlike security exceptions, the measures taken under the general exceptions are subject to three requirements: they must not be applied in a manner which would constitute a means of arbitrary or unjustifiable discrimination; nor must they constitute a disguised restriction on international trade; and they must be necessary to the ends pursued.

7.   Restrictions for balance of payments

As is widely accepted, trade and monetary policies are closely interrelated. It will be recalled that underlying the widespread quantitative restrictions of the pre- and post-World War II period were, notably, the financial difficulties of the countries concerned. Recognising that a contracting party may resort to trade measures for monetary reasons, the GATT sets out provisions principally in Articles XII and XVIII:B (concerning developing countries) by which contracting parties are authorised, subject to certain conditions provided therein, to take quantitative restrictions in order to safeguard their external financial position and their balance of payments. Co-operation with the International Monetary Fund is required regarding the ascertainment of certain facts and statistics.

8. Safeguard measures

Article XIX constitutes the principal 'escape-clause' of the GATT. By virtue of this provision, under certain conditions contracting parties are permitted to take protective ('safeguard') measures against a sudden surge of imports if they cause or threaten injury to domestic producers of like or competitive products. Withdrawal or modification of concessions or, most commonly, introduction of quantitative restrictions are the authorised protective measures. When taking safeguard measures a contracting party is under obligation to notify the CONTRACTING PARTIES in advance (or in urgent cases immediately after the action) of the measures concerned. More importantly, the safeguard measures must apply on a temporary basis and to the extent necessary (i.e. proportionately) to alleviate the injurious effects caused by unforeseen increase of imports. Obviously, this 'escape-clause' constitutes a severe derogation from the GATT basic principles and contains the intrinsic potential of being arbitrarily invoked as, in fact, has been repeatedly done. Arguably, it is one of the most controversial of the provisions of the GATT and for a long period has been – and still remains – in the negotiating agendas without a meaningful agreement having been reached.[60]

9. Export-restraint arrangements

Viewed in wide conceptual scope, safeguard measures are deemed to include bilateral export-restraint arrangements between exporting and importing contracting parties. Technically, however, they are quite distinctive in character in that they differ from them in several respects (transparency, duration, compensation, notification to the CONTRACTING PARTIES). Under a bilateral export-restraint arrangement the exporting country undertakes to impose, regulate or monitor public and/or private export restraints to the importing country at the request of or under threat from the latter. Such an

---

60. See generally M.C.E.J. Bronckers, *Selective Safeguard Measures in Multilateral Trade Relations – Issues of Protectionism in GATT, European Community and United States Law* (Kluwer, 1985).

arrangement usually takes the form of price undertakings, quantitative restrictions, surveillance systems or export forecasts.[61] 'Voluntary export restraints' (VERs), 'voluntary restraint arrangements' (VRAs) and 'orderly marketing arrangements' (OMAs) are the representative types of the generic term 'export-restraint arrangements'. They are considered inherently discriminatory and their consistency with the GATT is questionable.[62] There are various legal, economic and political reasons for reaching these agreements[63] but they clearly circumvent the basic tenets of the GATT law and fall in the category of so-called 'grey area' measures.[64] As a result of these measures, free market forces are suppressed and competition is distorted not only in the markets of the countries involved in the arrangement but also in third countries.[65] This 'managed' or 'results-oriented' trade is the antithesis of rule-oriented free trade and constitutes a systemic threat to multilateralism.[66] More alarming still is the proliferation of this kind of agreement. At present there are approximately 284 export-restraint arrangements in force[67] involving food and other agricultural products, textiles and clothing,[68] steel and steel products, electronic products, motor vehicles and equipment, footwear and machine tools.[69] Just over 60% of these measures have no expiry date.[70]

---

61. See E.-U. Petersmann, op. cit. supra n.24, p.28.

62. See generally J.H. Jackson, 'Consistency of Export-restraint Arrangements with the GATT' (1988) 11 World Economy 485; McGovern, op. cit. supra n.8, p.298.

63. Jackson, idem, pp.487 et seq.

64. See Petersmann, op. cit. supra n.24.

65. Such an agreement between the US and Japan, designed to open the Japanese market to US semi-conductors as well as to prevent dumping of Japanese semi-conductors in both the US and third markets, was successfully assailed by the EC under the GATT dispute settlement procedures. The Panel upheld the EC's contention in relation to the part of the agreement concerning price-fixing in third markets as inconsistent with Art.XI:1 of the General Agreement: Panel Report on *Japan – Trade in Semi-Conductors*, BISD 35S/116 at paras.117 and 118.

66. See J. Bhagwati, *The World Trading System at Risk* (Princeton University Press, 1991), pp.23 et seq.

67. *The Economist*, 21 Sept. 1991, p.112.

68. Apart from those concluded under the Multifibre Arrangement.

69. GATT Council Overview of Developments in the International Trading Environment. Annual Report by the Director-General, C/171, 5 Dec. 1989.

70. Ibid.

10. Multifibre Arrangement (MFA)

To the above exceptions should be added the *sui generis* MFA which, although concluded in the context of the GATT, departs from the basic GATT principles[71] for it authorises its signatories to enter into bilateral agreements establishing quotas with respect to trade in textile products. One of its basic objectives is to achieve the expansion and progressive liberalisation of world trade in textile products, 'while at the same time ensuring the orderly and equitable development of this trade and avoidance of disruptive effects in individual markets'.[72] It is doubtful, however, whether and to what extent the envisaged liberalisation can be achieved, given the explicit desire for the continuation of the MFA by both developed and developing countries.[73] The MFA was due to expire on 31 July 1991 but on that day the Textiles Committee decided to extend it for a further period of 17 months, from 1 August 1991 to 31 December 1992. This is the fourth extension of the MFA, which has governed most of the world's trade in textiles and clothing since 1974.[74]

11. Anti-dumping and countervailing duties

Contracting parties are authorised under certain circumstances to impose anti-dumping or countervailing duties on dumped or subsidised products imported into their commerce up to the margin of dumping or subsidy. In this sense, anti-dumping and countervailing duties are, technically, exceptions to the GATT basic rules.[75]

---

71. See Damian Chalmers, chap.VII infra and generally N. Blokker, *International Regulation of World Trade in Textiles,* (Nijhoff, 1989); H.G. Krenzler, 'The Multifibre Arrangement as a Special Regime under GATT' in H. Hilf, F.G. Jacobs and E.-U. Petersmann (eds.), *The European Community and GATT* (Kluwer, 1986), p.141.

72. Art.1 para.2 of the MFA.

73. See G. C. Hufbauer, *The Free Trade Debate* (Priority Press, 1989), p.116.

74. GATT Focus No.83, Aug. 1991, p.12; *Financial Times,* 1 Aug. 1991, p.6.

75. See Panel Report on *United States – Countervailing Duties on Fresh, Chilled and Frozen Pork from Canada,* DS7/R para.4.4. Of the voluminous bibliography on these subjects, see J. Jackson and E.A. Vermulst (eds.), *Antidumping Law and Practice: A Comparative Study* (University of Michigan Press, 1989); R.M. Bierwagen, *GATT Article VI and the Protectionist Bias*

III. DISPUTE SETTLEMENT

'We want to show the world that multilateral dispute settlement under the GATT works.'
Tej Bunnag, Thailand's Ambassador[76]

ONE of the real virtues of any legal system is its satisfactory handling of disputes arising therefrom. One might reasonably expect that an international institution subscribed to by 103 countries and regulating over four-fifths of the world merchandise trade would have an established elaborate supervisory mechanism to interpret the law, to secure compliance with the obligations thereof and, ultimately, to enforce them. Yet there is no such system institutionalised in the GATT: the ITO would have assumed this role, had it come into existence. Nonetheless, the GATT does provide, albeit crippled by institutional shortcomings, a forum for resolving disputes which is basically founded on GATT provisions but in fact has evolved through long practice. More particularly, there are several provisions throughout the General Agreement and the Codes pertaining to dispute settlement. The mechanism for resolving GATT disputes is principally based on the provisions of Articles XXII and XXIII of the General Agreement. Although most of the Tokyo Round Agreements provide for autonomous dispute settlement procedures, they are essentially drafted on the same pattern as that of Articles XXII and XXIII.[77] Thus, a common four-step sequential process is followed for disputes arising in either context.

A. Conciliation versus Adjudication

If there is an unassailable truth in the GATT dispute settlement mechanism, this is that it clearly and unswervingly favours conciliation over adjudication.

---

in Anti-Dumping Laws (Studies in Transnational Economic Law, vol.7, Kluwer, 1990); G.C. Hufbauer and J. Shelton Erb, *Subsidies in International Trade* (MIT Press, 1984); McGovern, op. cit. supra n.8, chaps.11–12.

76.   This statement was made before the GATT Council, on the adoption of the Panel Report on *Thailand – Restrictions on Importation of and Internal Taxes on Cigarettes*, BISD 37S/200, GATT Focus No.76, Nov. 1990, p.5.

77.   See generally Robert E. Hudec, 'GATT Dispute Settlement after the Tokyo Round: An Unfinished Business' (1980) 13 Cornell International Law Journal 145.

Article XXII:1 provides that contracting parties shall accord to one another 'sympathetic consideration' and afford 'adequate opportunity' for consultations regarding representations made with respect to any matter affecting the operation of the General Agreement. If no satisfactory solution can be reached the CONTRACTING PARTIES may, at the request of a contracting party, consult with any contracting party to this end (Article XXII:2).

Likewise, by virtue of Article XXIII:1 each contracting party may go through similar processes of consultations with other parties concerned if this contracting party considers that:

i. Any benefit accruing to it directly or indirectly under the General Agreement is being nullified or impaired, or that
ii. the attainment of any objective of the General Agreement is being impeded.

The overwhelming majority of the cases is concerned with nullification or impairment of benefits of a contracting party rather than the impediment to the attainment of the objectives of the General Agreement. Even in these cases there has always been an element of nullification or impairment. Contracting parties rarely assume the role of the guardians of the Agreement unless they suffer economic loss or wish to establish a legal precedent. In any event, nullification or impairment or impediment of the objectives must be the causal effect of:

(a) the failure of another contracting party to carry out its obligations under the General Agreement, or
(b) the application of another contracting party of any measure, whether or not it conflicts with the provisions of the General Agreement, or
(c) the existence of any other situation.

The first cause is the most commonly invoked whereas the third one has never been used. Clearly, the language of these provisions is vague to say the least. This, in turn, gives rise to several conceptual and practical problems.

B. Third-Party Adjudication

1. Panel procedures

If bilateral consultations under Articles XXII:1 and/or XXIII:1 have been exhausted without yielding a mutually satisfactory solution, the matter may be referred to the CONTRACTING PARTIES. In practice, this sets in motion the third-party adjudication procedures. The GATT does not expressly provide procedural rules for this purpose. But it has become customary practice through which comprehensive rules have been developed. Most of them were codified in the 'Understanding Regarding Notification, Consultation, Dispute Settlement and Surveillance'.[78] Under these procedures a contracting party may request the establishment of a working party or a panel whose task is to assist the CONTRACTING PARTIES to deal with the matter. It should be noted, however, that the establishment of such a body is not a formally entrenched right: but it is so well recognised that hitherto no such request has been turned down and the blocking power of any party involved can only produce a delay of the process.[79] A working party consists of a varying number of national delegations including the countries involved in the dispute. However, since 1952, the establishment of panels has become the standard practice. It is, therefore, the panel procedures that will be dealt with here.[80]

Depending on the case, a panel consists of three or five members acting in their individual capacity and not under the instructions of their governments. The establishment of the panel and its terms of reference are agreed

---

78. BISD 26S/210 (hereafter referred to as the 'Understanding'). The Understanding comprises a compilation of procedural practices which now operate as a useful guide or a kind of 'procedural code'. In 1966, special procedures were adopted relating to developing countries, BISD 14S/18.

79. Cf. R.E. Hudec, 'The FTA Provisions on Dispute Settlement: The Lessons of the GATT Experience' in D.M. McRae and D.P. Steger (eds.), *Understanding the Free Trade Agreement* (Institute for Research on Public Policy, 1988), p.33.

80. For an analysis of this subject see Rosine Plank, 'An Unofficial Description of How a GATT Panel Works and Does Not' (1987) 4(4) Journal of International Arbitration 53; Pierre Pescatore, William J. Davey and Andreas F. Lowenfeld, *Handbook of GATT Dispute Settlement* (Kluwer, 1991).

upon between the interested contracting parties and approved by the Council. Three significant issues emerge at this stage. First, the specification of the terms of reference. This is power-conferring and frequently determines the outcome of the case,[81] for it circumscribes *ad hoc* the jurisdiction of each panel, thereby delineating its competence to examine a certain number of matters. Panels never entertain questions not included in their terms of reference. Indeed, there have been cases wherein matters having a bearing on the case were not examined because they fell outside the terms of reference.[82] To the extent that the terms of reference determine whether the dispute will be dealt with under the General Agreement or a Code, the terms of reference may be regarded as an indicator of the 'forum' and 'law' applicable to the case. Second, great difficulties and delicate problems may arise in the process for the selection of panellists who are usually diplomats from national delegations in Geneva from countries not involved in the dispute.[83] However, academics, experts with relevant experience of the subject matter of the case, former judges and retired GATT Secretariat functionaries are increasingly being called upon to serve as panellists. Partly as a result of this, a legalistic element and professionalism are gradually being introduced into the panel procedures. In November 1984, the CONTRACTING PARTIES agreed to establish a roster of non-governmental panellists. The practice is to appoint at least one member from developing countries when a dispute is between a developing and a developed country. Third, time limits, rarely observed, are imposed in these procedures. Underlying all three issues are the difficulties associated with the decision-making processes in the Council. Since the decisions are generally taken by consensus, it is obvious that disagreements may lead to protracted and time-consuming debates.

81. It has been written characteristically: 'EC loses first round of Airbus dispute at GATT' referring to the EC's attempt to modify the terms of reference in the above dispute, *Financial Times* 12 Apr. 1991, p.5.

82. Panel Report on *Canada – Administration of the Foreign Investment Review Act*, BISD 30S/140 paras.5.3 and 6.2.

83. But see the composition of the Panels in the Panel Reports on *United States – Section 337 of the Tariff Act of 1930*, BISD 36S/345; *United States Customs User Fee* BISD 35S/245; *European Economic Community – Payments and Subsidies Paid to Processors and Producers of Oilseeds and Related Animal-Feed Proteins*, BISD 37S/86.

Once the composition and the terms of reference are established, the panel commences its work by first setting up its own working procedures. Disputants are invited to present written submissions and, if necessary, oral arguments. Both the parties to the dispute and also third parties which have notified the Council that they have a substantial interest in the matter have the right to be heard. Confidentiality dominates all the procedural stages. Obviously the written submissions are exchanged between the parties; counterarguments and defences may also be put forward. During the course of the dispute the panel repeatedly gives the parties an opportunity to reach a bilateral agreement. If this is achieved, a formal report is drawn up stating this outcome. If not, the proceedings continue leading to the panel's judgment contained in the panel report. The GATT Secretariat makes an enormously valuable contribution to the panel proceedings by providing the panels with legal services.

2. Nature and status of panel reports

The function of a panel is normally to review the facts of a case and the applicability of GATT provisions and to arrive at an objective assessment of these matters. In so doing a panel approaches the norms through interpretative criteria. In ascertaining the facts and interpreting and applying the law, this is reminiscent of a 'judge-like' approach. Indeed, although the panel reports fall short of a national court judgment, they virtually contain authoritative interpretations of GATT law in a legally consistent manner and they are essentially judicial in character.[84] This development is the result of a process evolved over 40 years. During this period of time there has been a remarkable shift from diplomatic negotiations towards objective, third-party adjudication procedures. In addition, if one looks perceptively at the way the disputes were handled throughout the GATT's history a dramatic change can be seen in the style of approaching disputes. A mere juxtaposition of an early case with a recent panel report is revealing. In the first ever complaint in the

---

84. See E. McGovern, 'Dispute Settlement in the GATT – Adjudication or Negotiation?' in M. Hilf, F.G. Jacobs and E.-U. Petersmann (eds.), *The European Community and GATT* (Kluwer, 1986), pp.75–81.

GATT, the Netherlands delegation, after unsuccessful consultations with Cuba over the latter's discriminatory consular tax, requested a ruling from the Chairman of the CONTRACTING PARTIES as to whether Article I (the MFN obligation) applied to consular taxes. The Chairman ruled 'Yes'. That was all.[85] In stark contrast to this, most of the recent panel reports contain articulate, legally based and carefully reasoned findings. Procedural rules, methodological principles and interpretative canons are amply utilised by the panels in reaching their conclusions. Thus, impartiality of the panellists and the right of the parties to have a fair hearing, both principles of the 'rule of natural justice', are closely observed.[86] Participation in the proceedings is open to any third party having a substantial interest in the case. Although the panels have specifically circumscribed jurisdiction, they enjoy a considerable freedom to use any source of information (consult with other international organisations, ask for statistics, seek technical assistance) they consider appropriate. More than one contracting party can join their complaints and/or defences arising out of the same factual and legal bases.[87] All the reports are drawn up on a standard pattern: introduction, factual aspects, arguments of the disputants and third parties and findings and/or conclusions. The overwhelming majority of cases are decided unanimously. If there is any dissenting opinion, it is reported anonymously.

It should be noted that, despite the declared contemplation in the Understanding to the effect that 'requests for conciliation and the use of the dispute settlement procedures of Article XXIII:2 should not be intended or considered contentious acts', many disputes are based upon acrimonious complaints leading to confrontational positions of the parties and finally to panel rulings which, if adopted, impose legally binding obligations. It is submitted, therefore, that this stage of the dispute settlement procedures in particular is adversarial in nature and contentious in character.[88] In this context, it is

85.   Cited in Hudec, op. cit. supra n.43, p.75.

86.   See McGovern, op. cit. supra n.83, p.77.

87.   See e.g. Panel Report on *United States – Taxes on Petroleum and Certain Imported Substances* (Canada, the EEC and Mexico co-applicants), BISD 34S/136; Panel Report on *United States Customs User Fee* (Canada and the EEC co-applicants), BISD 35S/245; Working Party on *Uruguayan Recourse to Article XXIII* (against 15 developed countries), BISD 11S/95.

88.   Panels usually speak of parties' 'contentions' and numerous complaints have culminated

interesting to observe certain salient methods and tests by which the panels approach the substance of a case. Although the *stare decisis* principle of common law is not enshrined in the GATT dispute settlement procedures, reference to previous panel reports is now a well established principle.[89] Furthermore, when a measure under examination is judged to be in breach of a GATT rule, such finding will *prima facie* constitute a case of nullification or impairment because it is presumed to have an adverse impact on other contracting parties. This presumption in essence transfers the burden of proof to the defendant and it is difficult to rebut. Enacted rules rank highest in GATT law. A long-standing practice relating to a measure inconsistent with the GATT is not legitimised by the fact that it has not been challenged under Article XXIII:2.[90] In addition, the principle referred to as 'the law-creating force deriving from the circumstances' can only be relevant in the absence of law.[91] And social and economic conditions cannot be considered unless reference to them is provided in the law.[92] Furthermore, the panels have articulated the 'non-violation' principle, essentially based on Article XXIII:1(b), whereby a measure can be prejudicial to the trade of another contracting party even though it does not *de jure* conflict with any GATT provision.[93] In practice, however, in this kind of case, a legal principle is usually violated. The fact that a measure inconsistent with the GATT has only minimal trade distorting effects does not suffice to immunise it (*de minimis* principle not applied). The panels can entertain questions regarding not only the actual infringement of GATT law but also the examination of mandatory national legislation without it being actually in operation in a particular case.[94]

---

in so-called 'trade wars' ('chicken war', 'pasta war', 'wheat flour war' and, recently, 'Airbus war').

89. But see the Panel Report on *European Economic Community – Restrictions on Imports of Dessert Apples – Complaint by Chile*, BISD 36S/93.

90. Panel Report on *EEC – Quantitative Restrictions against Imports of Certain Products from Hong Kong*, BISD 30S/129 para.28.

91. Idem, para.27.

92. Idem, para.21.

93. See McGovern, op. cit. supra n.8, pp.39–42.

94. Panel Report on *United States – Taxes on Petroleum and Certain Imported Substances*, BISD 34S/136 para.5.2.2.

C. Adoption of Panel Reports

With the completion of its work the panel draws up the report and distributes
it to the parties with a view to giving them a final opportunity to reach a
bilateral settlement.   If it proves unavailing, the chairman of the panel
submits the report to the CONTRACTING PARTIES or to the Code
Committee as the case may be.[95] It is normally put on the agenda of the
next Council meeting. It may be adopted immediately. But given that the
decisions are taken on the basis of consensus it is evident that the adoption
of a report is not an easy matter. The loser can simply block adoption for
various reasons. It may, for instance, be dissatisfied with the findings; or the
subject-matter may be based on highly sensitive political – whether domestic
or international – or economic issues. It is at this stage of GATT dispute
settlement procedures that legal rules cease to apply and diplomatic exercises
instead come into play. Bargaining and disagreements between the parties
concerned can result in protracted discussions within and out of the Council.
Partly because of this, and partly as a result of the request of the parties for
more time to 'consider' it, the report is often deferred for the next or subsequent Council meetings. Until these fraught circumstances are resolved, it is
difficult for the report to be adopted. Hitherto an overwhelming majority of
the panel reports has been adopted, a handful of them have not and one has
simply been 'noted'.[96] With its adoption a report obtains a legally binding
character and it is added to the collection of the GATT 'case law' which
forms part of the GATT jurisprudence. Apart from a very few reports which
have been set aside, the non-adopted reports remain virtually in limbo and
are technically 'pending'. Their status is unclear. Certainly they are neither
binding nor enforceable. But should the adoption procedures with their
inherently high political dimensions suffice to negate the entire legal validity
of non-adopted reports? Furthermore, their non-adoption may be based on
reasons entirely extraneous to their findings. In fact, this occurred when the

95.   For an appraisal of the institutional status of these Committees, see J.H. Jackson, 'The
Birth of the GATT–MTN System: A Constitutional Appraisal' (1980) 12 Law & Policy in
International Business 21, esp. pp.51, 52.

96.   Panel Report on *Spanish Measures Concerning Domestic Sale of Soyabean Oil*, L/5142.

US blocked the Panel Report on *United States – Definition of Industry Concerning Wine and Grape Products* because the EC opposed the adoption of the Panel Report on *European Economic Community Subsidies on Export of Pasta Products.*[97] Devoid of formalised legal status though they may be, they are certainly not without importance.

D. Enforcement

Assuming that the complainant has won the case before the panel and then succeeded in having the report adopted by the CONTRACTING PARTIES, how can the winner enforce the report? This is avowedly a difficult question and also relates to the more general issue of the enforcement of judgments in international law, given the absence of a central policing authority. The GATT is no exception to this problem. Once the report is adopted it becomes enforceable. First the CONTRACTING PARTIES may make recommendations on the basis of the findings or give a ruling on the matter. The primary objective is usually to secure the withdrawal of the measures concerned if they are found to be inconsistent with the General Agreement. Compensation can be awarded if the immediate withdrawal of the measures is impracticable and as a temporary measure pending the withdrawal. The loser does not always comply with the report. Second, the CONTRACTING PARTIES may authorise a suspension of concessions or other obligations if they consider that the circumstances are serious enough to justify such an action.[98] A *prima facie* case of nullification or impairment would *ipso facto* require consideration of whether the circumstances are serious enough to justify such an authorisation. Clearly, the enforcement mechanism falls far short of being completely effective. Several panel reports await implementation long after their adoption.

Not always unjustifiably, the GATT dispute settlement machinery has attracted much criticism from many sources. However a distinction should be made as to the different stages of the procedures. It is true that it can be

---

97. SCM/71 and SCM/43 respectively.
98. This has occurred only once in the GATT's history. The Netherlands was formally authorised, in 1952, to retaliate against US import restrictions on dairy products, BISD 1S/62.

difficult to reach agreement on many issues such as terms of reference, members of the panels, adoption and implementation, with the concomitant result of protracted processes. This is due to constitutional deficiencies. But the panel procedures themselves are flawed in very few respects. This is not because of the inadequacy of the panels: it is rather because the substantive rules are vague, ambiguous and subject to open-ended interpretations, which, in turn, is attributable to the failure of the contracting parties to lay down precise and clear rules.[99] For example, concepts such as 'more than an equitable share of world export trade' of Article XVI:3 are hard to define. Notwithstanding the above criticism, and, in stark contrast to occasional inactivity of the dispute settlement machinery, there has been recently, and particularly in 1991, a marked increase of cases brought under Article XXIII and the Codes' dispute settlement procedures.[100] This is a corollary not only of the increasing volume of international trade; it can also be attributed to growing confidence in the dispute settlement mechanism on the part of the contracting parties.

To recapitulate, 'the purpose of the dispute settlement procedures is to ensure the implementation of existing commitments'.[101] The panel adjudication mechanism plays a significantly conducive role to this. On the whole, however, the GATT legal system relies on the organised normative pressure rather than on the coercive force of economic sanctions.[102]

IV. GATT AS A FORUM FOR TRADE NEGOTIATIONS

APART from laying down an articulate rule system governing the conduct of international trade relations, the GATT provides a forum for periodic negotiations (rounds) on a major multilateral level with a view to facilitating the

---

99.   See also E.-U. Petersmann, 'Strengthening GATT Procedures for Settling Trade Disputes' (1987) 11 World Economy 55 at 69.

100.   Director-General of the GATT, GATT Focus No.83, Aug. 1991, p.8; see also GATT Focus No.84, Sept. 1991, p.2; and 'Dispute panels jump from 1 to 11', D.-G.'s Report, GATT Focus No.86, Nov.–Dec. 1991.

101.   Panel Report on *United States – Countervailing Duties on Fresh, Chilled and Frozen Pork from Canada*, DS7/R para.4.7.

102.   See Hudec, op. cit. supra n.44, pp.200–202.

substantial reduction of tariffs and other barriers to trade. To this end, seven such rounds have been completed hitherto, the eighth currently being in progress. These are: Geneva (1947), Annecy (1949), Torquay (1950–51), Geneva (1955–56), the Dillon Round (1960–61), the Kennedy Round (1964–67), the Tokyo Round of Multilateral Trade Negotiations (1973–79) and the Uruguay Round of Multilateral Trade Negotiations (not yet completed). The first five rounds were dominated by negotiations on reduction of tariffs and accession of new contracting parties. But in the Kennedy Round concern was expressed on non-tariff trade barriers, so negotiations were extended in that direction. As a result, the first Anti-Dumping Code was established. The growing concern over non-tariff barriers provided the impetus for a broader review of non-tariff measures in the succeeding round, the Tokyo Round.

A. Tokyo Round of Multilateral Trade Negotiations

The Tokyo Round of Multilateral Trade Negotiations, so called because the negotiations were launched at a Ministerial meeting in Tokyo, in September 1973, was the most ambitious and comprehensive round ever held. The Declaration envisaged that one of the Round's principal objectives would be to reduce or eliminate non-tariff barriers. Indeed, apart from securing a major reduction of tariffs it resulted in six agreements (referred to as 'Codes') concerning non-tariff measures and three sectoral agreements as follows:[103]

- Agreement on Technical Barriers to Trade ('Standards Code')
- Agreement on Government Procurement
- Agreement on Interpretation and Application of Articles VI, XVI and XXIII ('Subsidies Code')
- Agreement on Implementation of Article VII ('Customs Valuation Code')
- Agreement on Import Licensing Procedures
- Agreement on Implementation of Article VI ('Anti-Dumping Code' which revised and replaced the first Anti-Dumping Code)
- Arrangement Regarding Bovine Meat

---

103. They are published in BISD 26S.

- International Dairy Arrangement
- Agreement on Trade in Civil Aircraft

These agreements depart from the General Agreement in several institutional and substantive respects. Although they operate within the GATT system, each of them establishes its own Committee in charge of administering the respective agreement. Their membership varies considerably both from the General Agreement and from one to another. This, in turn, gives rise to numerous theoretical and practical problems.[104]

Additionally, four decisions were adopted – known as 'framework agreements' – aimed at improving the working of some of the fundamental provisions of the General Agreement. These are:

- Differential and More Favourable Treatment, Reciprocity and Fuller Participation of Developing Countries
- Declaration on Trade Measures Taken for Balance-of-Payments Purposes
- Safeguard Action for Development Purposes
- Understanding Regarding Notification, Consultation, Dispute Settlement and Surveillance.

The results of the Tokyo Round put the multilateral trading system into a new perspective. Compared to its predecessors, the Tokyo Round addressed, for the first time in the GATT history, questions relating to a whole range of non-tariff barriers thereby considerably improving and elaborating the GATT system.

---

104. See e.g. the Panel Report on *New Zealand – Imports of Electrical Transformers from Finland*, BISD 32S/55, where an anti-dumping case was examined under Art.VI of the General Agreement because New Zealand was not a signatory to the Anti-Dumping Code. See generally J.H. Jackson, J.V. Louis and M. Mathushita, *Implementing the Tokyo Round* (University of Michigan Press, 1984).

B. Uruguay Round of Multilateral Trade Negotiations

Of all the negotiating rounds, by far the most ambitious, comprehensive and significant multilateral trade negotiations ever undertaken were launched at a Ministerial Meeting in Punta del Este, Uruguay, on 20 September 1986. A Ministerial Declaration[105] was adopted addressing areas which fell indisputably under the GATT, i.e. merchandise trade, but also new questions, 'non-traditional' issues, such as trade-related aspects of intellectual property rights (TRIPs), trade-related investment measures (TRIMs) and, particularly, trade in services. Another distinguishing feature of the Uruguay Round is that its dynamics are different from previous Rounds. New groups, such as the Cairns Group, emerged, the collaboration of which proved to be instrumental to the progress of the negotiations;[106] furthermore it is the first Round in which developing countries are participating wholeheartedly.[107]

The continuous expansion of the GATT's competence from one Round to another in conjunction with its structural evolution towards an articulate legal system exhibits its inherent dynamism in two directions: in refining existing rules, and in expanding into new areas.[108] There are however certain issues, such as environmental issues which, although having a direct bearing on transnational trade relations, still escape the GATT disciplines. A revealing recent dispute between the US and Mexico concerned the prohibition of imports of canned Mexican tuna, imposed by the US under conservation legislation on the grounds that Mexican fishing methods killed dolphins which were caught in tuna nets. In so far as the GATT (save one provision in Article XX) does not lay down elaborate rules concerning environmental protection, the Panel of the case held that the US ban violated GATT rules because it interfered with fishing outside the 200 mile US exclusive offshore economic zone[109] and that 'a contracting party may not

---

105. BISD 33S/19; (1986) 25 ILM 1623.
106. See A. Oxley, *The Challenge of Free Trade* (Harvester-Wheatsheaf, 1990), pp.159–160.
107. Idem, p.101.
108. It should be noted however that this dynamism is restrained by countervailing forces in the GATT such as its large membership, the diversified economic and political interests, and the heterogeneity of national legal systems.
109. *Financial Times*, 23 Aug. 1991, p.6.

restrict imports of a product merely because it originates in a country with environmental policies different from its own'.[110] Nevertheless there is a growing concern over trade-related environmental issues within the GATT[111] in response to which the GATT Council decided to revive a working group on trade and environment that has never met since it was established 20 years ago. The working group is to examine how the trade provisions contained in existing international environmental agreements conform with GATT principles, to assess the transparency and trade effects of national environmental negotiations, and to look into the effects on trade of packaging and labelling regulations which are intended to protect the environment.[112] Characteristically, the Director-General has promised the US Congress that environmental issues will be addressed in the next GATT Round.[113]

The Punta del Este Declaration is divided into two parts. The first establishes the objectives and principles of the negotiations on trade in goods. Underlying these negotiations are 'standstill' and 'rollback' commitments according to which the participants agree in particular not to increase existing levels of protection as a means of improving their negotiating position; and also to dismantle progressively or bring into conformity with the GATT disciplines all the inconsistent trade restrictive or distorting measures. The Declaration sets out the subjects for negotiation, which are: tariffs, non-tariff measures, tropical products, natural resource-based products, textiles and clothing, agriculture, the GATT Articles, safeguards, the Tokyo Round Agreements and Arrangements, subsidies and countervailing measures, dispute settlement, trade-related aspects of intellectual property rights including trade in counterfeit goods, trade-related investment measures and

---

110. *The Economist*, 5 Oct. 1991, p.49. The Panel Report has been taken off the Council's agenda at the request of Mexico and the US, GATT Focus No.84, Sept. 1991, p.8.
111. The European Parliament 'attaches great importance to the assessment of environmental impact within GATT;' EP Resolution on the stage reached in the multilateral trade negotiations within the Uruguay round of GATT Doc.B3–905/90 of 17 May 1990, recital 26, OJ 1990 C 149/165; 'US Call for a GATT Code on Environment', *Financial Times* 18 Sept. 1991 p.6; the EFTA countries requested the activation of the 1971 Working Group on Environmental Measures and International Trade, GATT Focus No.82, July 1991.
112. *Financial Times*, 9 Oct. 1991, p.2.
113. *The Economist*, 5 Oct. 1991, p.49.

functioning of the GATT system. The second part of the Declaration deals with the negotiations on trade in services. It envisages the establishment of a multilateral framework of principles and rules for trade in services. A Group of Negotiations on Goods (GNG) and a Group of Negotiations on Services (GNS) were set up to supervise the conduct of negotiations respectively and report to the Trade Negotiation Committee (TNC), the supreme organ overseeing the Round as a whole.

The first half of the Round was marked by intensive negotiations and considerable progress was made culminating in the Mid-Term Review, held in Montreal in December 1988 and completed in Geneva in April 1989. This was a stock-taking exercise with a view to assessing the work already done and also injecting new impetus for further substantial negotiations. The Mid-Term Review generated a package of early results, the most important of which were two institutional novelties. First, the dispute settlement system was overhauled and streamlined and put into effect on a trial basis from 1 May 1989 to the end of the Round.[114]   Second, a Trade Policy Review Mechanism was established under which the impact of national trade policies on the international trade system were to be examined periodically, thus enabling the CONTRACTING PARTIES to assess and monitor all aspects of the trade policies and practices of each individual member, thereby enhancing transparency in the GATT system.[115]

The final Ministerial Meeting of the Uruguay Round was scheduled for December 1990. It was held in Brussels but reached an impasse, as is widely known, and the trade talks were suspended due to profound disagreement over agricultural reforms. Negotiations resumed in February 1991 and are now progressing through the final and most critical phase. The situation can best be described in the following words:[116]

---

114. See E.-U. Petersmann, 'The Mid-Term Review Agreements of the Uruguay Round and the 1989 Improvements to the GATT Dispute Settlement Procedures' (1989) 32 Germ.YBIL 299–306.

115. GATT Activities 1989, p.19.

116. Statement by the Chairman of the CONTRACTING PARTIES, Ambassador R. Ricupero (Brazil), speaking on behalf of the developing countries in the Trade Negotiations Committee on 30 July 1991, *News of the Uruguay Round* No.49, 6 Aug. 1991.

There is only one question we should put to ourselves today. Are we ready to give a chance to the democratic regimes and market economies that are changing the face of the earth in Central and Eastern Europe, in Latin America, Africa and Asia? Are we willing to allow trade once more to pull the world economy out of recession and unemployment and back to recovery? This, not less, is what is at stake now at the closing days, full of challenge and promise, of the Uruguay Round.

With its ramifications likely to extend well beyond the current century, a successful completion of the Round is bound to be a significant determinant to the survival of the multilateral trading system and, indeed, the GATT itself.[117] Political will and responsibility are needed to subject national trade policies to international legal disciplines and make international obligations justiciable. For, as at the national level law serves as an instrument of economic policy,[118] so at the international level law can serve as a means for co-ordination of national policies and at the same time as an instrument by which to pursue greater coherence on global economic policy making.

V. CONCLUSIONS

THE GATT is an international agreement laying down legally binding obligations. It has evolved into a hybrid international economic institution of legal rules and commercial diplomacy, though progressively gravitating towards the former. The symbiotic operation of 'law and order' and constructive pragmatism have proved to be instrumental to the world's economic growth[119] and have also served as a basis for the conduct of international trade relations. Since the latter are becoming increasingly complex by reason of strained economic rivalries in general and continually intensified competition in particular, the multilateral trading system needs enhancement now more than ever before. This can be achieved by strengthening and elaborating the GATT legal system. The legal fabric should not be eroded by a shift towards

---

117. Cf. A. Dunkel, 'The Uruguay Round and the World Economy' (1987) 42 Aussenwirtschaft 7 at 10.

118. See T. Daintith, 'Law as a Policy Instrument: Comparative Perspective' in T. Daintith (ed.), *Law as an Instrument of Economic Policy: Comparative and Critical Approaches*, (de Gruyter, 1987), pp.4–19.

119. Since World War II there has been a tenfold increase in the volume of the world trade.

the exercise of political power. For it is only adherence to agreed rules that can impose legal disciplines on trade relations. Unless GATT contracting parties subscribe to the rule of law and commit themselves to apply it in a consistent manner, creeping bilateralism, unilateralism or other steps away from multilateralism will undermine, in all likelihood irreparably, the international trading system.

Chapter VII

THE MULTIFIBRE ARRANGEMENT – RIPPING THE SHIRT OFF THE POOR MAN'S BACK?

Damian Chalmers

Chapter VII

THE MULTIFIBRE ARRANGEMENT – RIPPING THE SHIRT OFF THE POOR MAN'S BACK?

Damian Chalmers[1]

I. INTRODUCTION – THE MULTIFIBRE ARRANGEMENT, AN ALTERNATIVE LEGAL FRAMEWORK FOR INTERNATIONAL TRADE?

THE General Agreement on Tariffs and Trade (GATT) does not seem to inspire much enthusiasm amongst the lesser developed countries (LDCs). Only three days after the suspension of negotiations in the Uruguay Round the Indian Minister of Commerce threatened that his country might leave the GATT.[2] His comments were inspired not so much by the apparent failure of the Round as by the view that the Agreement itself did not adequately protect his nation's interests. LDCs are well represented in the GATT however.[3] Further, a variety of developments since 1947 has created what one commentator terms 'a one-sided legal relationship'.[4] Reciprocity is not

---

1.   The author wishes to thank Ambassador Rafaelli for so kindly providing some of the documents used in this study at such short notice. The author is solely responsible for any errors that occur.

2.   'India seeks Third World strategy on trade issues' *Financial Times*, 11 Dec. 1990, p.6.

3.   In 1947 there were 23 contracting parties, the majority of whom were developed countries. The growth in the number of contracting parties has led not only to a change in its nature but also to a shift in the interests of its constituents. At the end of September 1990 there were 99 States who were contracting parties to the GATT with a further nine who were negotiating entry. 74 of the Contracting Parties are either State-trading or lesser developed countries. All those negotiating entry are also either State-trading economies or lesser developed economies.

4.   Robert E. Hudec, *Developing Countries in the GATT Legal System* (London 1987), p.46.

expected from LDCs in tariff negotiations:[5] developed countries are authorised to extend differential treatment to LDCs on a non-reciprocal basis[6] and LDCs may enter preferential trading arrangements amongst themselves.[7] In the light of these developments the charge that the philosophy of the GATT is fundamentally flawed with regard to developing countries loses some of its strength,[8] or at least tells only half the story.

No one doubts the importance of export earnings to LDCs. The principal reason for the high number of States who are party to the GATT is the improved access to markets that it is supposed to offer. Import penetration by LDC goods into developed countries' markets has remained disappointingly low, however.[9] It is suggested that one reason for this situation is the non-application of the General Agreement to trade between LDCs and developed countries by the latter.[10] International trade is

---

5.   At the beginning of the Kennedy Round it was agreed that developed countries would not expect reciprocity from LDCs in tariff negotiations: GATT BISD 12S (1964) p.47 at p.48, para.8. This was carried forward into Part IV of the General Agreement, Art.XXXVI(8) and on into the present negotiations: cf. 'Ministerial Declaration on the Uruguay Round Part I B(v)' (1986) 25 ILM 1623.

6.   A decision of the Contracting Parties taken on 3 Dec. 1979 states: 'Notwithstanding the provisions of Article I of the General Agreement, contracting parties may accord differential and more favourable treatment to developing countries, without according such treatment to other contracting parties.' (GATT, Doc L/4903) BISD 26S/203 (1980). (See A. Yusuf, 'Differential and More Favourable Treatment: The GATT Enabling Clause' (1980) 14 JWTL 488; G. Espiel, 'GATT: Accommodating Generalised Preferences' (1974) 8 JWTL 342.

7.   The Enabling Clause (supra n.6) also permits LDCs to enter into preferential arrangements between themselves. See A. Yusuf (op. cit. supra n.6) at pp.498–501. It is within this framework that the Group of 77 Agreement on the Global System of Trade Preferences Among Developing Countries will apply: (1988) 27 ILM 1204.

8.   This former view was the central criticism of the GATT in the 1960s. R. Prebisch, *Towards a New Trade Policy for Development, Report by the Secretary-General of the UNCTAD*, (1964), p.66. For more recent advocates of this view see H. Espiell, 'The Most-Favoured-Nation Clause, its Present Significance in GATT' (1971) 5 JWTL 29 at 36. E. Piontek, 'The Principles of Equality and Reciprocity in International Economic Law' in Fox (ed.), *International Economic Law and Developing States* Vol.I, Some Aspects (London 1988) at p.93.

9.   In 1988 LDC manufactured imports accounted for just under 5% of the US market, just over 4% of the EEC market and under 3% of the Japanese market. UNCTAD, *Trade and Development Report* (1989), p.66.

10.   This criticism is not new, cf. the Leutwiler Report, *Trade Polices for a Better Future: Proposals for Action* (GATT Secretariat, 1985), p.44.

plagued by an increasing number of 'grey area' restrictions which take place 'outside' the GATT: administered trade whereby an exporter or exporting country will curb its exports at the instigation of an importer or importing country for fear of more onerous restrictions being placed upon it.[11] LDCs are especially vulnerable to this form of restriction as a result of their weak bargaining position brought about by their lack of economic strength.[12]

The Multifibre Arrangement,[13] the legal regime that effectively governs international trade in textiles and clothing, is the 'locus classicus for the global management of international trade'.[14] Trade in textiles was the first area in which this form of regulation took place.[15] Furthermore, most administered trade is administered behind closed doors and the details kept secret. The Multifibre Arrangement is far more institutionalised and, concluded under the auspices of the GATT, is open to greater multilateral surveillance than other areas of administered trade. As such, it provides greater insight into the mechanics and difficulties of such trade.

It also provides an alternative legal model to the MFN principle for the regulation of international trade. Changes in comparative advantage are occurring at a faster rate than previously and administered trade is to a

11. It was estimated in 1987 that 12% of non-fuel world trade was covered by these restrictions: M. Kostecki, 'Export Restraint Arrangements and Trade Liberalisation' (1987) 10 World Economy 425–429.

12. It should not be thought that such arrangements will always penalise the exporter. There may be cases where, depending on the elasticities of demand, the increased prices will more than compensate for the restriction on supply. Much will also depend on the terms of the arrangement. On the economics of administered trade see Hindley, 'VERs and the GATT's main escape clause' (1988) 11 World Economy 313; Jones, 'The Political Economy of Voluntary Export Restraint Arrangements' (1984) 37 Kyklos 82; Murray, Schmidt and Walter, 'On the Equivalence of Export Quotas and Voluntary Export Restraint' (1983) 14 J. Int'l Economics 191; Takas, 'The Non-equivalence of Export Quotas and Voluntary Export Restraint' (1978) 8 J. Int'l Economics 565.

13. The formal name of this Arrangement is the Arrangement Regarding International Trade in Textiles, GATT, BISD 21S/3 (1975). For convenience's sake it will be referred to as the Multifibre Arrangement.

14. Kessing and Wolf, Textile Quotas against Developing Countries (London 1980), p.2.

15. For a history of administered trade see Bernier, 'Les ententes de restriction volontaire a l'exportation en droit international économique (1973) Can.YBIL 48; Quick, Exportselbstbeschräpenkungen und Artikel XIX GATT (Cologne 1983), chap.1.

certain extent a reflection of that.[16] It might be perceived as more realistic to institutionalise administered trade to render it more transparent.[17] To that extent the MFA exemplifies the benefits and costs of such an approach.

Quantitatively the MFA also merits examination, for trade in textiles and clothing accounts for about 33% of LDC manufactured exports, by any standards a significant share.[18] It would thus be very difficult for any coverage of the legal regime governing the international trade of LDCs to ignore it. The MFA shows that the principle of non-discrimination to some extent rings hollow in the face of the reality of trade between LDCs and developed countries. An analysis of this alternate regime is not just necessary for completeness' sake but also to examine the underlying principles that govern the reality of a significant proportion of trade between LDCs and developed countries.

II. THE ORIGIN AND DEVELOPMENT OF THE MULTIFIBRE ARRANGEMENT

THE origins of the Multifibre Arrangement lie in the cotton industry. By the mid 1950s manufacturers in Western Europe and the United States were highly uncompetitive[19] and sought refuge in a host of protectionist instruments.[20] For mainly geopolitical reasons[21] the US pushed for a multilateral approach that would at the same time derogate from basic GATT principles by allowing discriminatory safeguard measures to be taken,[22] and

---

16. Kleen, 'The Safeguard Issue in the Uruguay Round – a Comprehensive Approach (1989) 23 JWT 73 at 75.

17. The argument that one should allow discriminatory safeguard measures to be taken is similar in that it regards the principle of non-discrimination as unrealistic, cf. Bronckers, *Selective Safeguard Measures in Multilateral Trade Relations – Issues of Protectionism in GATT, European Community and US Law* (The Hague 1985), pp.26–28.

18. UNCTAD, *International Trade in Textiles, with special reference to problems faced by developing countries* (1984), TD/B/C.2/215/Rev.1 p.1.

19. J.-L. Juvet, 'The Cotton Industry and World Trade' (1967) 1 JWTL 540 at 542–551.

20. Aggarwal, *Liberal Protectionism: the International Politics of Organised Textile Trade* (Los Angeles 1985), chap.3; Kessing and Wolfe, *Textile Quotas Against Developing Countries* (London 1980), pp.6–19.

21. Aggarwal, op. cit. supra n.20, p.78.

22. Safeguard action on protectionist grounds is authorised by Art.XIX of the General

in 1961 the Short-Term Arrangement in Cotton Textiles was signed.[23] This Agreement lasted for one year and authorised discriminatory quantitative restrictions on imports of cotton textiles that were causing or threatening 'market disruption'. This was replaced a year later by the Long-Term Arrangement in Cotton Textiles.[24] This was a slightly less restrictive continuation of its predecessor which lasted for five years and was extended for two further three-year periods, in 1967 and 1971 respectively.

American dissatisfaction with the Long-Term Arrangement grew in the 1960s as exporters switched to wool-based and multifibre products.[25] At US insistence and in the face of initial opposition from the EEC and Japan and fierce denunciation from the Group of 77[26] the Multifibre Arrangement was signed on 20 December 1973.[27] It was open to signature by States that were contracting parties to the GATT and States that were not.[28] The initial Arrangement took the form of a Protocol and had a life of four years.[29] It

Agreement but is subject, however, to certain procedural constraints and, although not explicitly stated, must be taken on a non-discriminatory basis and entitles the other contracting parties affected to compensation. Jackson, *World Trade and the Law of the GATT* (1969) chap.23; Bronckers, op. cit. supra n.17; Koulen, 'The Non-Discriminatory Interpretation of GATT: Article XIX:I – A Reply' (1983) LIEI 87.

23. GATT, BISD 10S/18 (1962). This Arrangement had 16 signatories.

24. GATT, BISD 11S/25 (1963). There were 19 signatories. Bardan, 'The Cotton Textile Agreement 1962–1972' (1972) 7 JWTL 8; Dam, *The GATT: Law and International Economic Organisation* (Chicago 1970), chap.17.

25. By 1968 imports of these products into the US exceeded those of imports of cotton. Aggarwal, op. cit. supra n.20, p.113.

26. Aggarwal, idem, pp.123–142.

27. The legal literature on the Multifibre Arrangement is quite extensive. Zheng, *Legal Structure of International Textile Trade* (Westport, US, 1988); Blokker, *International Regulation of World Trade in Textiles – lessons for practice, a contribution to theory* (Dordrecht 1989); Perlow, 'The Multilateral Supervision of International Trade: Has the Textiles Experiment Worked' (1981) 75 AJIL 93; Das, 'The GATT Multi-fibre Arrangement' (1988) 23 JWT 95; Majmudar, 'The Multi-Fibre Arrangement (MFA IV) 1986-1991: A Move towards a Liberalised System?' idem, p.109; Jacobs, 'Renewal and Expansion of the Multifiber Arrangement' (1987) 19 Law & Policy in International Business 7; Giesse and Lewin, 'The Multifiber Arrangement: "Temporary" Protection Run Amuck' idem, p.51.

28. Art.13. (When the author refers to a specific Article he is referring back to the initial Arrangement.)

29. Art.16.

was renewed in 1977,[30] 1981[31] and 1986,[32] each time for a period of four years, with the exception of MFA IV which is not due to expire until 31 July 1991.[33] As of July 1990 there were 40 participants.[34] The initial Arrangement applied to trade in textiles made from cotton, wool and most man-made fibres.[35] In 1986 this was extended to cover trade in textiles made from silk and vegetable fibres that were in direct competition with the above.[36]

III. THE INSTITUTIONAL STRUCTURE OF THE MULTIFIBRE ARRANGEMENT

THE only body established under the Long-Term Cotton Arrangement was the Cotton Textiles Committee which consisted of the representatives of the signatories and which met 'from time to time' to review trade in cotton textiles, the Arrangement and any differences between the signatories.[37] The institutional framework for the Multifibre Arrangement has been modified and revolves around two bodies, the Textiles Committee[38] and the Textile Surveillance Body (TSB).[39]

The Textiles Committee is modelled on the former Cotton Textiles Committee. It meets at least annually and consists of representatives of all the MFA signatories. It has not been successful and a significant gap has developed between the powers that the Committee has and the functions that it actually exercises. First, it is empowered to review textile trade and is obliged to review annually the operation of the Arrangement based upon the

---

30. GATT, BISD 25S/5 (1977).
31. GATT, BISD 28S/3 (1982).
32. GATT, COM.TEX/W/183. It is probably better to see these Protocols as amendments to the original Protocol rather than interpretations. Blokker, op. cit. supra n.27, pp.170–171.
33. The Arrangement has been extended for a further 17 months with the anticipation that the results of the Uruguay Round will come into effect at that time. 'MFA extended for 17 months' *Financial Times*, 1 Aug. 1991, p.6.
34. GATT, COM.TEX/SB/1490, p.8.
35. Art.12.
36. Para.24(i) of MFA IV. It should be noted that only the US and Canada have applied restrictions on goods from these materials. GATT, COM.TEX/SB/1490, p.108.
37. Art.8, Long-Term Cotton Arrangement.
38. Art.10.
39. Art.11.

review provided to it by the TSB and to report to the GATT Council.[40] Very little is achieved by this review as there is generally insufficient consensus for any universal conclusions to be drawn. Second, it is primarily the Textiles Committee that exercises control over the TSB. It appoints the members of the TSB. The TSB must also submit its annual reviews and recommendations to the Textiles Committee.[41] If problems continue to exist between parties following a recommendation of the TSB, the matter may be brought before the Textiles Committee.[42] The Textiles Committee, however, will be unlikely to resolve something that was not resolved in the TSB given its more diverse nature and the fact that countries will normally have the same representatives sitting on both institutions. Third, it is the Textiles Committee which is empowered to extend the Arrangement.[43] Finally, the Textiles Committee has the power to interpret the Arrangement and hear disputes regarding its application.[44] From the structure of the initial arrangement it would seem that primary power for the interpretation of the Arrangement was intended to lie with the Textiles Committee.[45] The wide membership of the Textiles Committee, its occasional nature and its lack of proper working procedures have hindered its ability to take decisions.[46] Thus whilst it has taken decisions which have touched on the interpretation of the Arrangement,[47] it has been largely superseded in this role by the TSB.

The TSB was hailed as a 'unique and innovative development in international relations'.[48] Unlike GATT dispute panels the TSB was a standing body that was not set up with reference to a particular dispute but to

40. Art.10(2) and (3).
41. Art.11(7), (11) and (12).
42. Art.11(9).
43. Art.10(5).
44. Art.10(3).
45. This is because in the initial Arrangement the TSB was only granted very limited explicit powers of interpretation by Art.12(4) over the narrow area of what textile products were covered by the Arrangement.
46. Zheng, op. cit. supra n.27, p.85.
47. E.g. the Textiles Committee implied that the rules of origin introduced by the US in 1984 were not compatible with the Arrangement. GATT, COM.TEX/W/154/Rev.1.
48. Perlow, op. cit. supra n.27, p.103.

administer and supervise a whole sector of trade. It thus marked a new form of multilateral discipline. It has been suggested that the TSB was also a compromise between the LDCs and the developed countries.[49] On the one hand the intervention of a supervisory institution would bolster the weak bargaining position of the LDCs when it came to the administration of restrictions. On the other the composition of the TSB has always favoured the developed countries in comparison with their numerical disadvantage within the GATT Council. The TSB originally consisted of a chairman and eight members. In practice the US, Japan and the EEC have permanent seats on the TSB, with medium-sized developed countries having another seat. This leaves only four seats for the 30 or so LDCs. The situation has been slightly improved by the decision to add a further two members to the TSB.[50]

TSB members are generally representatives of their governments.[51] Despite this the TSB contends that it does not look upon its members as representing purely national or sectoral interests.[52] The TSB works by consensus.[53] This has been criticised on the grounds that only weak decisions reflecting the lowest common denominator will be given.[54] Similarly it may be argued that any supranational qualities of the TSB are seriously weakened by its members being representatives of their respective governments. These criticisms overlook the feature that the TSB was probably only ever intended to be a representative body that helped administer bilateral or unilateral restrictions rather than some form of quasi-judicial organ.

---

49. Zheng, op. cit. supra n.27, p.54.

50. GATT, COM.TEX/63, p.2. The Chairman of the TSB is currently a Brazilian, Ambassador Rafaelli. Brazil, Canada, China, the EEC, Hong Kong, Indonesia, Japan, Pakistan, Sweden and the US are currently represented on the TSB. GATT, COM.TEX/SB/1550, p.5.

51. Zheng, op. cit. supra n.27, at p.55 points out that not only is this confirmed by State practice but Art.11 implies that government representatives are to sit on the TSB, stating as it does that membership should be 'broadly representative of the parties to this Arrangement'.

52. GATT, COM.TEX/SB/1 (1974), p.55.

53. GATT, COM/TEX/SB/1 (1974), p.1.

54. Zheng, op. cit. supra n.27, p.59; see also Blokker, op. cit. supra n.27, pp.209–211 on the US–Maldives dispute.

The functions of the TSB are threefold. First, it reviews annually all existing restrictions and reports its findings to the Textiles Committee.[55] Participating countries must take steps to ensure that the TSB has the necessary information and statistics.[56] It is important to note that this function involves no judgment on the legality of these restrictions but is just a collation of the restrictions that currently exist. This is not as unimportant as it sounds, for one of the problems facing legal regimes regulating international trade is that of ensuring transparency in international economic relations.[57] Whilst the TSB has had some problems with requiring States to provide adequate information,[58] it is probably fair to say that this collection of data has ensured a greater degree of transparency in textiles than in other areas that are dogged by protectionist measures.

The second explicit function of the TSB is supervisory. This function arises in various contexts and the effectiveness of the TSB varies correspondingly. Its initial task was to examine all restrictions that existed at the time of the entry into force of the original MFA and make recommendations as to their conformity with the Arrangement.[59] Furthermore, it is obliged to review all restrictions that are introduced either unilaterally or bilaterally by participating countries and to make recommendations.[60]

The TSB also has certain supervisory powers that may be instigated at the request of a participating country. This may arise in two situations. First, a participating country may feel its interests are being detrimentally affected by another participating country and if consultations do not produce a mutually

---

55. Art.11(12).
56. Art.7.
57. This is envisaged in Art.X of the General Agreement. See also E.-U. Petersmann, 'Strengthening the Domestic Legal Framework of the GATT Multilateral Trade System: Possibilities and Problems of Making GATT Rules Directly Effective' in Hilf/Petersmann (eds.), *The New GATT Round of Multilateral Tariff Negotiations* (Deventer 1988), p.33 at pp.72-74 for the political costs of failure to ensure transparency.
58. There have been cases where the TSB has been informed of restrictions only after their expiry. GATT, COM/S/610, p.65. This is especially relevant to the TSB's enforcement functions but the detail of most TSB reports suggests that it is fairly successful in keeping track of the majority of measures.
59. Art.2(5).
60. Arts.3(5), 4(4).

satisfactory result it may refer the matter to the TSB for discussion and, where necessary, recommendations.[61] Second, more specifically, if two parties fail to agree on the imposition of a restriction, one may refer the matter to the TSB to consider and make recommendations thereupon.[62]

From the above it is clear that the TSB only has the power to make recommendations. Whilst these recommendations are not binding upon participating countries the fact that participating countries 'endeavour to accept' them in full[63] indicates that they do have some legal force. Nevertheless there has been some questioning of the TSB's status. The EEC's view is that the TSB is conciliatory rather than arbitral in nature.[64] The TSB has issued recommendations however which suggest that participating country restrictions are not compatible with the Arrangement,[65] implying that it plays more than just a conciliatory role. The notion that the TSB performs a supervisory role has been strengthened by MFA IV which has given the TSB explicit powers to interpret the Arrangement.[66] Previously the TSB's powers of interpretation, except in one limited area,[67] were derived impliedly purely from its powers to issue recommendations. Despite this, however, the TSB had addressed itself to questions of interpretation.[68] This role has now been confirmed by MFA IV. On the other hand, if the TSB pursues a quasi-judicial function it does so with extreme timidity. The practice of the TSB has been characterised by an unwillingness to be guided by general principles.[69] Similarly, participating country behaviour has at

---

61. Art.11(5). This seems to be duplicated by Art.9(2). In the author's view it is difficult to envisage what role the latter plays. The role of Art.8(4) is similarly obscure.

62. Art.11(4).

63. Art.11(8).

64. GATT, COM.TEX/14 para. 29. This can be found at GATT, BISD 26S/340 at 347 (1980). For the background to this dispute see Perlow, op. cit. supra n.27, at pp.109–112.

65. E.g. in a dispute between the US and Turkey in 1984 the TSB stated that 'the US had not taken sufficient account of Turkey's position as a cotton supplier, developing country ...' (GATT, COM.TEX/SB/984 at p.69).

66. Para.22, MFA IV.

67. Art.12(4) gives the TSB powers to interpret what products were covered by the Arrangement. This has been superseded by para.22.

68. Perlow, op. cit. supra n.27, at p.108.

69. The TSB has repeatedly said that it will only interpret the Arrangement on a case-by-case basis. GATT, COM.TEX/SB/57 (1975) p.2; GATT, COM.TEX/SB/1490, p.17.

times shown a contempt for the provisions of the Arrangement that might not have been so evident in the face of a stronger supervisory body.

The TSB has been successful to the extent that it has brought relative transparency to textiles trade and introduced an element of supervision into the Arrangement. It is suggested that it is the Textiles Committee's inertia that has allowed the TSB to adopt its supervisory role. The nature of the TSB, its limited powers and the initial doubt over its role have however impeded it acting as an effective supervisory body. It only comments perfunctorily on the most flagrant violations of the Arrangement and it is unclear what effect its recommendations have had on participating country behaviour.[70]

IV. THE SUBSTANTIVE PROVISIONS OF THE
MULTIFIBRE ARRANGEMENT

A. An Equitable Development of Trade?

The objectives of the Arrangement go beyond the liberalisation of world textile trade and the avoidance of market disruption in both importing and exporting countries,[71] for the notion of 'orderly and equitable development of textile trade' is also mentioned as an objective of the Arrangement. The introduction of the notion of equity into the Arrangement resembles more the language of General Assembly Resolution 3281, the Charter on the Economic Rights and Duties of States,[72] than that of the GATT, suggesting a wider approach to accommodating States' needs than the MFN principle.

---

70. There are instances of participating countries following adverse TSB recommendations. E.g. the US modified its position on a ban on certain Thai products following a TSB recommendation (GATT, COM.TEX/SB/1550, p.35). Similarly Sweden revised a ban on certain products not covered by the MFA following a TSB recommendation (GATT, COM.TEX/SB/610 p.64). There are plenty of instances where States have not followed TSB recommendations, e.g. Sweden's persistent over-use of the minimum viable production clause despite repeated recommendations suggesting its over-use.

71. Art.1(2).

72. A/RES 3281 (XXIX). See (1975) 14 ILM 250. Art.8 of the Charter suggests also that States should co-operate in facilitating more rational and equitable international economic relations.

The notion of equity has been developed in two ways by the Arrangement. There is first a general obligation on participating countries to seek to preserve a proper measure of equity in the measures that they take.[73] Whilst this notion has never been extensively developed by the TSB, it has been interpreted to mean that a participating country cannot treat non-participating countries more favourably than participating countries. Consequently it is obliged to inform the TSB of any measures it takes *vis-à-vis* non-participants.[74] Furthermore, when the TSB finds particular measures incompatible with the Arrangement it will often refer, *inter alia*, to a breach of the equity provisions.[75] It is not clear whether in these circumstances this adds anything, a breach being already established.

Second, differential treatment may be applied in the case of certain exporting countries and certain importing countries who have special needs. The Preamble to the Arrangement recognises the importance of textiles trade to the economic and social development of LDCs, the importance for the expansion and diversification of their export earnings and that scope should be provided for them to have a greater share of world textile trade.[76] To this end Article 6(1) provides that:

> it shall be considered appropriate and consistent with equity obligations for those importing countries which apply restrictions under this Arrangement affecting the trade of developing countries to provide more favourable terms ...

An elaborate structure has been built around Article 6 with the evolution of the textile regime. Restraints should not normally be imposed upon exports from the least developed countries (LDCs) and, where they are, terms should be significantly more favourable than any other group contained within the Arrangement.[77]

---

73. Art.3(2).
74. GATT, COM.TEX/SB/296 para.9.
75. E.g. in a dispute between the US and the Dominican Republic in 1984 the TSB stated that 'the US had paid insufficient attention ... to the status of the Dominican Republic as an LDC and ... to the equity provisions': GATT, COM.TEX/SB/984, p.66.
76. This was reiterated in para.2, MFA III and para.4, MFA IV.
77. Para.13(a) and (b), MFA IV.

Furthermore the Arrangement pays attention to the structure of the trade by ensuring preferential treatment for new entrants and small suppliers.[78] Restraints on both should normally be avoided and where restraints are imposed the terms should take account of future possibilities for the development of the trade and the need to permit commercial quantities of imports in order to further the economic and social development of the suppliers.[79]

Suppliers in particular sectors also receive special treatment. Cotton suppliers should receive special consideration and account should be taken of the vulnerability of the importing country's industry as well as the importance of cotton textile exports to the exporting country.[80] A similar provision has been inserted in respect of restrictions on wool products where the exporter is an LDC whose economy is heavily dependent on the wool sector and whose volume of textile trade is comparatively small.[81]

A differentiation has also been made between importing countries' needs with special rules for those countries who have small markets, an exceptionally high level of imports and a correspondingly low level of production. Damage to their minimum viable production should be avoided.[82] These countries are entitled to administer restrictions in a more restrictive way than other importing countries in order to safeguard their minimum viable production. These provisions have been criticised on the ground that the justification for such a feature could only be on grounds of national security and textiles is not an area where this could be relevant.[83] An alternative rationale may however be that importing countries are perceived to be entitled to a domestic industry.

These provisions at first sight appear to provide a system of trade that goes beyond the basic safeguard mechanism in accommodating the exporting

---

78. The TSB has stated that new entrants are to be considered in relation to particular sectors and small suppliers in relation to the overall trading position of the country concerned. GATT. COM.TEX/SB/610, para.232.

79. Para.13(a) and (c), MFA IV.

80. Idem, para.13(d).

81. Para.14, MFA IV. This provision was proposed by Uruguay which may be the only country that will benefit from it. See Jacobs, op. cit. supra n.27, p.32.

82. Art.1(2). In practice these countries are Sweden, Finland and Norway.

83. UNCTAD, op. cit. supra n.22, at p.37; Kessing and Wolf, op. cit. supra n.14, p.173.

and importing countries' needs through a hierarchical system. They are undermined by a number of factors, however. First, the language is extremely vague.[84] Nowhere are specific and unconditional obligations laid down. In the absence of a strong supervisory body, this has resulted in concepts, which might have helped LDCs, instead remaining dormant and undeveloped, doing little to protect them, whilst importing countries have made full use of the concepts helpful to their interests.[85] Second, as shall be seen, this elaborate framework balancing competing interests is hung upon a safeguard mechanism that allows importing countries considerable discretion. Third, the notion of special and differential treatment is made a nonsense of when the vast majority of net exporting countries within the Arrangement are LDCs. Article 6 has consequently been virtually ignored.[86] In 1989 the TSB thus had to conclude that restrictions are used almost exclusively against products from LDCs.[87]

B. The Safeguard Mechanism

1. The safeguard provisions

The most noted feature of these two articles is that, unlike safeguard measures taken under Article XIX of the General Agreement,[88] they appear to allow safeguard measures to be taken in a discriminatory manner merely against imports from one country, thereby rendering protectionist action easier to take. It is necessary to add a proviso to this however, as whilst the Arrangement allows importing countries to discriminate between those countries that are causing market disruption and those that are not, partici-

---

84. Blokker, op. cit. supra n.27, pp.181, 189.

85. E.g. Sweden and Norway have invoked the MVP clause on all the restrictions on imports that they have imposed. GATT, COM.TEX/SB/1490 p.108.

86. In 1976 the TSB was already complaining that greater emphasis should be put on Art. 6. See Blokker, op. cit. supra n.27, pp.228–229.

87. GATT, COM.TEX/SB/1490 p.109.

88. See supra n.22.

pating countries 'endeavour to avoid discriminatory measures where market disruption is caused by more than one participating country'.[89]

The core provisions of the Arrangement that allow for a participating country to seek initial safeguard measures against imports are Articles 3 and 4. Article 3 permits an importing country to seek consultations with the exporting country concerned if it considers that its market is being disrupted[90] by imports from a product covered by the Arrangement.[91] If no agreement is reached within 60 days then the importing country can unilaterally impose restrictions for a 12-month period beginning the day the exporting country received the request for consultations.[92] In highly unusual and critical circumstances, when faced with serious market disruption the importing country may take restrictive measures prior to consultations.[93]

Article 3 is undermined by Article 4 of the Arrangement which allows an importing country to negotiate bilateral agreements with the exporting country restricting imports where there is a 'real risk of market disruption'.[94] Although greater use has been made of Article 3 in MFA IV,[95] it has to a large extent been pre-empted by Article 4.[96] Given that market disruption is a fairly hollow concept, a real risk of market disruption has proved to be almost unsusceptible to review. The different articles also have differing degrees of transparency. Under Article 4 the parties merely have to inform the TSB of the Arrangement, presenting it with a *fait accompli*.[97] Article 3 requires, however, that the importing country requesting consultations give a statement of the reasons and justification for the request prior to the restriction being taken.[98]

89. Art.3(2).
90. Annex A of the Arrangement defines when a situation of market disruption exists.
91. Art.3(3).
92. Art.3(5).
93. Art.3(6). This measure has only ever been used twice, the last time involving a restriction in 1989 by Canada on Brazilian bedlinen, (GATT, COM.TEX/SB/1490 Add.1 p.78) highlighting the restrictive nature of the other articles.
94. Art.4(2).
95. GATT, COM.TEX/SB/1490 p.97.
96. UNCTAD, op. cit. supra n.18, p.36 para.108. Art.4 still remains the predominant means of protection.
97. Art.4(4). Blokker, op. cit. supra n.27, pp.201-202.
98. Art.3(3). It should be noted however that under both articles participating countries are

2. The administration of Article 3 and 4 measures

The Arrangement, as previously mentioned, provides for a system of administration of trade rather than straightforward protection. As such, a series of conditions is imposed on the nature of restrictions that may be installed and under which they may be maintained.

(a) *Base levels:* Where a restriction is imposed, the imports are not permitted to be restrained below the level of actual imports for the 12-month period terminating two months or, where data is not available, three months before the request for consultations (the *base level*).[99]

There are two exceptions to this general rule. If the past year was especially adverse for a particular exporting country due to abnormal circumstances, then past performance in imports from that country over a period of years should be taken into account.[100] Second, if the imports subject to restraint were nil or negligible during the previous 12-month period then 'a reasonable import level taking account of future possibilities' should be established.[101] Whilst this is a more detailed threshold than Article XIX[102] it is more rigid and does not deal adequately with the instances where safeguard action is precipitated by a threatened rise in imports but the actual level of imports is still very low.

(b) *Growth rates:* At the end of the initial 12-month period parties may agree to renew the restraint.[103] Should agreement not be forthcoming it was agreed in 1986 that an importing country may unilaterally renew the restraint for a maximum of 12 months.[104] If the parties wish to continue the restraint, however, there is a basic obligation to increase the level of

---

required to provide the TSB with information as up-to-date as possible. Para.6 MFA IV. See Zheng, op. cit. supra n.27, pp.19–20.

99.   Art.3(4) and Annex B.
100.   Annex B(1)(c).
101.   Annex B(1)(d).
102.   Art.XIX merely states that safeguard action may be taken 'to the extent and for such time as necessary'.
103.   Art.3(8).
104.   Para.8, MFA IV.

imports by no less than 6% every 12 months.[105] There are three situations where this growth rate does not have to be implemented, first where there are clear grounds for holding that a situation of market disruption will recur or be exacerbated,[106] and second in the case of those importing countries who if obliged to implement the above growth rate would damage their minimum viable production.[107] Third, mutually acceptable agreements may be made with 'predominant suppliers' for lower growth rates.[108]

(c)   Flexibility provisions: Where more than one product is being restrained, a participating country within the aggregate restraint may export up to 7% above the agreed level in any one product[109] providing exports in other products are correspondingly reduced, save in 'exceptionally and sparingly used circumstances' in which case it is not to be less than 5%. Where a restraint lasts for more than one year, an exporter may carry over unused quotas and carry forward the subsequent year's quotas provided that the year's total is not exceeded by more than 10%.[110] These provisions will not apply in cases where imports from a particular source form a large part of the importing country's market or where damage might be done to an importing country's minimum viable production or where the exporter is a predominant supplier. In such cases parties are free to make mutually acceptable agreements.[111]

(d)   The anti-surge provision: MFA III also introduced the infamous anti-surge provision,[112] whereby participating countries already party to a restraint which was being under-utilised could agree to further limits on a

---

105. Annex B(2) and B(3).

106. Para.9 MFA III adds the possibility of exacerbation of market disruption being sufficient to justify market disruption. This widens the exception considerably.

107. Annex B(2) and para.12, MFA IV. These countries are still under an obligation to allow for positive growth, however.

108. Para.10 MFA IV.

109. The TSB has stated that this 'swing' provision applies to both products and product groups. GATT, COM.TEX/SB/198 p.30.

110. Annex B(5).

111. Paras.9 and 11, MFA III. See also paras.10 and 12, MFA IV.

112. Para.10, MFA III.

product to prevent a sudden surge in that product within the initial restraint. There was initially an obligation upon the importing country to pay compensation but this is now only required where appropriate.[113] There is also no multilateral supervision of these anti-surge arrangements, making it even easier for importing countries to impose restrictions on exporting countries.[114]

The account of this somewhat technical aspect of the Arrangement does show that once action has been taken the issue ceases to be one of protection against imports and becomes one of administration of trade. The percentages quoted are an entirely arbitrary result based upon political compromise.[115] The flexibility provisions envisage that it is unlikely that any producer in an importing country cannot afford further increases. Furthermore the Arrangement provides for further safeguard action in the form of derogation from the basic rules should market disruption recur or an importing country's minimum viable production be threatened.

Two problems have in practice manifested themselves in this area. First, the exceptions have been susceptible to abuse by importing countries. The amendments with regard to predominant suppliers have effectively prevented them from benefiting from the growth and flexibility provisions and, as mentioned earlier, the Nordic countries have consistently invoked the minimum viable production exception.[116] Indeed the TSB has had to remind Sweden that the minimum viable production clause is not a 'general waiver of particular obligations under the Arrangement'.[117] In MFA III there was furthermore found to be a generalised invocation of the exception clauses[118] and, whilst the situation has improved under MFA IV, the TSB has found their use still to be common.[119] Second, in the absence of any

---

113. Para.11, MFA IV.

114. It should be noted that despite this, use of the anti-surge provision appears to be rare: cf. Blokker, op. cit. supra n.27, p.224.

115. The figure of 6% for growth rates was based upon the figure of 5% in the Long-Term Cotton Arrangement. It was increased by 1% to entice the ldcs into the Arrangement – cf. Kessing and Wolf, op. cit. supra n.14, p.40.

116. GATT, COM.TEX/SB/984 pp.86–88; GATT, COM.TEX/SB/1490, p.108.

117. GATT, COM.TEX/SB/610 p.50. See Blokker, op. cit. supra n.27, p.219.

118. GATT, COM.TEX/SB/984 p.148.

119. GATT, COM.TEX/SB/1490 p.108.

form of supranational enforcement agency there has been a breakdown of legal discipline with restrictions being concluded which flout the rules in this area with regard to base levels, flexibility and growth rates that are lower than the minimum required.[120]

V. MARKET DISRUPTION

ALTHOUGH certain States are entitled to preferential treatment, the foundation upon which the whole Arrangement is based is the concept of market disruption. A participating country is not entitled to enter into any initial restrictions unless its market is being disrupted. A recurrence or exacerbation of market disruption is also relevant to the nature of the regime that may be maintained. If this notion is hollow, the system that provides for differing treatment similarly collapses like a castle in the sand.

There are three requirements for a situation of market disruption to exist under Annex A of the Arrangement. These are (a) serious damage to domestic producers, or actual threat thereof, must (b) be caused by (c) a sharp and substantial increase of imports at prices below those for comparable goods in the market of the importing country.[121] The most serious weakness is that only a subjective evaluation by the importing country of a situation of market disruption is required for restrictions to be imposed.[122] Only the question of whether a *bona fide* assessment has been made can be supervised.

A. Serious Damage to Domestic Producers

Paragraph 1 of Annex A lists a series of factors that are to be taken into account in assessing whether damage has been caused to the domestic

---

120. Instances of this are too numerous to mention. For a summary of the practice under MFA III see the conclusions of the TSB at GATT, COM.TEX/SB/984 pp.147–148.

121. One of the problems particularly pertinent to market disruption was the unwillingness of the TSB from an early stage to develop any general principles in this area. In 1975 it considered the matter and stated that situations of market disruption could only be decided on a case-by-case basis. GATT, COM.TEX/SB/57 at p.2.

122. Art.3(3) begins 'If, in the opinion of any participating country its market ... is being disrupted.'

industry. These are turnover, market share, profits, export performance, employment, volume of disruptive and other imports, utilisation of capacity, productivity and investment.[123] Decline in *per capita* consumption was added to this list in 1986.[124] It is stated that no one of these factors can give decisive guidance but damage should be based on the above and 'not by factors such as technological change or changes in consumer preference which are instrumental in switches to like and/or directly competitive products'.

The impression of detail here is superficial if one compares the notion of damage here with that contained in other areas of the GATT, notably dumping and subsidies. Whilst one finds considerable overlap between the description of damage in the Arrangement and that contained in Articles 3(3) and 6(3) of the 1979 Codes on the Interruption of Articles VI, XVI and XXIII of the GATT and on implementation of Article VI of the GATT (the Tokyo Round Codes on Subsidies and Dumping respectively)[125] the latter are considerably more detailed. Thus whilst the Multifibre Arrangement refers merely to 'production', the Codes refer to the effects on wages, growth, inventories and cashflow. Similarly 'investment' is mentioned in Annex A, but in the Codes on the other hand one finds the more detailed concepts of return on investment and ability to raise capital.

More worryingly, there are factors included in the above list whose role is perplexing. It is not seen how an increase in imports will readily lead to a decline in *per capita* consumption. Similarly, the volume of imports in a domestic market cannot constitute damage, unless one defines damage on the basis of market share.[126] Market share is listed as a separate factor in Annex A, however. If one were to move on to the factor of export performance,[127] this can be said to be relevant to the assessment of damage only

---

123. Annex A(I).
124. Para.5, MFA IV.
125. GATT, BISD 26S/56, 171 (1979). These provisions are identical and both state that the following should be taken into account – actual and potential decline in output, sales, market share, profits, productivity, return on investments or utilisation of capacity; factors affecting domestic prices; actual and potential negative effects on cashflow, inventories, employment, wages, growth, ability to raise capital or investment.
126. UNCTAD, op. cit. supra n.18, para.101 at p.35.
127. The criterion of market share has not merely not been abandoned: it has been reaffirmed in para.6, MFA IV.

if one regards an industry as having a traditional right of access to a third market.

The quantum of damage necessary for market disruption is similarly confused and vague. The original Arrangement states that the damage should be serious. This requirement seems to have been treated with a certain levity, however, as in 1981 it was added that damage must be serious and palpable.[128] The notion that you can have serious damage without its being palpable is clearly nonsensical. The softness of the obligation is stressed by the fact that market disruption does not merely apply to cases of serious damage to domestic industry but also to cases where there is an actual threat thereof. The vagueness of this notion compares once again unfavourably with practice elsewhere in the GATT.[129]

B. Sharp and Substantial Increase or Imminent Increase in Imports of Particular Products from Particular Sources Offered at Prices Substantially Below those Prevailing for Similar Goods of Comparable Quality in the Market of the Importing Country

Like much of the MFA this requirement is extremely loosely worded. It also undermines itself by allowing an 'imminent' increase of imports to suffice for a situation of market disruption to exist. Furthermore, importing countries have been permitted to introduce obscure systems of product classification which have made it difficult to see which domestic industry the imports are being compared with.[130] The consequence has been a virtual abandonment of this provision. This has happened on two planes. First, the TSB has noted a growing number of restrictions being enacted on products of which there were as yet no exports.[131] Second, major importers of textiles have adopted

---

128. Para.10, MFA III.

129. Under Art.3(6) of the Agreement of Implementation of Article VI of the General Agreement (see supra n.125) a threat of injury caused by dumping will only exist where the situation in which this will happen is clearly foreseen and imminent. It was stated in 1986 that this will only be the case where demonstrable trends in trade adverse to domestic industry continue or clearly foreseeable adverse events occur. GATT, BISD 32S/182 (1986).

130. Choi, Ying-Ik, Chung Hwa Soo and Nicholas, *The Multifibre Arrangement in Theory and Practice* (1985), p.28; Majmudar, op. cit. supra n.27, p.116.

131. GATT, COM.TEX/SB/1503. The TSB noted its preoccupation with the features of such

regimes whose compatibility with this provision is dubious. The US has adopted the 'trigger mechanism' device which presumes market disruption to exist if either the total growth of a particular product in a particular year exceeds 30%, or the ratio of total imports to domestic production in that product is 20% or, finally, if imports from a particular supplier exceed 1% of total US production.[132] These figures are totally arbitrary and the latter two are extremely low.[133] The EEC, on the other hand, has adopted the device of 'cumulative disruption', whereby once a certain level of imports has been reached any further imports no matter how small shall be considered disruptive.[134] This device tended especially to freeze out LDCs who were new entrants onto the market.[135] As such its compatibility with the Arrangement was dubious. Indeed the TSB said as much in 1989.[136]

C. Causation

From a classical economic viewpoint it is very difficult to say that one industry can cause harm to another if the consumer is perceived as free to buy whatever goods he wishes. The notion of causation only becomes meaningful in a safeguards context if one presupposes the right of a domestic industry to supply a domestic market, for then another industry is infringing that right by entering into that market and denying the domestic industry sales. In that sense any safeguard action involves the predominance of

restraints and urged against their proliferation.

132. For details see GATT, BISD 31S/309 (1985). There was considerable anger expressed by many LDCs within the Textiles Committee at the instigation of this measure.

133. For analysis of this measure see Zheng, op. cit. supra n.27, pp.23–25.

134. For analysis of the EEC's behaviour within the MFA see Koekkoek and Mennes, 'Liberalising the MFA: Some Aspects for the Netherlands, the EC and the LDCs' (1986) 20 JWTL 142; van Dartel, 'The EEC's Commercial Policy Concerning Textiles' in Völker (ed.), *Protectionism in the European Communities* (2nd edn 1987).

135. Zheng, op. cit. supra n.27, p.26.

136. GATT, COM.TEX/SB/1490 p.17. The TSB stated that such a device was incompatible with the Arrangement if it did not ensure an orderly and equitable development of trade and if it disrupted the export trade of such products. The TSB stated that the consistency of such limits could only be decided on a case-by-case basis. It is difficult to conceive of a situation where a device to prevent 'cumulative disruption' would comply with those requirements, however.

domestic political norms over classical norms.[137]   What distinguishes the MFA is that the notion of market disruption has been drawn so widely as to allow importing countries considerable leeway, free from any multilateral discipline, to restrict access to their domestic markets quite heavily, rendering classical economic norms the exception rather than the rule and allowing importers to act in furtherance of their strategic interests rather than in pursuit of a more equitable economic order.[138]

VI. CONCLUSIONS

IN one sense it is easy to draw a line under the Multifibre Arrangement as there is near-consensus that it has worked unsatisfactorily. Its economic effects are by now well known: whilst certain exporting countries have gained from the high 'rents' generated by the Arrangement, many LDCs, especially new entrants and middle-level exporters, have been penalised.[139]   In 1986 it was formally stated that one of the aims was to reintegrate textiles back into the main framework of the GATT on the basis of strengthened GATT rules and disciplines.[140]   It also appears that, subject to the Uruguay Round being concluded, a framework agreement for the dismantling of the Arrangement has been reached.[141]   If the Arrangement dies it may still prove to be of more than historical interest, however. The death of the Arrangement does not signify the conceptual death of administered trade. The Arrangement's problems arose partially from the weakness of its substantive provisions but, above all, from its inadequate institutional structures.   Any future system will clearly need multilateral supervisory institutions which have strong enforcement and interpretative powers. The

137. UNCTAD, *Trade and Development Report*, p.71 makes this accusation about the MFA as if it were somehow alone in this respect.

138. A good example of this was the relaxing of restrictions on Turkish textile imports into the US as a result of Turkey's support in 1990 during the Kuwaiti crisis.

139. For the most recent reviews of the economic effects of the MFA on LDCs see Trela and Whalley, 'Unravelling the Threads of the MFA' and Erzan, Goto and Holmes, 'Effects of the Multifibre Arrangement on Developing Countries' Trade: An Empirical Investigation' in Hamilton (ed.), *Textile Trade and Developing Countries* (1990).

140. Punta del Este Declaration launching the Uruguay Round, (1986) 25 ILM 1623.

141. 'Developing World feels Cheated on Textile Trade', *Financial Times*, 5 Dec. 1990, p.7.

MFA offers another lesson for LDCs. This is that the notion of 'differential and preferential' treatment may only be able to exercise a weak corrective function. Progress is far more likely to be achieved through the adoption of enforceable ground rules in international economic relations that will enable LDC advancement.

Chapter VIII

THE SOVEREIGN DEBT CRISIS: A LAWYER'S PERSPECTIVE

Jonathan M. Clark, Jr.

Chapter VIII

THE SOVEREIGN DEBT CRISIS: A LAWYER'S PERSPECTIVE

Jonathan M. Clark, Jr.

I. HISTORICAL OVERVIEW

FROM the late 1940s until the early 1970s, most sovereign states seeking to borrow money from abroad (to supplement tax revenues and amounts borrowed through domestic capital markets) to finance domestic projects or to cover balance of payments shortfalls relied principally on funds provided by multilateral institutions such as the IMF and the World Bank, on loans extended by other sovereign states and on funds raised through the public issuance of bonds in the international capital markets.[1] Those commercial banks which extended loans to sovereign states during this period did so with little concern for the risk involved, as there had been since the end of the Second World War virtually no instances of sovereign borrowers defaulting on their external debt (although delays in servicing external debt were not uncommon).

The decade from 1972 to 1982 saw a fourfold expansion in the outstanding medium- and long-term indebtedness of developing countries owed to foreign

---

1. J. Hurlock, 'Advising Sovereign Clients on the Renegotiation of their External Indebtedness' (1984) 23 Columbia J. Transnat'l L. 29. For compilations of articles discussing various legal implications of lending to sovereign states, see generally M. Gruson and R. Raisner (eds.), *Sovereign Lending: Managing Legal Risk* (1984) and L. Kalderen and Q. Siddiqi (eds.), *Negotiations with Commercial Lenders* (1984).

public or private creditors (often referred to as 'external debt'), with the share of such debt owed to private creditors rising simultaneously from one-half to two-thirds of the total amount.[2] This expansion can be attributed to several factors, the principal of which being the damage to the balance of payments of the developing countries as a group occasioned by OPEC's decision to triple oil prices in 1973. Coming as it did at a time of increasing competitiveness and regulation in the domestic banking markets of the developed countries, these balance of payments difficulties presented commercial banks with an opportunity to diversify their loan portfolios by increasing the level of sovereign lending. This process of 'recycling' the OPEC oil surpluses to developing countries has been concisely described by one commentator as follows:[3]

> Over the four years to 1978 the average annual surplus of the Middle Eastern oil exporters was $33.8 [billion] and the average annual deficit of the developing countries was $39.5 [billion]. The international banks came in useful as intermediaries between these two groups. They received much of the oil exporters' surplus in the form of deposits and were able to on-lend, or 'recycle', them to the developing countries. The smooth circulation of funds from the newly rich Arab nations to the potentially rich nations of Latin America seemed, at the time, a signal achievement.

Governments and central banks in the developed countries further encouraged this trend, largely because they viewed the increase in private lending to sovereign borrowers as the best way to counteract the global payments imbalance caused by the increase in oil prices. Coupled with such other factors as increased demand for credit in developing countries to fund development projects and to finance existing external debt, the boom in sovereign lending by the end of the 1970s had left the developing countries in a highly vulnerable position.

The loans extended by commercial banks to developing countries during this period (and into the 1980s) typically were made directly to the sovereign government or to public sector agencies and instrumentalities (with central government and/or central bank guarantees). The loans were repayable within five or seven years, usually in a single 'bullet' payment at maturity.

---

2. Hurlock, op.cit. supra n.1, at n.1.
3. T. Congdon, *The Debt Threat* (1988), p.112.

The majority of the loans were denominated in US dollars and bore interest at a floating rate equal to a spread over the London Inter-bank Offer Rate (LIBOR), the base lending rate which reflects the cost to banks of funding their loans by taking deposits from first-class banks in the London inter-bank market. In most loan agreements LIBOR was reset every three or six months, thus exposing many sovereign borrowers to the macroeconomic risk of interest rate fluctuations in developed countries (and particularly in the United States). By contrast, the 'spread' element of the interest rates charged to sovereign borrowers (out of which the banks covered their administrative overhead and took their profit from the loan transaction) was typically modest, rarely more than 1 or 1.5% per annum, reflecting the banks' assessment that there was little risk in lending to sovereign borrowers.

Particularly during the 1970s, when US dollar interest rates were relatively low and hard-currency revenues derived by developing countries from their commodities exports were growing steadily, the ratio of debt service (being the total amount of principal and interest on outstanding loans required to be paid by a sovereign borrower during a given period) to export earnings of the developing countries (on which the commercial banks based their credit analysis) remained fairly constant.[4] As a consequence, the banks generally discounted the possibility that unsustainable levels of debt were being incurred. Further, the general view of the commercial banks at this time was that it was not possible for a country to go bankrupt in the commercial sense because the country would always 'own' more than it owed (and would be able to gain access to its assets through exercise of its power of taxation).[5] The potential risk involved in lending on an unsecured, floating-rate basis to developing countries was only fully apprehended by the banks in the wake of the events of the late 1970s and early 1980s.

In 1979, the occurrence of the second 'oil shock' occasioned by the overthrow of the Shah of Iran led to a second round of recycling of OPEC oil surpluses to the developing countries to finance their balance of payments deficits. In itself this was not a cause for concern, as the experience of the mid-1970s had demonstrated that developing countries could sustain

---

4.   Idem, p.109.
5.   Idem, p.114.

increasing levels of debt so long as their export earnings expanded faster than real US dollar interest rates. The difference this time was that the expansion of sovereign lending was accompanied by a dramatic increase in domestic US interest rates (with a corresponding increase in US dollar LIBOR), which increase was occasioned by the decision of the US Federal Reserve in late 1979 to tighten monetary policy in an effort to reduce domestic inflation. The greatly increased amount of debt service required to be paid by sovereign borrowers as a result of these two events, combined with stagnation or decline in commodity-based export earnings throughout much of the developing world during the 1980s, brought on the current phase of the sovereign debt crisis.[6]

The initial reaction of the commercial banks to the events of 1979 was to expand the credit available to sovereign borrowers in order to help them get through what was then seen as a temporary crisis of liquidity. The banks evidently anticipated that US dollar interest rates would soon return to the levels prevailing in the mid-1970s, and that growth in export earnings in debtor countries would again generate sufficient revenues to service external debt. Moreover, the banks apparently believed that the governments of the United States and the other developed countries, in conjunction with the IMF and other multilateral institutions, would be unwilling to stand by in the event any sovereign debtor repudiated its obligations. It was not until 1982, with the announcement by the Mexican government that it was unable to service its external debt, that the commercial banks stopped expanding their lending to developing countries. By then, of course, the damage had been done.

II. CONVENTIONAL DEBT RESCHEDULING TECHNIQUES

IN the years following Mexico's default in 1982 and as a result of continuing high US dollar interest rates and relatively low worldwide commodity prices, many heavily indebted developing countries have found it necessary to renegotiate the terms of their external indebtedness with a view to alleviating (or at least ameliorating) their debt service burden. Although the creditors

---

6.   Idem, pp.116–117.

potentially affected by such renegotiation include multilateral institutions (such as the IMF), public bondholders, official (government) creditors and commercial banks, as a practical matter only the last two categories are included in most renegotiations. Multilateral institutions are typically excluded (and the credits extended by such institutions are generally repaid on time and in full) because most developing countries simply cannot afford to see these sources of funding disappear. This is the case not only because credits from the IMF in the form of technical assistance and performance programmes provide essential liquidity support to cover balance of payments shortfalls and help finance essential development projects, but also because the successful completion of a debt renegotiation with official and commercial bank creditors is usually conditional upon the sovereign having reached agreement with the IMF on the terms of an austerity programme (consisting of performance criteria and targets) and a standby credit facility.[7] Public bondholders (i.e. holders of securities publicly issued by the sovereign) are typically excluded for other reasons. On a practical level, since most bonds issued by sovereign states are issued in bearer form (with the result that the sovereign has no way of ascertaining the identities of the holders of the bonds), negotiation with public bondholders to change the terms of the bonds is impractical or impossible. More importantly, the international capital markets tend to have 'long memories', and most sovereigns have concluded that the long-term loss of access to such markets which would result from a default on its public obligations (as opposed to a default on its debt service obligations owed to foreign banks, which will not necessarily prevent it from tapping the international capital markets) makes such a course inadvisable.[8]

Although in theory the situation of each debtor country is considered by its official (government) and commercial bank creditors on a case-by-case basis, in practice most sovereign debt renegotiations have followed a common pattern. At the heart of the renegotiation is the agreement reached between the sovereign borrower and the IMF alluded to above, which is considered

---

7.   Hurlock, op. cit. supra n.1, pp.37–38. The conclusion of a successful debt renegotiation is often also conditional on there being no outstanding defaults under structural adjustment loans and other credit facilities provided by the World Bank.

8.   L. Buchheit, 'Of Creditors, Preferred and Otherwise' (June 1991) International Financial Law Review 12–13.

essential by the bank creditors in so far as it lends credibility to the claim that the sovereign is undertaking structural economic reforms to ensure that it will be able to comply with its ongoing contractual obligations. The second component of a successful renegotiation is the agreement reached between the sovereign borrower and its official creditors, which agreement is evidenced by a 'minute' initialled by the members of the committee of official creditors known as the Paris Club. A Paris Club 'minute' is not a legally binding document, but instead serves as the basis for and is implemented by bilateral negotiations between the sovereign debtor and individual official creditors.[9] The final and most complex component of a sovereign debt renegotiation, and the component on which the remainder of this chapter will focus, is the agreement reached between the sovereign borrower and its commercial bank creditors. In view of the fact that 500 or more individual banks may have made loans to the sovereign borrower that need to be restructured, the borrower normally appoints a representative group of 10 to 15 banks to act as a 'steering committee' for the bank syndicate as a whole. Negotiations on the terms of the debt restructuring are thereafter conducted directly between the sovereign borrower and the steering committee, although each individual bank must ultimately decide whether to accept or reject the package negotiated by the steering committee on its behalf. As a practical matter, however, the terms of the deals struck by steering committees over the past decade have attracted high degrees of participation and approval by the international banks.[10]

Consistent with the view of the banks throughout most of the 1980s that the debt crisis was fundamentally a problem of liquidity that could be overcome by granting sovereign borrowers a temporary respite in which to put their financial and economic houses in order, the first round of debt renegotiations provided no forgiveness or reduction of debt but merely a deferral of obligations currently overdue. The basic components of most early rescheduling packages included the following: (i) principal maturities of

9. Hurlock, op. cit. sipra n.1, p.38. For a description of the Paris Club and its procedures, see 'A Nightmare of Debt: A Survey of International Banking', *The Economist* 20 Mar. 1981, p.27.

10. L. Buchheit, 'Advisory Committees: what's in a name?' (January 1991) International Financial Law Review 9–10.

defined categories of commercial bank debt falling due within a narrow window (typically no more than one or two years) were rescheduled to become due in five or six years; (ii) interest owing on outstanding debt was required to be paid currently, often at a slightly greater 'spread' than in the original loan agreements; (iii) outstanding short-term trade finance and similar lines of credit extended by the commercial banks remained in place; and (iv) the 'financing gap' of the sovereign borrower (representing interest currently due or overdue which the sovereign could not afford to pay) was covered through a combination of borrowings from multilateral institutions and official sources and through 'new money' loans rendered by the existing syndicate of commercial banks.[11] Each bank taking part in the rescheduling was expected to participate in the provision of such 'new money' loans to the extent of its ratable share of the outstanding sovereign debt.

If the sovereign borrower's position did not improve by the end of the period covered by the initial rescheduling agreement, the process was typically repeated with an additional year or two of principal maturities being rescheduled into the medium term. The basic philosophy underlying this approach was that temporary debt relief and limited infusions of 'new money' would give the sovereign borrower a breathing spell in which the beneficial effects of an IMF-sponsored structural adjustment programme could begin to take hold. The hope was that the introduction of domestic fiscal and monetary reforms, combined with the expected resurgence of commodity-based export earnings and decline of US dollar interest rates over the medium term, would have the net result of restoring the relatively stable balance of payments position that had prevailed in the mid- to late-1970s. Whether or not such hope was realistic at the time, experience has proved that conventional debt reschedulings of the type described above did little to improve or even stabilise the position of the most heavily indebted developing countries.

The driving force behind the early debt rescheduling agreements was the understandable desire of the commercial banks to reduce or at least minimise any increase in their sovereign debt exposure while at the same time avoiding the necessity of creating loan-loss reserves or writing down the value of

---

11. L. Buchheit, 'Alternative Techniques in Sovereign Debt Restructuring' [1988] University of Illinois Law Review 371, 372–373.

existing loans on their balance sheets (which would adversely affect their capital-to-assets ratios and depress the market value of their equity).[12] Regulatory and accounting treatment of underperforming sovereign loans differ from jurisdiction to jurisdiction, but the treatment afforded such loans in certain key jurisdictions proved critical in determining the structure of early agreements. In the United States, for example, commercial banks were able to treat sovereign loans as 'performing' assets for accounting and regulatory purposes (and thus carry the loans on their books at 100% of their face value) so long as interest was being paid on a current basis.[13] The fact that principal payments currently due were being rescheduled well into the future did not affect this regulatory treatment, so the banks typically placed enormous pressure on sovereign borrowers to stay current on their interest payments. Such pressure resulted in the diversion of scarce resources from development-oriented programmes to debt service, with the result that economic growth necessary to restore a manageable balance of payments was stunted.[14]

Indeed, faced with a marked reduction in hard-currency export earnings due to the decline in the price of certain key primary commodities during the 1980s, many developing countries found themselves unable even to service

12.   Banks are typically subject, in each jurisdiction where they accept deposits, to extensive regulation of the amount and nature of their loans and investments. Such regulation is intended to ensure, among other things, that there are always sufficient assets available to meet the banks' obligations to their depositors. To the extent a loan extended to a sovereign is not being paid currently or is being renegotiated, the value of such asset is diminished and, depending on the rules of the relevant jurisdiction, may have to be 'written down' to its actual market value (reflecting the risk of nonpayment). Alternatively, reserves may have to be established to protect the bank against the risk of nonpayment. Such 'writing down' of assets or establishment of reserves weakens the financial position of the bank, and can as a consequence depress the share price of the bank or increase its cost of borrowing. Because of this, banks are very sensitive to the accounting and regulatory treatment of their sovereign loans, and are reluctant to enter any arrangement which could lead to a more unfavourable classification of such loans.

13.   J. Hurlock, 'Domestic Regulation of Institutions and Markets; Implications for Reducing Developing Countries' Liabilities' (unpublished paper delivered at the Oxford Roundtable Conference on International Capital Markets, 20–27 Feb. 1988), pp.10–12. See also *Accounting by Debtors and Creditors for Troubled Debt Restructurings, Statement No.15* (Financial Accounting Standards Board 1977).

14.   Buchheit, op. cit. supra n.11, p.374. See generally H. Lever and C. Huhne, *Debt and Danger: The World Financial Crisis* (1985).

their interest obligations without further financial support. Accordingly, virtually all of the 'new money' loans and bilateral credits extended to sovereign borrowers after 1982 were earmarked for debt service, with the result that the external debt burden of many developing countries actually grew during the 1980s without any significant portion of the proceeds of the new loans being applied to stimulate internal growth. As one commentator observed about this trend, 'between the two evils of making an involuntary loan to a less-than-creditworthy borrower, or allowing existing loan assets to slip into the 'non-performing' category, most banks tend to prefer the former.'[15] These unhealthy developments were further exacerbated by the fact that during the first round of sovereign debt renegotiations, proposals put forward by various sovereign borrowers to place a 'cap' on the interest rate payable on outstanding loans (to limit the borrower's exposure to fluctuations in US dollar interest rates) or to reschedule the payment of interest arrears were successfully resisted by the banks on the grounds that any such concession would result in adverse regulatory and accounting treatment. It was also argued that forcing the banks to accept a below-market interest rate would discourage further extensions of credit and thus have the undesirable effect of making it more difficult (and thus more expensive) for the sovereign borrower to obtain new loans, although the experience of the 1980s showed that banks were unwilling to render new credits to heavily-indebted sovereign states even at market rates of interest except where such credits were used to finance current interest payments.

The net result of these developments was that net resource transfers (defined as the excess of new loans over debt service charges) into the developing world became negative in 1982 and have remained so ever since.[16] In order to cover the shortfall between the amount of new credits being provided by the developed world and the amount of interest owed on existing obligations, many developing countries found themselves forced to boost hard-currency exports, cut back on imports and adopt politically unpopular fiscal policies to deal with government deficits that had previously been financed from external sources. The reduction of such deficits through

15. Buchheit, op. cit. supra n.11, p.375.
16. Congdon, op. cit. supra n.3, pp.134–135.

tax increases and sharp reductions in the level of government expenditure (rather than through the inflationary but more politically palatable technique of increased domestic borrowing) were typically required by the IMF as a condition to the availability of its standby credit facilities, and most often resulted in a decrease in the standard of living for the ordinary citizens of the affected countries.[17] Because of the web of 'cross-conditionality', whereby the commercial bank creditors of sovereign borrowers required that an IMF programme be in place as a condition to renegotiating the terms of outstanding debt or providing 'new money' loans, the implementation of an IMF-approved 'austerity' budget and the monitoring of the sovereign borrower's compliance therewith came to be fundamental components of most debt rescheduling packages. Predictably, such policies caused widespread social and political resentment in developing countries whose limited resources were being increasingly diverted to service external debt rather than to promote economic growth and finance infrastructure development (thus further undermining their long-term prospects for improving their balance of payments through domestic economic expansion). By the end of the 1980s, sovereign borrowers who had already been through several rounds of debt renegotiations with their external creditors but had seen little improvement (and often a marked deterioration) in their economic position began to question openly the soundness of the accepted approach to the sovereign debt crisis.

The most radical alternative to the conventional rescheduling approach was outright repudiation of the obligation to repay the external debt. Somewhat surprisingly, no major sovereign borrower (regardless of the extent of its indebtedness) has opted for this alternative during the current debt crisis, although a number of smaller borrowers have declared temporary moratoria on the payment of debt service or taken similar unilateral actions in the face of short-term liquidity crises.[18] The reluctance of most sovereign borrowers to repudiate their external obligations (no matter how politically attractive such option might be) is largely attributable to the concern that repudiation would have adverse long-term consequences for the country in

17. Idem, p.138.
18. Idem, pp.150–151.

question. Not only might foreign creditors attempt to seize assets of the repudiating sovereign that were located abroad, but access to the international capital and financial markets would almost certainly be interrupted for a period of time (or would be made so expensive as to be impractical).[19] In such an environment, the repudiating sovereign could find it impossible to obtain hard-currency export trade credits or external financing for development projects. For these reasons, during the 1980s most sovereigns concluded that it served their interests better to renegotiate the terms of their external debt and reach a consensual understanding with their creditors rather than take unilateral action which could prompt a harsh response. Nevertheless, by the end of the decade even the principal creditor countries began to acknowledge publicly that a fresh approach to the problem was required.

III. THE BRADY INITIATIVE

THE basic philosophy underlying the most recent round of sovereign debt negotiations was first articulated by US Secretary of the Treasury Nicholas Brady in a speech given on 10 March 1989 at the annual meeting of the Bretton Woods Committee. Prior to that time (at least since 1985), the official US government position was that the debt crisis could be overcome through a combination of market-oriented structural reforms in the developing countries (under the auspices of the IMF and other multilateral organisations) and fresh extensions of credit by the developed countries to ease the pain initially associated with such reforms.[20] While this approach at least acknowledged that the problem was more than a temporary crisis of liquidity caused by the concurrence of high US dollar interest rates and low worldwide commodity prices, it did not advocate or even encourage the negotiation of substantial reductions in the debt burden of the developing countries.

Nicholas Brady's speech to the Bretton Woods Committee signalled a fundamental change in the US government's approach to the debt crisis. For the first time, the US government threw its support behind the idea that

19. Ibid.
20. Idem, pp.155, 209–210.

macroeconomic and fiscal reforms alone would not be sufficient to restore the stability and creditworthiness of heavily indebted developing countries without the tonic of systematic debt reduction:[21]

> Commercial banks need to work with debtor nations to provide a broader range of alternatives for financial support, including greater efforts to achieve both debt and debt service reduction and to provide new lending. The approach to this problem must be realistic. The path towards greater creditworthiness and a return to the markets for many debtor countries needs to involve debt reduction. Diversified forms of financial support need to flourish and constraints should be relaxed.

Brady went on to identify specific elements in existing sovereign loan documentation which, in his view, acted as impediments to the negotiation of meaningful debt reduction packages. Principal among these are 'negative pledge' clauses which restrict the ability of the sovereign to grant mortgages or other security interests over its assets to secure its obligations under present or future debt obligations (unless all the bank creditors participating in the renegotiation are similarly secured), and 'sharing' clauses which provide that each bank participating in a renegotiation has an obligation to share with the other banks so participating all payments received from the sovereign borrower in excess of its rateable share.[22] These clauses are intended to ensure equality of treatment among the existing and future creditors of the sovereign borrower (in other words, to prevent the sovereign from negotiating a special arrangement with certain favoured banks), but the net result is to make it impossible, without obtaining waivers of such clauses from all or a very high percentage of the affected banks, to put into place voluntary debt-reduction schemes of the sort discussed below. Brady specifically encouraged the banks to grant general waivers of these clauses 'to permit an orderly

21.   Remarks of US Secretary of the Treasury Nicholas Brady on 10 Mar. 1989 to the Brookings Institution and the Bretton Woods Committee Conference on Third World Debt, quoted in P. Kuczynski, 'Brady and Beyond', *Debt Equity Swaps in the 1990s*, Vol.1 at p.3 (S. Rubin ed., 1989).

22.   Ibid. For a discussion of these clauses and their practical implications, see generally L. Buchheit and R. Reisner, 'The Effect of the Sovereign Debt Restructuring Process on Inter-Creditor Relationships' [1988] University of Illinois Law Review 493.

process whereby banks which wish to do so, negotiate debt or debt service reduction transactions.'[23]

The fundamental goal of a debt renegotiation conforming to the Brady initiative is to achieve a sufficient reduction in the debt stock of the sovereign borrower to enable the borrower, going forward, to service its remaining debt on a current basis without the necessity of further restructuring. As a *quid pro quo* for such reduction, the Brady initiative requires the sovereign borrower to undertake growth-oriented structural reforms under IMF and World Bank auspices and to provide guarantees or other collateral to backstop its obligations under the remaining debt. The Brady initiative proposes that the cost to the borrower of such guarantees be covered, if appropriate, through loans on concessionary terms from the IMF and the World Bank. Although marking a philosophical break from the 'short leash' approach to debt renegotiation which characterised most of the 1980s, the Brady initiative is careful to emphasise that any debt-reduction package must be voluntary and must recognise and be responsive to the specific regulatory and other requirements of the creditor banks. Accordingly, in most of the sovereign debt renegotiations since 1989, the preferred route has been to present the bank creditors with a 'menu' of debt-reduction options from which each bank can choose the option or options most amenable to its particular circumstances. Some of the more popular and/or innovative debt-reduction options that have appeared in recent transactions include the following:

1. *Debt Buybacks:* In a debt buyback, the sovereign borrower purchases its debt from the banks at a discounted price reflecting the debt's secondary market value. Thus, if a particular country's debt is trading at a 40% discount, the sovereign buys the debt back at a price of $60 for each $100 face amount of debt. Debt buybacks are appealing from the perspective of the sovereign because they result in an absolute reduction in the amount of debt outstanding, although the disadvantage is that the up-front cash cost can be substantial. Such cash cost can be funded either from the sovereign's hard-currency reserves (if those reserves are adequate for the task) or with the

23.   Kuczynski, op. cit. supra n.21, p.3.

proceeds of further borrowings (in some cases from the IMF or the World Bank at concessionary rates of interest). From the perspective of a typical bank, debt buybacks have the desirable effect of reducing the bank's sovereign debt exposure. However, debt buybacks may also force it to recognise for accounting and bank regulatory purposes the 40% diminution in the value of the loans (with adverse effects to its balance sheet to the extent the loans have not already been written down). Thus, debt buybacks, like the 'collateralised principal reduction bonds' discussed next, tend to appeal to banks which have already recognised on their books the diminished value of the debt in question and are looking to reduce their sovereign debt exposure by cashing out.

2. *Collateralised principal reduction bonds:* Another favoured debt-reduction technique is to exchange the sovereign's existing debt for securities having a discounted face value equal to the secondary market price of the original debt. Using the above example, a bank would receive a bond with a face value of $60 for each $100 of original debt which it tendered. Such bonds would typically bear interest at a market rate (i.e. a spread above LIBOR), and payment of the principal and/or interest on the bonds would be partially or totally secured so as to ensure that the bonds would trade at or close to 100% of their face value. Security for the sovereign's obligation to pay the principal of the bonds at maturity (often 15 or more years following the date of the restructuring) can take the form of zero-coupon bonds (debt instruments which do not pay interest on a current basis but which entitle the holder to receive a lump sum, consisting of a principal and interest component, at maturity) or other assets purchased by the sovereign with its hard-currency reserves or with the proceeds of new loans and placed in a collateral account for the benefit of the bondholders. The sovereign's obligation to pay interest on the bonds is typically also secured by depositing in a collateral account for the benefit of the bondholders highly-liquid assets with a market value at all times sufficient to pay 12 to 18 months of interest on the bonds. Upon the occurrence of a default under the principal reduction bonds, the holders of the bonds would be entitled to liquidate the relevant collateral account to raise funds to pay the overdue amounts of principal and/or interest. Such collateralisation enhances the marketability of the bonds, and makes them attractive to banks which have already written down the value of

the sovereign's debt on their books and are thus attracted by the prospect of exchanging a highly volatile, unsecured asset for one of equivalent value but with much greater security and liquidity. From the country's perspective, the exchange of existing debt for collateralised principal reduction bonds is relatively cheap up front (the only significant cost being associated with acquiring the necessary collateral), although its debt service obligations will continue at a reduced level reflecting the discount on the face amount of the bonds. Obviously, to the extent the sovereign is able to negotiate a collateralisation package that provides less than full security for the holders of the bonds, the up-front cost to the sovereign will be reduced (though the bonds will be less marketable and thus less likely to be taken up by the banks).

3. *Collateralised interest reduction bonds:* The third principal debt-reduction technique involves the exchange of existing sovereign debt for securities having the same face value but bearing interest at a fixed, below-market rate of interest. A bank selecting this option might, for example, exchange debt with a face value of $100 and bearing interest at a floating rate equal to 1% above LIBOR for bonds also having a face value of $100 but bearing interest at a rate of 6% per annum. Principal and interest payments on the bonds would be collateralised in the same manner as with the principal reduction bonds, similarly enhancing their marketability. In so far as the principal amount of the new bonds is the same as the face amount of the debt for which it is exchanged, this option is attractive for a bank which, due to bank regulatory and accounting rules in its home jurisdiction, has not been required to write down the value of the original sovereign debt on its books and does not want to see a deterioration of its balance sheet as a result of its selection of one of the debt-reduction options. Although on an ongoing basis the interest a bank will receive on the interest reduction bonds will generally not be sufficient to cover such bank's cost of funding its loan, and the bank will thus have to recognise a loss on its earnings statement, for certain banks this could be a more desirable outcome than seeing the value of their assets written down by opting for the debt buyback or principal reduction bonds. From the perspective of the sovereign, the benefit of the interest-rate reduction bonds (as with the principal reduction bonds) flows from the reduced level of debt service that will be required on an ongoing basis.

4. *Value recovery instruments:* In order to make principal reduction bonds and interest reduction bonds more attractive to the banks and thus more likely to be selected from the 'menu' of debt-reduction options, sovereign borrowers occasionally attach instruments to such bonds which enable the holder to recoup under certain circumstances part of the losses which it incurred by participating in the sovereign's debt-reduction programme. A typical value recovery instrument might provide, for example, that the holder is entitled to receive an amount determined by reference to the then market price of a commodity (such as oil) on which the sovereign borrower's economy depends for a significant percentage of its export earnings.[24] To the extent the market price of the commodity does not exceed a stated strike price during the life of the instrument, the holder would not be entitled to receive any payment. The virtue of value recovery instruments is that they provide the banks with a limited stake in the future economic recovery of the sovereign borrower (but do not place an extra burden on the country if the recovery does not occur), much as a creditor who receives equity as part of the reorganisation of an insolvent company under the US Bankruptcy Code may be able to recoup some of its losses by participating as an equity holder in the company's future earnings stream.[25]

5. *Debt for Equity Conversions:* Another form of debt reduction given overt support by the Brady initiative is debt for equity conversions. In such transactions the holder of eligible sovereign debt exchanges such debt for new bonds denominated in the local currency of the sovereign, which bonds are then used to finance equity investments in public or private enterprises.[26] The purchase price for sovereign debt exchanged in such manner is typically set at a premium to the secondary market price (though at a discount to the

24. L. Buchheit, 'No Easy Route to Recovering Value' (September 1991) International Financial Law Review 7–8.

25. Ibid. For discussions of the merits of applying bankruptcy principles in the context of the debt crisis, see Silard, 'International Law and the Conditions for Order in International Finance: Lessons of the Debt Crisis' (1989) 23 International Lawyer 963, 971–975 and D. Suratgar, 'The International Financial System and the Management of the Debt Crisis' in D. Suratgar (ed.), *Default and Rescheduling: Corporate and Sovereign Borrowers in Difficulty* (1984).

26. Buchheit, op. cit. supra n.11, p.398. See also J. Sachs, 'Making the Brady Plan Work' in S. Rubin (ed.), op. cit. supra n.21, Vol.1 at p.13.

face value) in order to give both the holder and the sovereign a financial incentive to enter the transaction. The net result of a debt for equity conversion is that the sovereign has reduced its stock of external debt (though at the cost of increasing its stock of domestic debt), and has also stimulated foreign investment in its economy. As a consequence of the likely impact of debt for equity conversions on the local economy, most debt for equity conversion programmes give the sovereign wide-ranging discretion to approve or disapprove particular transactions (and to vary the level of the discount at which the bonds are to be exchanged) depending on whether or not the proposed investment would be in a priority sector of the economy. By making its debt for equity conversion programme accessible to its citizens with hard currency deposited abroad, a sovereign can also if it so desires use its programme as a magnet for attracting back 'flight capital'. While a number of leading economists have criticised debt for equity conversion programmes as expensive (especially when compared to 'straight' debt buybacks) and inflationary, such programmes are likely to continue to play an important role in debt reduction packages for the foreseeable future.[27]

One of the central premises of the Brady initiative is that debt reduction, however essential it might be for the heavily indebted developing countries, must be implemented on a strictly voluntary and consensual basis. In particular, Brady stressed that banks must not be coerced into accepting options that do not suit them. In the absence of a requirement that banks participating in a debt renegotiation adopt one or more of the debt-reduction options presented to them, however, the risk exists that certain banks will behave strategically by refraining from selecting any of the options (in essence opting to hold on to their original debt obligations) in the hope that the improved creditworthiness of the sovereign following the debt reduction will enable them to receive payment in full of the amounts owing under the original obligations. As Professor Sachs has pointed out, this is a variation on the ubiquitous 'free-rider' problem, and taken to an extreme could undermine the efforts of heavily indebted sovereigns to put together workable debt-reduction schemes.[28] Only if sovereign borrowers are allowed to

---

27.   Ibid.
28.   Idem, p.14.

penalise non-participating banks without incurring sanctions from the holders of their new debt instruments (or from the rest of the international banking community) can this problem be overcome; though tolerating such penalties, which could include non-payment of the contractual rate of interest on the original debt obligations, would run contrary to the letter (if not the spirit) of the Brady initiative. Further refinement of the meaning and limits of 'voluntariness' in the context of debt reduction programmes will thus be required if such programmes are not to fall victim to strategic behaviour by the banks.

IV. CONCLUSION

THE current phase of the sovereign debt crisis is gradually working itself out through consensual restructurings of the external indebtedness of those developing countries that borrowed heavily at floating rates of interest during the 1970s and early 1980s. In the absence of an international bankruptcy procedure which could serve to formalise the process by which sovereign debtors and their commercial bank creditors resolve their differences, the pattern to date has been characterised by highly individualised (and often protracted) negotiations in which consensus is ultimately achieved. Contract rather than coercion has proven the key to halting and in some cases reversing the spiralling debt burden of such countries. Insofar as the inability (or unwillingness) of a sovereign to pay its debts implicates issues of a political and macroeconomic nature as well as of a legal nature, it is perhaps not surprising that no international institutions have developed to deal with the crisis. Each sovereign must evaluate its own situation and decide for itself how it will allocate its limited resources. However, if it fails to convince its external creditors that such decision represents the most realistic and equitable avenue available to it, the sovereign debtor could find itself without support in and access to the international financial community. From the banks' perspective, failure to support a realistic and consensual restructuring plan can result in the sovereign defaulting on its debt or imposing a unilateral solution that is not in the banks' best interest (such as a debt moratorium or cap on the aggregate amount of debt service that it is willing to pay).

The basic truth of the interdependence of the sovereign debtors and the commercial banks goes far to explain the success of recent restructurings of the external commercial debt of Mexico, Venezuela, Costa Rica, the Philippines and (most recently) Nigeria. It also helps explain the absence (to date) of a significant free-rider problem in those countries which have successfully negotiated debt reduction packages. Participating banks have shown themselves to be entirely unsympathetic to those banks which 'opt out' in the hope of receiving payment on their existing debt at full contractual rates as a result of the improved financial position of the sovereign debtor. Indeed, participating banks often (quietly) encourage sovereign debtors not to service the debt of such 'rogue banks', or at least encourage the sovereign not to pay the rogue banks more than what the holders of the restructured debt are receiving, in order to discourage such behaviour in future restructurings. The economic pressures militating toward consensus have thus proven a formidable bar to strategic behaviour of this sort in the international banking community.

The great merit of the consensual approach is that it has – particularly in the years since Secretary Brady formulated his initiative – spawned a wide variety of creative solutions to the problems confronting both sovereign debtors and the commercial banks. Although not always an efficient or entirely amicable process, it is reasonable to predict that this approach will prevail for so long as governments in the developed world and multilateral institutions continue to lend their support. Support by governments is manifested not only by public statements endorsing the process, but also by a willingness and ability to reach agreements with the relevant sovereign debtor (through the auspices of the Paris Club or otherwise) on substantial reductions in its inter-governmental debt. The perception that governments are 'sharing the burden' of debt reduction makes it easier for banks to agree to participate in restructurings which often require substantial write-offs and have other adverse accounting consequences. Equally important, the international banking community has shown itself unwilling to undertake comprehensive Brady Plan restructurings where the sovereign debtor has not implemented (or is not attempting to implement) an IMF-approved budgetary programme.

Relief from the crushing debt burden which continues to weigh on a large number of developing countries can thus be seen to require the active participation and support of a wide variety of private, multilateral and governmental bodies. Further, success in obtaining meaningful debt relief is only achievable where *all* the parties agree to accept an appropriate share of the pain associated with debt reduction. Despite the unpredictability and inefficiency of the consensual approach, it has (in the last few years at least) shown itself capable of producing solutions acceptable to the broad spectrum of interested parties. So long as it continues to do so, there will be little pressure to create more formal international structures for resolving the issues posed by the sovereign debt crisis.

FURTHER READING AND
SELECTED BIBLIOGRAPHY

INDEX

FURTHER READING AND
SELECTED BIBLIOGRAPHY

CHAPTER I
Introductory - The Definition and Sources of International Economic Law
The following provide an introduction to the theory and structure of this branch of law:

G. SCHWARZENBERGER
'The Principles and Standards of International Economic Law' (1966-I) 117 Hague Recueil 7
P. VER LOREN VAN THEMAAT
The Changing Structure of International Economic Law (1981)
I. SEIDL-HOHENVELDERN
'International Economic Law' (1986) 198 Hague Recueil 1, reprinted and updated in *International Economic Law* (1989)
E.-U. PETERSMANN
'International Economic Theory and International Economic Law: on the Tasks of a Legal Theory of International Economic Order' in R.St.J. Macdonald, D.M. Johnson (eds), *The Structure and Process of International Law* (1983) at p.251
F. SNYDER AND P. SLINN
International Law of Development: Comparative Perspectives (1987)
FOX (ed)
International Law and Developing States, Vol.I, Some Aspects (1988)
P. SARCEVIC AND HANS VAN HOUTTE
Legal Issues and International Trade (1990)

CHAPTER II
The New International Economic Order: Principles and Trends

Primary materials are indicated in the notes to the chapter, the principal sources being:

Declaration on the establishment of the New International Economic Order, UNGA Res.3201 (S-VII) May 1974

The Charter of Economic Rights and Duties of States, UN Res.3281 XXIX Dec. 1974, Brownlie, *Basic Documents in International Law* (3rd edn), p.235

Secondary Sources

The Challenge to the South: The Report of the South Commission (OUP 1990)

J.E. SPERO

The Politics of International Economic Relations (4th edn 1990)

S. GEORGE

A Fate Worse than Debt (Penguin Books 1988)

ILA

Report of 62nd Conference 1986, Seoul Declaration on the Progressive Development of Principles of Public International Law relating to a NIEO

Report of 63rd Conference 1988, Warsaw, Committee on Legal Aspects of a NIEO, Committee on International Monetary Law

S.K.B. ASANTE

'International Law and Foreign Investment, A Reappraisal' (1988) 37 ICLQ 588

A. AKINSANYA

'International Protection of Direct Foreign Investments in the Third World' (1987) 36 ICLQ 58

OECD

Report on Development Cooperation (annual)

Financing and External Debt of Developing Countries – 1989 Survey (1990)

Promoting Private Enterprise in Developing Countries (1990)

University of Liverpool Library

Name: WU,Liying
University ID: ******2440

Title: International economic law and developing states: an introduction
Barcode: 012786029
Due: 21-10-09

Total items: 1
20/10/2009 14:57

Please short loan books on due date as given above.

UNCTAD
Trade and Development Report (annual)
VIII Final Act of the Conference

CHAPTER III
Extraterritorial Jurisdiction in Economic Transactions
Of the extensive literature on this subject generally, the following are
especially useful:

SIR A. NEALE AND M.L. STEPHENS
International Business and National Jurisdiction, Oxford (1988), a good
general survey, with bibliography (cited as 'Neale')
A.V. LOWE
Extraterritorial Jurisdiction, Cambridge (1983), giving annotated extracts of
cases and legal acts (cited as 'Lowe')
F.A. MANN
'Doctrine of Jurisdiction in International Law' (1964) Hague Recueil 1
C.J. OLMSTEAD (ed)
Extraterritorial Application of Laws and Responses Thereto, Papers given at
a Conference of the International Law Association in 1983, giving views
from all around the world, including the EEC (cited as 'Olmstead')
AMERICAN LAW INSTITUTE
The Restatement (Second) of the Foreign Relations Law of the United States
(1965) and *The Restatement (Third)* (1986), which revised and replaced
it
GRIFFIN AND CALABRESE
'Coping with Extraterritorial Disputes' (1988) 22 JWT 5

CHAPTER IV
The International Monetary Fund

M. AINLEY
The General Arrangements to Borrow, IMF Pamphlet Series, No.41,
Washington DC, IMF (1984)

E.M. BERNSTEIN
'Strategic Factors in Balance of Payments Adjustment', *Staff Papers*, IMF, Washington DC, vol.5 (August 1956) pp.151-169
'The History of the International Monetary Fund, 1966-71', *Finance and Development*, vol.14 (December 1977) pp.15-17

M.G. DE VRIES
'Multiple Exchange Rates: Expectations and Experience', *Staff Papers*, Washington DC, IMF, vol.12 (July 1965) pp.282-311

J. DE LAROSIÈRE
'Debt Strategy must be Flexible, Managing Director Tells Bankers', *IMF Survey*, vol.15 (june 1986) pp.164-167

I.S. FRIEDMAN
The Emerging Role of Private Banks in the Developing World, New York, Citicorp (1977)

SIR JOSEPH GOLD
Interpretation by the Fund (Pamphlet Series) No.11, Washington DC, IMF (1968)
The Reform of the Fund (Pamphlet Series), No.12, Washington DC, IMF (1969)
Special Drawing Rights: Character and Use (Pamphlet Series) No.13, Washington DC, IMF (1971)
The Fund's Concepts of Convertibility (Pamphlet Series) No.14, Washington DC, IMF (1971)
Voting and Decisions in the International Monetary Fund Washington DC, IMF (1972)
Membership and Non-membership in the International Monetary Fund: A Study in International Law and Organisation, Washington DC, IMF (1974)
Voting Majorities in the Fund: Effects of Second Amendment of the Articles (Pamphlet Series) No.20, Washington DC, IMF (1977)
Floating Currencies, SDRs and Gold: Further Legal Developments (Pamphlet Series) No.22, Washington DC, IMF (1977)
SDRs Currencies and Gold: Fourth Summary of New Legal Developments (Pamphlet Series) No.33, Washington DC, IMF (1980)
The Fund Agreement in the Courts in 2 volumes, Washington DC, IMF (1980)

G.K. HELBEINER (ed)
Africa and the International Monetary Fund, Washington DC, IMF (1986)
A.W. HOOKE
The International Monetary Fund: Its Evolution, Organisation and Activities
(Pamphlet Series) No.37, Washington DC, IMF (1982)
INTERNATIONAL MONETARY FUND
Annual Report of the Executive Directors
'Deputies of the Group of 10 Issue Report on Functioning of the
Monetary System', *IMF Survey*, Supplement on the Group of 10
Deputies' Report (Washington) vol.14 (July 1985) pp.1-16.
'Deputies of Intergovernmental Group of 24 Call for Major Changes in
Monetary System', *IMF Survey*, Supplement on the Group of 24
Deputies' Report (Washington) vol.14 (September 1985) pp.2-16.
LEAGUE OF NATIONS
International Currency Experience: Lessons of the Inter-War Period, Geneva
(1944)
J.J. POLAK
Some Reflections on the Nature of Special Drawing Rights (Pamphlet Series)
No.16, Washington DC, IMF (1971)
Valuation and Rate of Interest of the SDR (Pamphlet Series) No.18,
Washington DC, IMF (1974)

CHAPTER V
The World Bank

K.J. HAVNEVIK (ed)
The IMF and World Bank in Africa, Uppsala, Scandinavian Institute of
African Studies (1987)
B.S. HURNI
*The Lending Policy of the World Bank in the 1970s: Analysis and Evalu-
ation*, Boulder, Westview Press (1980)
H. MEHRAN (ed)
External Debt Management, Washington DC, IMF (1985)
I.F.I. SHIHATA
MIGA and Foreign Investment, Dordrecht, Martinus Nijhoff (1988)

CHAPTER VI
Structure and Operation of the GATT
Primary Materials

Basic Instruments and Selected Documents published by the GATT
Secretariat and cited as GATT, BISD

Secondary Literature

M.C.E.J. BRONCKERS
Selective Safeguards Measures in Multilateral Trade Relations - Issues of Protectionism in GATT, European Community and US Law (The Hague 1985)
KENNETH W. DAM
The GATT: Law and the International Economic Organization (Chicago: University of Chicago Press 1970)
ROBERT E. HUDEC
Developing Countries in the GATT Legal System (London 1987)
The GATT Legal System and World Trade Diplomacy (2nd edn, Salem, NH: Butterworths 1990)
JOHN H. JACKSON
World Trade and the Law of GATT (Charlottesville, VA: Michie 1969)
The World Trading System: Law and Policy of International Economic Relations (Cambridge, MA: MIT Press 1989)
Restructuring the GATT System (Royal Institute of International Affairs, London: Pinter 1990)
M. KOULEN
'The Non-Discriminatory Interpretation of GATT: Article XIX:I. A Reply' [1983] Legal Issues of European Integration 87
EDMOND MCGOVERN
International Trade Regulation: GATT, the United States and the European Community (2nd edn, Exeter: Globefeld 1986)

CHAPTER VII
The Multifibre Arrangement - Ripping the Shirt off the Poor Man's Back?
Primary Materials

There are two principal sources:
1. The *Basic Instruments and Selected Documents*. These are published by the GATT Secretariat. They are available at most university libraries and at any UN Depository Library. They will contain the discussions of the Textiles Committee and any relevant decision by Dispute Panels or the Contracting Parties. They are normally cited such: e.g. GATT, BISD 25S/7 (1977).
2. The deliberations of the Textiles Surveillance Body are published separately. These are not confidential but access to them is more restricted. Those interested in obtaining copies are advised to write directly to the GATT Secretariat. They are cited thus: e.g. GATT, COM.TEX/SB/1490 p.108.

Secondary Literature

The following literature is especially informative on this area:
NIELS BLOKKER
International Regulation of World Trade in Textiles - Lessons for Practice, a Contribution to Theory, Dordrecht (1989)
HENRY ZHENG
Legal Structure of International Textile Trade, Westport (US) (1988)
UNCTAD
International Trade in Textiles with Special Reference to Problems Faced by Developing Countries (1984) TD.B.C.2/215/Rev.1, p.1
GARY H. PERLOW
'The Multilateral Supervision of International Trade: Has Textiles Experiment Worked' (1981) 75 AJIL 93
BRENDA A. JACOBS
'Renewal and Expansion of the Multifiber Arrangement; Temporary Protection Run Amuck' (1987) 19 Law & Policy in International Business 7

CHAPTER VIII
The Sovereign Debt Crisis: A Lawyer's Perspective

T. CONGDON
The Debt Threat (1988)
H. LEVER AND C. HUHNE
Debt and Danger: The World Financial Crisis (1985)
D. SURATGAR (ed)
Default and Rescheduling: Corporate and Sovereign Borrowers in Difficulty (1984)
M. GRUSON AND R. RAISNER (eds)
Sovereign Lending: Managing Legal Risk (1984)
L. KALDEREN AND Q. SIDDIQI (eds)
Negotiations with Commercial Lenders (1984)
L. BUCHHEIT
'Alternative Techniques in Sovereign Debt Restructuring' [1988] University of Illinois Law Review 371
'No Easy Route to Recovering Value' (Sept. 1991) International Financial Law Review 7 and see generally articles published from time to time in the International Financial Law Review

INDEX

INTERNATIONAL ECONOMIC LAW AND DEVELOPING STATES: AN INTRODUCTION